Three Plays by Squint & How Th

CW00493512

Three Plays by Squint & How They Were Made

Long Story Short

Molly

The Incredible True Story of the Johnstown Flood

SQUINT THEATRE

methuen | drama

LONDON • NEW YORK • OXFORD • NEW DELHI • SYDNEY

METHUEN DRAMA
Bloomsbury Publishing Plc
50 Bedford Square, London, WC1B 3DP, UK
1385 Broadway, New York, NY 10018, USA
29 Earlsfort Terrace, Dublin 2, Ireland

BLOOMSBURY, METHUEN DRAMA and the Methuen Drama logo are trademarks of
Bloomsbury Publishing Plc

First published in Great Britain 2023

Proprietor © Squint Theatre Company Ltd, 2023
Squint Theatre have asserted their right under the Copyright, Designs and Patents Act, 1988, to
be identified as author of this work.

For legal purposes the Acknowledgements on p. 269 constitute an extension of this
copyright page.

Cover design: Rebecca Heselton

All rights reserved. No part of this publication may be reproduced or transmitted in any form or by
any means, electronic or mechanical, including photocopying, recording, or any information
storage or retrieval system, without prior permission in writing from the publishers.

Bloomsbury Publishing Plc does not have any control over, or responsibility for, any third-party
websites referred to or in this book. All internet addresses given in this book were correct at
the time of going to press. The author and publisher regret any inconvenience caused if
addresses have changed or sites have ceased to exist, but can accept no responsibility for
any such changes.

No rights in incidental music or songs contained in the work are hereby granted and performance
rights for any performance/presentation whatsoever must be obtained from the respective
copyright owners.

All rights whatsoever in this play are strictly reserved and application for performance etc.
should be made before rehearsals to Squint Theatre at mail@squinttheatre.com. No performance
may be given unless a licence has been obtained. No rights in incidental music or songs
contained in the Work are hereby granted and performance rights for any performance/
presentation whatsoever must be obtained from the respective copyright owners.

A catalogue record for this book is available from the British Library.

A catalog record for this book is available from the Library of Congress.

ISBN: HB: 978-1-3502-8996-3
       PB: 978-1-3502-8995-6
       ePDF: 978-1-3502-8998-7
       eBook: 978-1-3502-8997-0

Series: Methuen Drama Play Collections

Typeset by RefineCatch Limited, Bungay, Suffolk
Printed and bound in Great Britain

To find out more about our authors and books visit www.bloomsbury.com
and sign up for our newsletters.

Contents

ABOUT

Squint is an award-winning devised theatre company that stages stories about the here and now. They collide new writing, choreography and genre in unexpected ways to create thrilling nights at the theatre.

They develop projects through in-depth primary research and create collaboratively in spaces that are welcoming and playful. They also offer learning opportunities with a focus on inspiring and empowering those who feel theatre is not for them.

Squint was founded at the University of Reading in 2009 by Artistic Director Andrew Whyment. Today, they're London-based but work internationally.

Website: squinttheatre.com.

TEAM

Andrew Whyment | Artistic Director
Andrew is a stage and screen director. He stages new writing, devised work and adaptations. He is an Associate of the National Youth Theatre and formerly Resident Assistant Director at Leeds Playhouse. Over the years, he has developed countless scripts with acclaimed writers including Brad Birch, Chris Bush, Isley Lynn and Ross Willis and worked with tens of notable companies including English Touring Theatre, Good Chance Theatre, Guildhall School of Music and Drama, Headlong, National Theatre, The PappyShow, Royal Welsh College of Music and Drama and Synergy Theatre Project.

Lee Anderson | Literary Associate
Lee is a writer, dramaturg and educator. He creates new writing, devised work and adaptations. He is board member of the Dramaturgs' Network and has worked with companies including Lyric Hammersmith, Bush Theatre, Sheffield Crucible, Arcola Theatre, New Diorama Theatre, Park Theatre, Pleasance Theatre and South Hill Park. He has delivered courses and masterclasses in writing and theatre-making for The Mono Box, Royal Welsh College of Music and Drama, Guildhall School of Music and Drama, University of West London and Carnegie Mellon University School of Drama.

Adam Foster | Artistic Associate
Adam is a writer, theatre maker and facilitator based in Margate. He has previously been a member of writers' groups at Soho Theatre, Bush Theatre and HighTide as well as the Oxford Playhouse Playmaker programme. His work has been performed at leading venues and festivals across the UK. He has delivered courses and workshops for The BRIT School, Open School East, The Margate School, The Mono Box and University of East London as well as corporate organisations across Europe.

Claire Gilbert | Associate Producer
Claire is an Essex-based independent producer who has worked on over ten international tours and worked on productions at the National Theatre, Royal Court Theatre and Barbican Centre. With extensive experience working in arts for social change she has delivered projects for Good Chance Theatre, Deafinitely Theatre and Cardboard Citizens.

Kane Husbands | Associate Artist
Kane is a director and facilitator who specializes in movement and choreography. He is Artistic Director of The PappyShow, where his practice is focused on movement, physical theatre and training, with an emphasis on play and a physical, therapeutic approach to making work.

Louise Roberts | Education Associate
Louise is a drama teacher and facilitator who previously studied musical theatre at the Royal Academy of Music. She has performed in a number of Squint productions including *Molly* and *The Daily Plays*. Her work focuses on empowering young people on and off stage and the importance of the arts within learning experiences.

Ash J. Woodward | Associate Artist
Ash is an award-winning video and projection designer and director. He has won a Drama Desk Award and Outer Critics Circle Award and has designed and animated content for large-scale shows on Broadway, the West End, and around the world. His work includes 2D and 3D animation, cinematography, editing and visual effects. Ash also designs work for other live performance genres such as live music, exhibitions, and art installations and has directed short-form work for film and exhibitions.

Foreword

My name is Amit Lahav, I'm the artistic director of Gecko and I make and devise theatre that is visual, poetic, emotionally expressive and musically rich.

I first encountered Squint through their show *Molly* at the Edinburgh Festival in 2015 and was struck by the rigour and imagination of their work. It's been fascinating to read this generous and detailed articulation of the tools and methods of their theatre making and reflect on a few shared ideas in our approaches.

I've identified some fundamentals of Squint's work outlined in this book and – inspired by them – would like to share four short stories which reflect on experiences that have shaped my journey and style of making theatre with Gecko over the last twenty years.

'We plan and manage our time rigorously. It helps us stay focused, productive and, most importantly, creative'.

In 2001, I was still working solely as an actor, often with companies interested in devised work. Whilst it was very fulfilling, I couldn't stop the feeling that I wanted to bring my own ideas to life.

A new creative journey started, and my main intention was to get making. I wasn't really worried about having a company or funding or about a fully finished production. I just wanted to meet a few like-minded, brilliant human beings who were also interested in exploration.

It was a humble beginning, with no money, which created an opportunity to find out who really had a hunger to create as I did. Our intention was to make the best work possible, and we were determined not to compromise when it came to the amount of time we felt we needed on a particular moment. Crafted scenes with ropes, harnesses, puppets, percussion, and exciting choreography emerged and a production – *Taylor's Dummies* – was born. I think it's worth saying that everyone involved at that time was mid-career, highly skilled and energised. This is an important point about ingredients and expectations – if you want to make an impressive meal, start by getting the best ingredients possible and then take the time needed to create the best dish you can.

Many of the principles and values put in place during that first frugal process are the same today, twenty years later. Great humans, talented artists, expansive time, making the best work now, reducing expectations/pressures where possible, and an organic, playful, serious creative atmosphere in which everyone is empowered and encouraged to be rigorous in every moment of the process and performance.

Squint talk about being rigorous in managing time but I've no doubt this rigour permeates their entire process and their productions.

'Take care of your collaborators'.

In 2001, I was I invited to co-facilitate a two-week creative process for a group of disenfranchised and marginalised young people in Bangkok, Thailand as a member of the David Glass Ensemble. Half of the group were boys who lived on the street with access to a drop-in centre and half were girls who lived in care having experienced trauma and abuse at a very young age. The rest of the room comprised carers, support workers, translators and local artists. The premise of our intervention was to devise a piece of theatre and train the local artists and carers in a creative methodology. The encounter was a process of listening, looking and feeling with every fibre of my being. No common spoken language, no common cultural or societal references; almost everything was stripped back bare to the absolute essence of human connection, authenticity and presence. In an environment where people don't feel safe and their trust in human relationships is broken, you really are beginning with the simplest forms of being human; breathing, rhythm, seeing, listening, moving.

I remember feeling an enormous sense of responsibility for each human in the room, and the great desire to take care to listen and watch every moment from every child. As each of them began to feel safer, physically and unconsciously, they moved closer and closer into the circle. As facilitators, we elicited ideas from the children through tasks, games and exercises and built on themes that emerged, devising a piece of theatre together. We were endlessly exploring this emerging story, continually asking, 'what happens next?'. The children essentially told us the story of their lives through metaphor, drawings and emotion-led physicality. It was extremely playful and creative, and a small world with its own rules evolved that contained this extraordinary and unlikely gathering.

I remember the severity and care in the room, the laughing and playfulness, the fragility and pain, the enormous sense of responsibility and privilege, the wonder and awe at all the blossoming possibilities, from tiny, shattered stones into brave shouting volcanos. This was shocking and thrilling for me.

The experience changed me because it happened at exactly the moment it needed to in my life, it set some templates in me and enabled me to formulate fundamental ideas about what I was interested in and exhilarated by. It also gave me a grounding in how to create a safe environment and a culture of care in which everyone can feel empowered to create and connect. It inspired me to never be afraid to explore and ask deep and difficult questions of myself and of a room of people.

Every time I start a weeklong residency with twenty new faces, or at the beginning of a new create voyage, I treat the room and everyone in it with enormous care and I watch and listen to everything I see and feel. I don't always immediately understand what I'm experiencing (intellectually), but I have developed a sense and taste for what feels right and an ability to organise, nurture and interrogate these moments whilst keeping a culture of care alive in the room.

'Find the game'.

Lindsay Kemp is the most irreverent, playful, decadent artist I've ever known, who truly lived every second of every day as an artist. A walk around the supermarket was an opportunity; everything was inspirational and every moment danced as if loud delectable music was playing.

I worked for Lindsay over a number of years, and I lived with him in Italy for a short time where I also studied the language. Lindsay was absorbed and immersed in an endless theatrical landscape, and he was uncompromising about where and how he played; he could light up any room and sparkle the eyes of anyone he met within seconds. By example, Lindsay gave me huge courage to be bold and uncompromising and to use and be propelled by one's own beautiful burning fire, nothing can extinguish that.

'Follow your North Star'.

In 2017, I felt a huge urge to go to Israel and ask my grandmother about the journey the family took from the north of Yemen to Palestine in the 1930s. I asked her questions and talked this through with other members of my family. The conversation wasn't as revealing as I'd hoped; my grandmother by that time was around ninety years old (she never knew her age), living in a care home and living with dementia. Nonetheless some important provocations had begun inside me, raising questions about the migration stories of all my grandparents and great-grandparents, and this led me to a fascination in the broader human story of migration and how we are all connected through a complex web of journeys and stories. The impact of that was empowering and, through a number of residencies and workshops, I found that the conversation provoked feelings of compassion and empathy in each group, but also for each individual, self-empathy and a sense of connection with others in the group and, by extension, the world. The fundamentals of those initial feelings remain.

How I get from migration stories, both personal and societal, to a theatre show is certainly not easy to explain but I wanted to give you a sense of how and where a starting point might emerge. Every piece I make begins in this way; I have a feeling, a provocation and then begin to view the world through this lens.

For Squint, this is their North Star – in Gecko, I call it a 'Seed' idea – but it acts as a similar guide and reference that provokes and compels you.

If you have the nerve, the rigour, the joy of play, the patience, the drive, the eye for detail, an open heart, a childlike wonder, a hopeful spirit, if you love people, if you can express your most private fragilities, if you can protect and defend your beliefs and ideas, if you can give up everything you thought you knew, if you can listen and learn and change your mind in front of a group of people, if you can convince strangers to trust you with their feelings, if you can stay calm and friendly on an empty stomach, if you are all of these things and more, then devising theatre is for you. I love making theatre, I love devising theatre, it is my life and my passion and my expertise; I don't fully understand how it happens or quite how the pieces I make emerge, but it still fires me every day.

I applaud the endeavour and clarity of this book and its generous gift of signposts, exercises, starting points and provocations, and I hope they set you free and inspire you to explore and create with care, rigour, joy and connection.

Amit Lahav

Introduction

If you're reading this, there's a good chance you want to make a play.

Maybe you've got an idea but haven't started yet? Perhaps you've begun making something but can't make head or tail of it? Maybe you've made a play before, but you need fresh tools for your latest endeavour?

Whatever your experience or discipline there's probably one thing we can all agree on: getting started is hard.

We've deleted and rewritten the opening lines of this introduction more times than we care to admit, hoping to find a more felicitous phrase or a more fitting analogy. Taking those first few tentative steps into the unknown, poking and prodding at the edges of a new idea, is full of promise and risk. If we're very lucky, a bolt of inspiration will strike out of nowhere, zapping us with an absolute belter of an idea, sparking our imagination with something fully formed, demanding to be put on stage. Sadly, it's rare. What usually happens is altogether more piecemeal and imprecise with an idea revealing itself in fits and starts, taking shape slowly and irregularly over a long period of time.

While we're on starting points, it's worth considering how we first began making work as a company over ten years ago.

Despite having very little money and no Arts Council England funding, a couple of us who had recently graduated from the University of Reading – Artistic Director Andrew Whyment and Literary Associate Lee Anderson – began searching for a play and a venue to stage it in. We were recent graduates with a haphazard sense of how to go about getting our work in front of a live audience beyond the walls of a university. We already had an Edinburgh Fringe production of Bryony Lavery's *Frozen* (2009) under our belts and we now found ourselves calling in a lot of favours from friends, family and anybody kind enough to throw us a couple of quid or lend us some space to rehearse for a few hours. What it amounted to was an Off-West End production of Simon Stephens' *Bluebird* (2010). The experience of bringing that play to life is one that we look back on with real fondness. We staged it because we liked it and wanted to make something with our friends. It's as simple as that. No grand vision or company mission statement; just an impulse to put something in front of an audience with like-minded collaborators. Who knows, perhaps when it comes down to it, that's the reason we continue to do it today. Whatever the case, we learned an awful lot about what it takes to collaborate and produce work as an independent company on that project and it's impossible to imagine this book existing without that first leap into the unknown.

It was three years later that we began to experiment with new writing, producing a one-off night of short plays from early-career writers entitled *Love Thy Neighbour* (2011) at The Cockpit in London. The pleasure of producing, developing and staging entirely new work was a real discovery. It served as a practice run for what would later become the three full-length plays collected in this book, but it was also the beginning of building a company ethos and the team attached to Squint today. We don't make all our work together, but we have a shared interest in the sort of work that Squint creates. Between us we represent the disciplines of directing, facilitating, writing, movement directing, producing, teaching and video designing. Each associate offers a different set of perspectives and experiences and brings them to everything the company does on and off stage.

Today, we have a shared ambition to make work that engages with the here and now. Through a collaborative process that involves artists from a range of disciplines we aim to activate an audience's empathy, tell provocative stories and, above all, offer a thrilling night out. Our work is theatrical, ensemble-led, often physical and embraces genre.

In the first part of this book are the three full-length, original plays we've made since our inception as a company: *Long Story Short* (2014), *Molly* (2015) and *The Incredible True Story of the Johnstown Flood* (2021). Our hope is that, by sharing the plays as a collection, you'll see something of the journey we've been on over the last ten years.

At the heart of all three plays is a character struggling to process their personal trauma under the intense glare of the public eye.

The story of *Long Story Short* concerns sixteen-year-old, Jamie, who's forced to confront the loss of his older brother – a soldier in the British Army – while navigating a public media storm; his grief transformed into a television news bulletin seen by millions of viewers.

In *Molly*, our titular protagonist is someone with a history of violence, but it's the narrators who reveal their own appetite for cruelty, relishing the power they wield over her story while extracting confessions of guilt to sate the appetite of a live audience. Trauma transformed into television. Grief as entertainment. Private pain as public spectacle.

Meanwhile, in *The Incredible True Story of the Johnstown Flood*, Ken survives a devastating flood that tears through his entire community, only to find himself working with actors to reconstruct the events leading up to the disaster. A well-meaning act of drama therapy mutates into a masochistic ritual and Ken is compelled to relive his trauma in the name of justice.

The same anxiety returns again and again to haunt these plays and the characters that populate them; when does the desire to tell someone else's story become a compulsion to control their voice?

Storytelling is not a neutral act. Stories are shaped as much by the desires, fears and prejudices of the storyteller as they are by the facts or events contained within them. For us, the impulse to tell a story starts by imagining the life of another, with whom we hope to empathize. But telling stories is also about power and control, exacting control over narrative, characters, and events. Shaping and sculpting content for a specific audience. When we bend a story to our will and force it to obey a particular design, are we exploiting those it belongs to? This conflict is something that speaks as much to our own role as theatre artists as it does to the specific subject matter of these plays.

One of the narrative threads running through *Long Story Short* concerns the meteoric rise of an ambitious media mogul nicknamed Red. The story of Red's rapacious drive to monopolize the British press runs in tandem with Jamie's journey. Throughout the play, Red cloaks his ambition in silky rhetoric and superficial charm, casting himself as a bullish outsider whose crusade against the media establishment will democratize news and give a voice to the voiceless. But as Red's journey to the top unfolds alongside Jamie's descent into notoriety and scandal, the play presents its audience with the human cost of Red's legacy.

Meanwhile, *Molly* deploys a chorus of Actors who tell the titular character's life story across childhood, adolescence and adulthood. When the play begins, the Actors address us in a collective voice, acting as the bridge between the protagonist and the live audience in the theatre, reassuring us that their sympathy resides with the protagonist of the story. But when Molly's own version of events begins to diverge from the narrators', a conflict opens up between subject and storyteller. When the Actors assert their control over Molly, they begin to intervene directly in the narrative itself.

The Incredible True Story of the Johnstown Flood uses a similar device. The Troupe of nineteenth-century theatre actors collaborate with their subject, Ken, in the name of justice but, when differences emerge around the vision for how Ken's own story should be told to create the greatest impact, the Troupe use the trapping of the melodrama they are staging to literary trap Ken within the form of their play.

The starting points for these plays varied considerably.

Long Story Short was born of a set of conversations and an extensive period of research. As reports of the phone-hacking scandal began to dominate newspaper headlines and evening news bulletins, we started asking each other questions about our relationship with the news media. Where do we get our news from? Who makes the decisions about what we see and how we see it? What is the human cost of the ever-increasing speed at which we deliver news? There were no characters, settings or scenes at this point. We followed our noses and soon found ourselves wandering the corridors of ITV News, experiencing first-hand the frantic energy of the editors, journalists and presenters who spend their working lives nipping, tucking and squeezing world events into neatly packaged bulletins for our daily consumption. Conversation became research and research began to take on a dramatic shape. Soon, characters, settings and scenes began to suggest themselves.

For *Molly* we started with a question: what drives someone to commit a seemingly random and atrocious act of violence? The question emerged in the wake of a spate of grisly news stories that saw journalists, psychologists and the general public trying to understand the possible motivations behind the murderous actions of teenage offenders, including the BBC documentary series *Life on Death Row* and a horrific mass shooting in LA committed by the teenage son of a Hollywood film director. We knew we wanted to tell a story about a young person's capacity for violence while interrogating the sensationalized treatment of such cases in the media. However, it wasn't until we happened upon M. E. Thomas's book *Confessions of a Sociopath* that we were able to add story to the initial idea which, in turn, inspired the form of the show: a reality television show.

For our most recent project, *The Incredible True Story of the Johnstown Flood*, the starting point was wide-ranging research in the so-called Rust Belt of America during the 2016 US presidential election. Reeling from the aftershock of the UK's vote to leave the European Union in 2016, while watching our screens with growing horror as Donald Trump mounted an 'America First' nationalist campaign for the US presidency, we started asking questions about the possible connections between these two events. These questions evolved into a fact-finding journey across America, in which we met with communities on all sides of the debate in a fraught attempt to understand the appeal of Trump's particular brand of right-wing populism. Initially, this had nothing whatsoever to do with the Johnstown Flood, but as these research-led conversations unfolded across numerous different states, we were forced to confront our own prejudices and misplaced assumptions, and in doing so the project began to change in all kinds of fascinating and fundamental ways. It forced us to look inwards and ask, why are we telling this story? We ended up making our most personal project to date. The play looks at the ethics of appropriating someone else's story, the responsibilities you have when you choose to do so and how harmful it can be when you get it wrong.

The second part of this book pops the bonnet on our practice and unpacks how we get started and grow our projects. We hope offering up some exercises from the Squint Toolkit will empower you to make plays of your own.

The word 'practice' is a little mystifying. What does it mean in the context of writing or devising a play? Is it a set of fixed principles that one calls upon to make something? Or does practice evolve and change to meet the unique demands of a new project? While some artists remain famously tight-lipped when it comes to divulging their methods, others have built second careers on revealing their secrets in books, lectures and masterclasses. The simple fact is that what works for one person won't necessarily work for another. Not all practice is replicable and, unlike other art forms, making theatre is a uniquely social practice. It demands the presence of other people for it to exist. Unlike writing a novel or painting a landscape, putting something together for live performance requires a level of ongoing collaboration to solve problems and make discoveries. The practice of making theatre is always a negotiation. When artists working in the theatre share their practice to impart lessons or trade tips, like we're doing in this book, those of you seeking them out should be ruthlessly selective in your approach; steal what you find useful and dispense with what feels counterproductive.

There are tools in this book for every stage of the creative process; from fleshing out a new idea and getting to know your collaborators to making scenes, structuring stories and growing characters. There are no grand theories or carefully calibrated formulas – our time spent making work is defined by experimentation, playfulness, a lot of trial and error, working together in and out of the rehearsal room, trying stuff out, making mistakes, starting over – and these are simply the exercises we used that bore fruit.

A lot of our work involves text – working with writers to develop scripts – but our projects rarely begin this way. When we step into a rehearsal room together for the first time, equipped with only the seeds of an initial idea, we start exploring through practical exercises. It's a process that centres the actor and enables us to make shows in a variety of ways. It creates equality between all the collaborators working on a project and dismantles the supremacy of the writer.

During early development on *The Incredible True Story of the Johnstown Flood*, we went into the rehearsal room with a group of actors and a list of possible scenes inspired by the rough narrative outline for the story we wanted to tell. There was no script, only a very loosely sketched treatment that included a breakdown of characters and some key events. We scribbled the events down on small pieces of paper and invited the actors to improvise scenes inspired by each one. Naturally, some improvisations worked while others failed; some soared, some sunk. This is always the case with improvisation; embracing failure as a precondition for making discoveries is crucial to this process. Eventually, some exciting possibilities and interesting discoveries began to emerge, and these began to spark the imaginations of the other creatives in the room. Whether it was a line of text, a physical gesture or a moment of action, each improvisation produced a surfeit of material that galvanized our imaginations. Sometimes we'd have the actors repeat the same improvisation several times, each time applying a new game that would alter the dynamic of the scene in some unexpected way. Games are invitations to the actors to play with the scene and these can take different forms, such as only allowing each actor to speak one word of text at a time or having all the actors vocalize their inner thoughts to the audience. Inevitably, the games enlivened the improvisations by pushing the action beyond a sense of default realism, and into a realm that is altogether more surprising, imaginative and theatrical. We record these improvisations and use the recordings to create more crafted versions of the scenes on the page, attempting to capture the fleeting immediacy of the original improvisations.

We offer this as one of many examples of how we use tools to get a diverse set of artists collaborating in and out of the rehearsal room, working towards a shared vision for a show rather than a script, from the outset.

We hope the plays and tools in this book will inspire and empower you to make your own work.

Long Story Short

This play was first performed at Charing Cross Theatre, London in September 2014.

Created by Lee Anderson, Adam Foster and Andrew Whyment
Text by Lee Anderson, Adam Foster and Andrew Whyment

Neil | Tom Gordon
Tweeter 1/Soldier 3/Red | Kevin Phelan
Tweeter 2/Soldier 1/Jamie | Cole Edwards
Tweeter 3/Anna/Sarah/Steward 1/Melissa/Journalist 1 | Eva-Jane Willis
Tweeter 4/Mary/Journalist 2 | Cliodhna McCorley
Tweeter 5/Inspector/Sam/Amy/Journalist 3 | Fern McCauley
Tweeter 6/Soldier 2/Drew/Traveller/Scott/Gavin/Journalist 4 | Sam Jenkins-Shaw/
Ekow Quartey
Tweeter 7/Woman/Steward 2/Julie | Louise Roberts

Director | Andrew Whyment
Writers | Lee Anderson, Adam Foster
Designer | Georgia De Grey
Lighting Designer | Aaron J. Dootson
Sound Designer | Jay Jones, Chris Tarren
Composer | Rhys Lewis
Musical Director | Josh Sneesby
Movement Director | Kane Husbands

Producer (Squint) | Alex McCorkindale
Producer (Charing Cross Theatre) | Steven M. Levy
Assistant Producer | Fiona Steed
Production Manager | Jordan Whitwell
Stage Manager | Jasmin Hay

Characters

Soldier 1
Soldier 2
Soldier 3
Neil
Tweeter 1
Tweeter 2
Tweeter 3
Tweeter 4
Tweeter 5
Tweeter 6
Tweeter 7
Red
Anna
Astronaut
Sarah
Jamie
Reporter
Drew
Tannoy
Woman
Inspector
Steward 1
Traveller
Steward 2
Mary
Sam
Scott
Julie
Melissa
Amy
Gavin
Journalist 1
Journalist 2
Journalist 3
Journalist 4

Notes

The action takes place in multiple locations in the 1960s, 2012 and 2015.

The design should embrace the non-literal and lean into the fact that the story is being told through the prism of Twitter.

The characters can be distributed amongst the cast in any way and genders can be changed but the actor playing **Neil** *should only play that role.*

Prologue

20:41, Tuesday 24 July 2012. A warehouse in Helmand Province, Afghanistan.

Three British **Soldiers** *enter; their faces covered by masks, their guns and torches raised.*

Soldier 1   Clear.

Soldier 2   Clear.

Soldier 3   Clear.

The **Soldiers** *relax their weapons.*

Soldier 1   Oi, boys, watch this . . .

Soldier 1 *takes aim, fires and hits a can.*

Soldier 3   Fuck's sake.

Soldier 2   Nice one, babycakes.

Soldier 1 *takes aim, fires and hits a second can.*

Soldier 2   That's really good mate.

Soldier 1   Fuck off.

Soldier 3   Stop pissing about.

Soldier 2   Aw, schnookums . . .

Soldier 1   Lighten up. There ain't much chance of waking the neighbours is there?

Soldier 1 *takes aim, fires and hits a third can.*

See that? Mad skills. That's some *Metal Gear Solid* shit right there.

Soldier 3   We've gotta get back to the convoy.

Soldier 3 *goes to leave.*

Soldier 2   Three in a row is it? Right. Let's have a pop.

Soldier 3   There's no time –

Soldier 1   'Good luck, 007.'

Soldier 2   Three in a row. Watch 'em drop . . .

Soldier 2 *takes aim.*

Neil *enters and watches.*

Soldier 2 *fires and hits a first can.*

Soldier 1   One.

Soldier 2 *takes aim, fires and hits a second can.*

Soldier 1   Two. It all comes down to this final shot . . .

Soldier 2 *takes aim and, suddenly, a shot rings out from another direction.*

Soldier 3   Fuck me.

Soldier 1 *to* **Soldier 2**   What the fuck you playing at!

Soldier 2   I didn't shoot!

Voices and machine-gun fire.

Move –

Soldier 1   Unit under fire –

Soldier 3   Contact – contact –

Soldier 1 *and* **Soldier 3** exit.

2015.

Neil   Report the event. It's the first thing I learnt. Report the event. Tell it straight. Don't speculate. Don't interfere. Don't do anything that could make a bad situation worse than it already is.

Tweeters *enter.*

Tweeter 7   Do you feel like a big man?

Tweeter 6   Call yourself a journalist?

Tweeter 2   How much did they pay you?

Tweeter 7   Did it make you feel good?

Tweeters 4 & 5   You'll never live this down –

Tweeter 3   How do you sleep at night?

Neil   I made an informed decision in –

Tweeter 6   Couldn't believe what I was watching –

Tweeter 7   Watched it thirty, forty times –

Tweeter 1   Hashtag car-crash TV –

Tweeter 2   It was everywhere.

Tweeter 1   Hashtag –

Tweeters 2 & 3   Literally –

Tweeter 7   Watched it forty, fifty times –

Tweeter 6   Hashtag cringe –

Tweeter 5   Scum of the earth –

Tweeter 7   Watched it sixty times –

Tweeter 3   LOL.

Tweeter 6   Hashtag prick –

Tweeter 2   Cunt –

Tweeter 3   Monster –

Tweeter 5   Hashtag P45 –

Neil   I didn't have a choice –

Tweeter 2   You did it for the ratings –

Tweeter 2   You all have an agenda –

Tweeter 6   You're a prick –

Tweeter 2   You all are –

Tweeter 5   A manipulative fucking prick.

Tweeter 6   Hashtag prick –

Tweeter 2   Cunt –

Tweeter 3   Monster –

Tweeters 5 & 7   P45 –

Tweeter 2   Hashtag –

Tweeters   Most hated man in Britain.

Neil   Do you think I wanted this?

Tweeter 7   It's people's lives –

Tweeters 2 & 4   Real people's lives.

Tweeter 6   Don't you regret it?

Tweeter 2   Aren't you sorry?

Tweeter 3   Don't you have an ounce of fucking remorse?

Neil   I made an informed decision in extremely challenging –

Tweeter 2   You're disgusting.

Neil   I made –

Tweeter 2   No you are . . .

Tweeter 4   You're disgusting –

Tweeter 2   He was just a kid –

Tweeter 6   A vulnerable kid –

Tweeter 5   Sixteen –

Tweeter 7   Barely out of nappies –

Tweeter 3   It's disgusting –

Tweeter 6   Hashtag prick –

Tweeter 2   Cunt –

Tweeter 3   Monster –

Tweeters 4 & 5   P45 –

Tweeters   Most hated man in Britain.

Tweeter 2   Hashtag –

Tweeters   Justice for Jamie.

Neil   What do you know without context? It's headline without copy. And the planet's drowning in it. Around the clock, twenty-four-seven, limitless. It's everywhere. We're addicts. Every last one of us.

Tweeter 7   Do you feel like a big man?

Tweeter 6   Call yourself a journalist?

Tweeter 2   How much did they pay you?

Tweeter 7   Did it make you feel good?

Tweeters 4 & 4   You'll never live this down.

Tweeters 2, 3 & 6   How do you sleep at night?

Tweeters   Hashtag –

Neil   I'll tell you the story. The full story. But I need you to understand . . . You need to listen to me. Okay . . .?

Tweeters   . . .

Neil   It begins long before I became a journalist. In Australia, 1968, on a farm, just outside Sydney.

Scene One

06:18, Tuesday 24 December 1968. A farm, Sydney.

Red *sits on a deckchair listening to the Apollo 8 mission on a portable radio while* **Anna** *stands wearing a nightgown and holding a gift bag.*

Astronaut   We're now approaching lunar sunrise and, er, for all the people back on earth, the crew of Apollo 8 have a message that we would like to send to you. In the beginning, God created the heaven and the earth and the earth was . . .

Anna   Why, Red . . .?

Red   Why what?

Anna   Why's your suitcase still unpacked?

Red *listens.*

Anna   So this is your plan, is it?

Red   Yes.

Anna   Really?

Red   Yes, I thought I'd spend days preparing presentations so I could sit here at six-thirty in the morning and stare at the stars.

He listens.

Anna   Red, I'm trying, really trying not to take this personally. It's your decision. But we've been in this together for well over a year now and I just – I love you Red, but I need to know why you're not getting on that plane.

Red *listens.*

Anna *places the gift bag beside* **Red** *and goes to leave.*

Red *switches off the radio.*

Red   Three questions.

Anna   . . .

Red   You've got three questions.

Anna   . . .

Red   We're not going to debate this, Anna.

Silence.

Anna   Who's told you this is a bad idea?

Red   No one.

Anna   Red.

Red   I'm serious. The shareholders love it. It's a win–win deal as far as they're concerned. Things are running themselves here. I'm free to 'flee the nest'. 'We support your next endeavour wholeheartedly.' Next question.

Anna   Who's got into your head?

Red   Me.

Anna   I think you're bored of winning.

Red   Bored of winning *easy.*

Anna   You want a graze or two so you know you've fought for it. Well, don't worry about that, Red, you're gonna be standing in front of a crowd waving pitchforks and you're going to get hurt . . . and then you're going to win.

Red   But what if I don't?

Anna   . . .

Red   There's a side of me you won't like.

Anna   What's that?

Red   The losing side.

Anna   . . .

Red   Don't like the taste of that, aye?

Anna   Look, you're a stubborn fuck and you'll do whatever you want anyway but I'm damned if I'm going to be looking at you twelve months from now, full of regret, because, what? You didn't get on a plane because you were afraid you'd lose?

She buttons **Red***'s shirt and does up his tie.*

Anna   You're right. Being married to a loser isn't sexy. But being married to someone who didn't run the race . . . Hell, Red, give me the divorce papers and I'll sign them now.

She puts the gift bag down and goes to leave.

Red   I can't go, Anna.

Anna   *Can't?* Or *won't* because you're too scared?

Red   That's four questions.

Anna *exits.*

Car headlights glare on **Red***'s face.*

Scene Two

02:31, Friday 27 July 2012. The kitchen of **Sarah***'s house, Watford.*

Sarah *enters brandishing a hockey stick.*

Sarah   Who's there? I know someone's there!

Jamie   Sarah, it's me.

Sarah *turns on the light revealing* **Jamie***; he has a deep gash down his right arm, his sweatshirt is torn and he's covered in mud.*

Sarah   What are you doing here?

Jamie   Keep your voice down –

Sarah   You scared me to death.

Jamie   Sarah –

Sarah   How did you get in?

Jamie   Window –

Sarah   You broke in?

Jamie   It was open –

Sarah   Is that blood?

Jamie   Turn off the light.

Sarah   You're bleeding.

Jamie   Sarah, turn it off.

Sarah   What the fuck happened to you?

Jamie   Calm down.

Sarah   It'll get infected. Jesus, you look terrible –

Jamie   TURN OFF THE FUCKING LIGHT!

Sarah *turns off the light; blue lights stream through the window.*

Jamie *ducks.*

He pulls **Sarah** *to the floor with him.*

The blue lights disappear.

Sarah   Tell me that wasn't the police.

Jamie   That wasn't the police.

Sarah *hits* **Jamie**.

Sarah   What the actual fuck, Jamie!

Jamie   I'm sorry. I'm really sorry –

Sarah   Have you hurt someone?

Jamie   No!

Sarah   Tell me!

She gets **Jamie** *in an arm lock.*

Thirty seconds.

Jamie   Agh! What?

Sarah   You've got thirty seconds to explain why you're bleeding all over my house or I'll snap your arm out of its socket.

Jamie   You won't.

Sarah   Try me.

Jamie   Ah! Alright. Okay. I'll tell you, I'll tell you!

Sarah *releases* **Jamie**.

Jamie   I did a runner.

Sarah   You broke curfew?

Jamie   They have this wire fence. I got a good run-up, jumped, caught it and climbed over. My sleeve got caught and the wire sliced my arm on the way over. Didn't feel it at the time –

Sarah   You could've died.

Jamie   No chance, I'm fast.

Beat.

You've seen me.

Sarah   Show me.

Jamie   It's not even that bad.

Sarah *rolls back* **Jamie**'s *sleeve*.

Jamie   Sarah . . . When was the last time you spoke to my brother?

Sarah   It's deep. It might be infected. You need a doctor.

Jamie   Your mum's a nurse.

Sarah   Don't even think about it. If she sees you down here she'll go ballistic.

Jamie   You could do it.

Sarah   You need a hospital.

Jamie   There's police all over.

Sarah   They'll take you to hospital and then drive you back home.

Jamie   It's not 'a home'. I fucking hate it when people say that.

Sarah   I didn't say 'a home'. I said 'home'. As in, 'this is my home and you're not welcome' –

Jamie   When did you last speak to my brother?

Beat.

Sarah   You're shaking all over. What is it?

Beat.

Jamie, please tell me what's wrong.

Jamie   It's Andy. He's missing.

Sarah   What?

Jamie   Where's the remote?

Sarah   Jamie –

Jamie   Give me the remote.

Sarah   Tell me what's going on –

Jamie   Sarah, just turn on the TV!

Sarah *gets the remote, switches on the television and flicks through the channels.*

Jamie   Wait. Back.

Sarah *flicks back a channel.*

Jamie   There.

Reporter   Two of the three British service personnel reported as missing in Afghanistan two days ago have been named. Officer Alex Astin and Lance Corporal Andy Glover of the Third Battalion Grenadier Guards. There is still no further information as to the whereabouts of the missing personnel. The MoD are refusing to comment as to whether intense ground fighting in the northern region earlier this month had anything to do with the incident. Back to Olympic news now and the London 2012 opening ceremony is just hours –

Jamie *takes the remote from* **Sarah** *and switches off the television.*

Jamie   Sarah . . .?

Sarah   When did you –

Jamie   Yesterday.

Sarah   . . .

Jamie   Family Welfare Officer.

Sarah   Do you think something's happened to him?

Jamie   I don't know. They said they've lost contact. That's all they kept saying, over and over, they just kept repeating it –

Sarah   Slow down. Who said?

Jamie   I got a visit. Family Welfare Officer. They check up on us from time to time. Mostly, it's just routine, like maybe once or twice a month, y'know? But I could tell straight away it wasn't regular because they phoned ahead. Now they never do that because they always visit at the same time; the first and last Thursday of the month –

Sarah   When was this?

Jamie   It's hard to map it all out in my head.

Sarah   Soldiers don't just go missing.

Jamie   I haven't slept.

Sarah   Are they trying to find him?

Jamie   I don't know.

Sarah   Do you think something's happened to him?

Jamie   I don't know.

Sarah   Do you think he's hurt?

Jamie   I don't know.

Sarah   Stop saying that!

Jamie   What do you want me to say?

Sarah   I want you to tell me he's alive.

Jamie   . . .

Sarah   I'm sorry.

Beat.

I'm so sorry.

Jamie   Have you heard from him?

Sarah   We broke up, Jamie. The last time we spoke . . . I haven't spoken to him in over a year.

Blue lights stream through the window.

Jamie   I've gotta go, Sarah.

Sarah   Where?

Jamie   Train station.

Sarah   Jamie –

Jamie   Can I borrow some money?

Sarah   . . .

Jamie   I'll pay you back.

Sarah   . . .

Jamie   Sarah, can I borrow some money?! Please.

He takes a bundle of cash out of a jar.

Don't tell anyone I was here.

Jamie *and* **Red** *put on their jackets, grab their bags and depart.*

Scene Three

10:03, Tuesday 24 December 1968. The offices of the Daily Mirror, *Sydney.*

Red *stands with the suitcase and gift bag by his side; he listens to the Apollo 8 mission beside a desk piled with newspapers, a telephone and a radio.*

Drew *enters clutching a stack of papers; busy office noise blares as the door swings open.*

Drew   Honeysuckle Creek – NASA tracking station two miles from here – beaming that signal around the world right now. Two miles from here! They almost lost communication, but Honeysuckle kicked in and bob's-your-uncle we have an Australian hero in our midst. Martin Pemberton is the duty engineer. Sean's getting shots. Tomorrow the world's press'll lead with an international story. But not here. No sir. At the Sydney *Daily Mirror* it's a local story. No Yankee heroes on these pages. It's a big news week!

He kisses the papers he's holding.

Thank you, Martin Pemberton, you beauty!

Red   Drew –

The telephone rings.

Drew   Yes? Sean, don't say a word. Go around the back, stick your fucking tripod over the fence, I don't care, just get me a shot of Martin-bloody-Pemberton.

He slams the telephone down.

Christ!

He pours two glasses of bourbon.

Come on, mate, 'An Australian Hero' . . .

He hands **Red** *a bourbon.*

Red   It's nine in the morning.

Drew *insists.*

Red *accepts.*

Red   I fired Sean.

Drew   What?

Red   I fired Sean.

Drew   But he just –

Red   I saw him on his way out. He told me about the tracking station. I fired him.

Drew   . . .

Red   You need to stop giving jobs to morons.

Drew   Morons? He's not some vagrant. He came from Adelaide, and Melbourne before that –

Red   I don't want him working for my newspaper.

Drew   Fair enough.

Red   I need to know this place is in good hands when you're not around. Sean's idea of home affairs is cats up trees and senators kissing babies. Dead stories, Drew. Public interest, waste-of-fucking-column-inch crap.

Drew   Are you . . .?

Red   What?

Drew   When I'm 'not around'?

Red   I'm not firing you / Drew –

Drew   Well, thank God for that . . . It's just the last time I saw you like this was the day you gave me this job and the guy sitting here back then didn't come off so well.

Red   I need you to keep your foot on the gas.

Drew   All right then.

Red   I want you to meet me somewhere next week.

Drew   Where?

Red   I'm going away and if things go to plan then I'll want you to join me. If not I'll see you back here in seven days.

Drew   What are you up to?

Red   Drew –

Drew   I'll be there. Seven days. I'll bring Sean – no you fired Sean – I'll bring Brian up to speed on everything here and can join you for as long as you need.

Red   Good.

Drew   I could at least do with knowing where we're off to though, mate?

Red *goes to leave.*

Red   Oh and Drew, don't send another one of those clowns to cover that tracking station bullshit. It'll be news when we walk on the moon. Until then keep it off my front page.

Drew   This stuff sells papers, Red.

Red   We're not the *Reader's Digest*. I mean 'An Australian Hero'? How old are you?

Drew   Thirty-two.

Red   Would your friends read this?

Drew . . .

Red We're the young men in this game, Drew. Act like it.

Drew Red, I've gotta be honest, I'm struggling here. If the world's standing up and cheering they want us cheering along with them. It's post-war patriotism, mate.

Red *and* **Jamie** *grab their bags.*

Red Yeah? Well, we'll soon change that.

Scene Four

16:18, Tuesday 24 December 1968. Sydney Airport. It's sunny.

and

07:31, Friday 27 July 2012. Train station, Watford. It's raining.

Jamie *counts cash from his pocket.*

Tannoy All passengers for the seven thirty-one service to London Euston, please board the train now as it is ready to leave.

Jamie *sees a train ready to leave.*

He jumps the barrier and boards the train.

Red *gets a new coat out of the gift bag and changes into it.*

Woman *approaches.*

Woman Spare some change?

Red Excuse me?

Woman Spare change?

Red Here, take this.

He wraps his old coat around **Woman** *and goes to leave.*

Woman It's not cold nights, mate, it's my stomach that needs your generosity.

Red You're wearing a four-thousand-dollar Armani jacket. Pawn it.

Red *and* **Jamie** *are engulfed by crowds.*

Jamie *boards the train and walks down the aisle lugging his bag.*

Tannoy This is a London Midland service calling at all stations to London Euston.

Jamie *finds a seat and slumps down.*

Inspector *enters.*

Inspector Tickets, please.

Jamie *glances at* **Inspector**.

Inspector   Tickets!

Jamie *runs*.

Jamie *and* **Red** *weave through crowds*.

Red *arrives at the check-in area of Sydney Airport*.

Tannoy   The next flight to depart from gate number twelve . . .

Red *approaches* **Steward 1** *with his passport*.

Steward 1   Smoking or non, sir?

Red   Smoking.

Steward 1   Row thirty, sir. Boarding now.

Red *boards the flight*.

Tannoy   Ladies and gentlemen, welcome aboard this British Overseas Airways flight to Hong Kong . . .

Red *is sandwiched between two other passengers as the plane takes off*.

The seat-belt sign pings off.

He lights a cigarette.

The seat-belt sign pings on.

The plane lands at Hong Kong Airport.

Jamie *arrives at London Heathrow Airport*.

Scene Five

09:15, Friday 27 July 2012. Heathrow Airport, London.

and

18:18, Thursday 26 December 1968. Hong Kong Airport.

Jamie *stands at the head of a queue where* **Steward 2** *is serving and* **Traveller** *is waiting behind*.

Red *stands beside* **Traveller**; *they are holding identical bags*. **Traveller** *speaks in a language (*) foreign to* **Jamie** *and* **Red**.

Jamie   I'd like to purchase a ticket to Kabul, please.

Steward 2   I'm sorry?

Jamie   I want to buy a ticket. I have money. How much do you need?

Steward 2   It isn't a question of money, sir.

Jamie   It's my clothes, isn't it?

Steward 2   Your clothes?

Jamie   I know I'm a mess.

Steward 2   No, sir, it's not –

Jamie   I was running here and fell over cos I was late and I didn't want to miss the flight.

Beat.

Steward 2   Where are you flying to?

Jamie   Kabul. Afghanistan.

Steward 2   I see.

Jamie   I have a passport.

He shows **Steward 2** *his passport.*

Jamie   Look, that's me in the picture. Jamie. Jamie Glover. See?

Steward 2   I'm afraid there are no direct flights to Kabul.

Jamie   No direct . . .?

Steward 2   There are no direct flights to Kabul from this airport, sir.

Jamie   I didn't think of that.

Steward 2   I'm sorry but you'll need to step aside, sir. There are other people waiting.

Traveller *approaches the desk.*

Traveller   Are there still business seats available to Kabul at midday?

Steward 2   Of course, sir. With a transfer in Dubai?

Traveller   Please.

Steward 2   Of course, sir.

Jamie   Oi, I'll get what he's getting. I'll get the transfer thingy.

Steward 2 (*to* **Traveller**)   I apologize. (*To* **Jamie**.) Do you have eight hundred and sixty pounds, sir?

Jamie *takes out more crumpled fifty-pound notes.*

Steward 2   I am very sorry, sir, but we don't accept cash payments of over three hundred pounds.

Jamie   You're just making that up!

Steward 2   It's our policy, sir.

Jamie   I can pay. I have a passport.

Steward 2   Please calm down, sir.

Jamie   I am being calm.

Steward 2   You're shouting.

Jamie   No I'm not. I'm not shouting. This isn't shouting. You must have very sensitive ears – Lesley Ann – if you thought that was shouting.

Steward 2   Unless you can organize another form of payment, I cannot authorize you to fly.

Jamie (*to* **Traveller**)   Can you buy me a ticket?

Traveller   Leave me alone.

Jamie   I have money. I can pay you. They won't let me do it myself.

1968.

Red (*trying to get at the opposite bag.*)   If you just –

Traveller   No touch.

Red   I can prove to you –

Traveller   No touch.

Red (*waving a key at* **Traveller**)   There's a lock.

Traveller   *What?

Red (*showing* **Traveller** *the key*)   My key, for my bag. Not your bag.

Traveller   *I don't speak English.

Red   Very similar bags. We've got confused. Mixed up.

Traveller   *Why are you talking to me like I'm an idiot?

Red   Look, it's my fucking bag, so if you don't mind –

Traveller   *On my mother's grave I swear I will call the authorities. Police! Police! This man is stealing my bag. Police!

2012.

Jamie *hands money to* **Traveller**.

Jamie   Please –

Traveller   Is this a drug thing?

Jamie   No, I need to get to Kabul so I can find my brother.

Steward 2   Is this man bothering you, sir?

Jamie   I just want to get on that plane.

1968.

Red   Look. How much do you want? Money. I have money. I buy the bag.

Mary *enters and watches from a distance.*

Traveller   *Money?

Red   Yes. Money. Australian Dollars.

2012.

Traveller   He's trying to bribe me.

Jamie   I'm not. He's lying.

Steward 2   Calm down, sir. I'm not going to ask you again.

1968.

Red   How much do you want?

Traveller   . . .

Red   I'll buy you a gift.

Traveller   *You give me money?

Red   I'll buy you a present. I buy you present, and you give me bag. This is very important to me. It has important papers inside. For big meeting.

Traveller   *Meeting. (*Miming.*) Business meeting. Businessman.

Red   Yes, businessman!

2012.

Traveller   I think he's involved in drugs.

Steward 2   Will you come with me, sir?

Jamie   I have money. I have a passport.

Steward 2   Why don't you come with me and we can discuss this matter privately?

1968/2012.

Traveller   *You buy me present?

Red   You give me my bag and I'll buy you a bloody gift, alright?!

Traveller   *Don't insult me. How dare you! This man is a thief! He's a liar and a thief! Police! Police!

Red   Jesus Christ.

Jamie   The flight is boarding soon!

Steward 2   You're distressing the other customers, sir.

Mary *steps in.*

Mary   Wow, you know how to cause a scene.

Red   He's got my bag.

Mary   If that's your bag then why don't you open up the bag you have there and prove it to him?

Steward 2   Security to Terminal 5 please.

Red *unzips the bag.*

Traveller   *First he steals my bag, now he tries to insult me with his money!

Mary   He's Australian.

Red *pulls out a pair of underwear and waves them at* **Traveller**.

Red   These are not mine. These are yours. Yes?

Traveller   *You have my bag.

Red   Yes! (*Pointing.*) Your bag. My bag.

Traveller *grabs his underwear and bag and exits.*

Red *retrieves his bag.*

Red   Thank you!

Mary   *Thank you very much.

Red   Thanks for nothing.

Mary   Don't be rude.

Red   I offered him a gift!

Mary   Flaunting your wealth is an insult in his culture.

Red   'Flaunting'?

Mary   'When money talks, truth shuts up.' Russian proverb.

Red   I see.

Mary   Roughly translated; there's some things you can't solve with your wallet.

Beat.

First time in Hong Kong?

Red   I'm just passing through.

Mary   Where you heading?

Tannoy   Last call for passengers boarding British Overseas Airways flight 103.

Red & Mary   That's my flight.

Jamie *and* **Red** *weave through crowds.*

Red *and* **Mary** *find their flight.*

Jamie *runs through residential London streets looking for a house.*
He finds the house.

Scene Six

12:15, Friday 27 July 2012. The front door of **Sam** *'s house in Highgate, London.*
Jamie *stands on the doorstep while* **Sam** *leans out of an upstairs window.*

Sam   Go away.

Jamie   Five minutes, that's all I'm asking for.

Sam   If you're not gone in five seconds, I'm calling the police.

Jamie   I'm not a reporter.

Sam   One . . .

Jamie   You're not listening to me –

Sam   Two . . .

Jamie   My name's Jamie –

Sam   Three . . .

Jamie   My name's Jamie Glover.

Sam   Four. I'm dialling.

Jamie   My brother's name is Andy Glover.

Sam   I don't know who that is. Five! I'm calling them now.

Jamie   Alex Astin.

Sam   . . .

Jamie   Alex Astin. That's your brother, isn't it?

Sam   You a friend of Alex's?

Jamie   Let me in and I'll explain.

Sam   . . .

Jamie   Please.

Beat.

Sam   I can't let you in until my parents are home.

Jamie   I can't do that. Please, it's important.

Sam   . . .

Sam *opens the door.*

Jamie   Thank you.

Jamie *enters.*

Sam   What did you say your name was again?

Jamie   Jamie. Jamie Glover.

Sam   And you know Alex?

Jamie   Yeah. Well, no. Not directly. My brother, he's . . . he and Alex . . . they were friends. Are friends. Fuck. Sorry. This is . . . all a bit weird, you know?

Jamie *takes out his phone, scrolls through his photos and shows a picture to* **Sam.**

Jamie   That's my brother. He's a lance corporal in the British Army. Him and Alex . . . they're in the same regiment. They're friends. When was the last time you spoke to him?

Sam   We haven't Skyped for a while.

Jamie   I know it's hard . . .

Sam   We usually talk all the time, but we haven't had broadband for three days now. Dad says it's to do with the subscription.

Jamie   What?

Sam   No Sky either.

Beat.

Jamie   When are your parents back?

Sam   A couple of hours.

Jamie   I need to speak to them.

Sam   I can pass on a message if you like?

Jamie   I just need to speak to them for a couple of minutes.

Sam   You're being weird.

Beat.

Jamie   Have you been watching the news?

Sam   No signal. Told you.

Jamie   When was the last time you had the TV on?

Sam   Three days ago. The Xbox still works.

Jamie   Jesus . . .

Sam   Is something wrong? You look pale.

Jamie   I don't how to tell you . . .

Sam   Tell me what?

Jamie   Your brother . . . Our brothers are . . .

Beat.

Andy told me to get in touch if I was ever in the area. That's all.

Sam   Right.

Jamie   Listen, I should go. I can come back another time. Sorry to bother you.

Sam   You forgot your phone.

Jamie *notices a framed picture on the shelf.*

Jamie   Do you know when this was taken?

Sam   We got it in the post two weeks ago. That's my brother on the left there, see?

Jamie   Yeah. I see him.

Sam   Is that your brother?

Jamie   That's him, yeah.

Sam   Are you alright?

Jamie   Huh? Yeah. Yeah, everything's fine.

He takes out his phone and takes a photo of the picture.

Sam   Fancy a game before you go?

Jamie   Sorry?

Sam   It's the only thing that works and I'm bored.

Jamie   I've gotta meet someone.

Sam   Oh, come on. One game.

Jamie   What we playing?

Sam   *Call of Duty: Modern Warfare 3*. We'll play co-op.

Jamie   Okay. Sure. Sounds good.

He and **Sam** *play.*

Scene Seven

19:18, Thursday 26 December 1968. The cabin of a British Overseas Airways plane, Hong Kong.

Red *and* **Mary** *sit either side of an aisle.* **Red** *reads the* Financial Times.

The seat-belt sign pings on.

Mary   Buckle up.

Red   Huh?

Mary   Put your seat belt on or they'll get you.

Red   Who?

Mary   Plane Jane and her friends.

Red   Don't worry about me.

Mary   More fool you if this thing goes down . . .

Red   I've flown a hundred and fifty thousand air miles this year and drawn the conclusion that a twenty-inch strip of strengthened nylon across my waist will do me no good if this thing goes down.

Mary   You don't know that.

Red   We're sat in a two hundred and fifty-tonne metal tube that cruises at thirty-five thousand feet –

Mary   Worth the click. Just in case.

Red   Do you fly a lot?

Mary   Second time.

Red   Wow. How was the first?

Mary   Hated it.

Red   And now?

Mary   Petrified.

Red   You stay buckled up then.

Mary   And you keep tempting death.

Red   You can't flummox fate.

Mary *(gesturing to the* Financial Times*)*   What you reading that thing for, then?

Red   This? This puts me in control.

Mary   Play around on the markets, do you?

Red   I dabble –

Mary   My dad was a gambler.

Red   I don't gamble.

Mary   Oh no, you're an 'investor'.

Red   Kind of.

Mary   You don't gamble, you 'take risks'.

Red   Yes.

Mary   How do you know where to lay your chips?

Red (*gesturing to the* Financial Times)   I read this.

Mary   I wouldn't believe everything you read. Trust me, those things are poison.

Beat.

So what are you travelling for? A new investment?

Red   Perhaps.

Mary   Well I hope it works out. I've seen people fall hard. If I were you I'd –

Red   – you'd keep your chips in the bank?

Mary   The house always wins.

Red   Not always.

Beat.

Mary   What's your name?

Red   Rupert.

Mary   Well, Rupert, be careful. It's not too late to turn back, you know?

The seat-belt sign pings off and on.

I'd put a seat belt on if I were you.

The engines fire up.

Scene Eight

16:15, Friday 27 July 2012. A cafe in Piccadilly Circus, London.

Jamie *sits at a table with* **Scott***; he sips from a can of Tizer while* **Scott** *drinks a cup of tea.*

Scott   No, Jamie. Before you ask. There's – all I can tell you because there's fuck-all I know.

Jamie   . . .

Scott   Don't look at me like that, mate, I'm not trying to be a cunt.

Jamie   You're just being one anyway.

Scott   Do you understand the shit I'd be in?

Jamie   Why the fuck you being like this?

Scott   Because there's nothing I can do, mate. Look, I'm sorry, yeah? Honestly, I am. But you saw the statement. If anything changes, then you'll know, when they know. It all goes above my head anyway. I couldn't tell you anything even if I wanted to.

Jamie   So that's it, is it? Don't you even care?

Scott   You know I do.

Jamie   Doesn't seem like it, bruv.

Scott   Andy's a top bloke. But this is a professional matter so leave it to the professionals, yeah?

Jamie   Not for me. For me it's family. For me it's blood. I don't have much of that left, Scott.

Scott   Look, do you fancy a breakfast?

Jamie   Why?

Scott   Because I want to get you a breakfast. You must be starving.

Jamie   I DON'T WANT A FUCKING BREAKFAST.

Scott   Alright, alright. Keep it down yeah? Fuck's sake . . .

Jamie   You were out there with him.

Scott   Yeah, so?

Jamie   What do you mean 'so'? So you've been out there. So you must be able to tell me something.

Scott   . . .

Jamie   Fuck this. You're a coward.

He goes to leave.

Scott   He was in Helmand. That's where it happened.

Jamie   I know that already.

He takes his seat.

Scott   There'd been these airstrikes. Our lot had fucking flattened the place. Kajaki District, it's called. Shithole. Dusty. Air feels like sandpaper in your eyes. Andy and me hated it.

Jamie   Go on.

Scott   Your brother was sent in to sweep it. Nothing fancy. Piece of piss most of the time. Kids' stuff.

Jamie   For all I know he's staring down a camera with a machete at his neck. Doesn't sound like 'kids' stuff' to me. What went wrong?

Scott   They didn't go in expecting contact. Looks like they found it.

Jamie   That's it? Fuck's sake, I could have got all that off the BBC homepage.

Scott   Why didn't you then?

Jamie   Cos you're supposed to be a mate. You're supposed to be Andy's mate.

He shows **Scott** *the photo from* **Sam**'s *house.*

Jamie   Look at this.

Scott   What am I looking at?

Jamie   There. Bottom left.

Scott   I can't make it out.

Jamie   Recognize any familiar-looking faces?

Scott   Should I?

Jamie   That's you. That's Andy. And who's that, aye?

Scott   That was ages ago, mate.

Jamie   Do I look stupid to you, Scott?

Scott   . . .

Jamie   It was two weeks ago. Camp Bastion.

Scott   Jamie, listen to me. I need to know you're not planning on doing something stupid.

Jamie   . . .

Scott   Where did you get that picture?

Jamie   . . .

Scott   There's an operation under way Jamie. They wouldn't be doing anything unless they thought the three of them were alive.

Jamie   You're good mates. He deserves better than this.

Scott   Fuck this. I'm gone.

He goes to leave; he's on crutches.

Jamie   That's nice. Turn your back. You're good at that. Don't wanna be seen upsetting your superiors.

Scott (*pulling a twenty-pound note out of his wallet*)   Get yourself fed and go home. Let the big boys do their job.

Jamie   I don't need your money.

Scott   Andy knew what he was getting himself into.

Jamie   It's like he's being erased.

Scott   They're trying to find him. But the world's not going to stop turning. People turn on the telly for diamond-fucking-jubilees. Not soldiers scraping about in some desert hole.

Jamie   . . .

Scott   I know you don't believe me but I am sorry. You gonna be alright?

Jamie   . . .

Scott   Jamie?

Jamie   . . .

Scott   Take this . . .

He takes off his hoodie and gives it to **Jamie**.

Scott   You look a state. I'll leave the money there. Do what you want with it. But take it.

He throws some money on the table.

Take care of yourself.

He exits.

Jamie *stares at the photo.*

Neil *enters and watches.*

Jamie   Take care of yourself.

He tweets the photo.

2015.

Tweeter 6   Have you seen this?

Tweeter 4   Just came up on my feed.

Tweeter 6   Where's it from?

Tweeter 5   Is that who I think it is?

Tweeter 2   Looks like –

Tweeter 3   Who's he with?

Tweeter 2   OMG.

Tweeter 6   Retweet –

Tweeter 5   Retweet –

Tweeter 4   Favourite –

Tweeter 2   Retwee –

Neil   Stop. You see this. Here. This is where it starts to unravel. Jamie Glover, phone in hand, tweets a photograph and –

Tweeter 5   Too long.

Tweeter 6   Word limit reached.

Tweeters 5 & 6   A hundred and forty characters.

Neil   I'm trying to explain. If you'd let me –

Tweeter 2   You could have ignored it.

Tweeter 4   You didn't have to shine a spotlight on it.

Tweeter 2   Tell us, then –

Tweeters 2, 4 & 6   Tell us what happened next.

Tweeter 2   The full story.

Tweeter 3   Hashtag false promises.

Tweeter 5   Context –

Tweeter 3   Truth –

Tweeter 4   Report the event.

Tweeter 6   Tell it straight –

Tweeter 7   Hashtag –

Tweeter 2   Last chance.

Tweeters   Tell us!

Scene Nine

16:30, Friday 27 July 2012. The newsroom at NSC News, London.

and

05:32, Friday 27 December 1968. The cabin of a British Overseas Airways plane, somewhere over Germany.

Neil *(editor)*, **Julie** *(director)*, **Melissa** *(anchor)* and **Amy** *(online editor) gather for a meeting.*

Neil   Sky, the Beeb, CNN, they're all leading with the opening ceremony.

Amy   The Beeb are monopolizing the coverage. We can't compete with that.

Melissa   It's the Olympic Games . . .

Gavin *(researcher) enters with coffees.*

Gavin   Have you seen that billboard of Jessica Ennis? It's fucking massive.

Neil   Nice of you to join us.

Julie   Are we leading with it or not, Neil?

Neil   We're leading with it. Of course we're leading with it. I'm just not willing to regurgitate what the Beeb have been saying since nine o'clock this morning.

Julie   So what are we doing?

Amy   I still say we go with Afghanistan.

Neil   We're not leading with bloody Afghanistan.

Amy   Why not?

Neil   There are no new developments.

Amy   We've got the names of two of the missing soldiers.

Neil   They were released this morning.

Amy   So?

Neil   It's been on the website all day.

Amy   Well, exactly. There's a lot of public interest. And it's all over Twitter.

Neil   I'm sorry, Amy. It's not happening.

Julie   What's our peg for the Olympics?

Melissa   'Excitement builds with just hours until the Games get under way.'

Neil   That's it?

Melissa   Yeah.

Neil   That's our peg?

Melissa   Yes.

Neil   'Excitement builds'?

Melissa   Yes, Neil.

Neil   We're not using that.

Melissa   Why not?

Neil   We need another angle on it.

Melissa   Well, what else is there to say?

Neil   You tell me.

Melissa   The public are excited.

Neil   But they don't want to be told how excited they are. They know how excited they are. Everyone's been telling them how excited they are for the last six months.

Gavin   We're getting the VT from the team on the ground in the next half hour.

Julie   We can't wait that long.

Neil   Have we sifted through the footage from the end of the torch relay?

Melissa   Most of it, yeah.

Neil   And?

Melissa   Largely uneventful. Matthew Pinsent lit the cauldron on the Royal Barge. Jeremy Hunt nearly hit someone with a bell.

Gavin   Why don't we use that?

Julie   What are we doing, then? We're live in an hour and a half and we don't have a lead story, Neil . . .

Neil   Yes, I'm aware of that, Julie. Does anyone have something?

Amy   What about the details of the ceremony?

Neil   We don't know the details.

Amy   We could find out? Talk to some of the volunteers.

Neil   They won't talk.

Gavin   I was thinking we could look at the environmental sustainability and legacy policy of the games?

Neil   The environmental, what now?

Gavin   The Olympic Park was designed to incorporate forty-five hectares of wildlife habitat, five hundred and twenty-five bird boxes and one hundred and fifty bat boxes. Local waterways and riverbanks have been enhanced. Not to mention –

Neil   I'm gonna stop you there, Gavin.

Melissa   What about the financial angle?

Neil   That's hardly exciting either is it?

Melissa   The original budget for the games was two point four billion. That's increased fourfold to about nine point three billion.

Neil   It's all a bit negative.

Gavin   Well, maybe that's our angle?

Neil   What, negativity?

Gavin   Well, look, all the noises from the government suggest that the games are going to be a rip-roaring success. There's every chance they won't be.

Neil   On what basis?

Gavin   Heathrow will be running way over capacity. So will London Underground.

Neil   It's not really a story though is it, Gavin?

Amy   What about security concerns? Three thousand seven hundred British soldiers across London. Surface-to-air missiles on rooftops. An aircraft carrier on the Thames.

Gavin   What about this? Despite the heightened security, an eleven-year-old was still able to board a flight from Rome to Manchester yesterday without a passport or boarding pass.

Neil   Okay . . .

Gavin   Okay, so the kid didn't have a passport, didn't have a ticket, didn't have a boarding pass, but was able to get all the way from Italy to one of Britain's largest airports, no questions asked.

Neil   That's more like it.

Julie   What's the peg?

Melissa   Embarrassing breach of security days before the start of London 2012.

Neil   That's it. That's our story. Didn't think to mention that before, Gavin?

Julie   Polish the copy and send it downstairs in the next ten minutes.

Gavin   I'm on it.

Neil   Can set up a two-way with someone from the airline?

Julie   We're cutting it a bit fine.

Neil   Or even a statement?

Gavin   There's one on the Jet2 website.

Amy   I'll have a look.

Julie   What's next then?

Melissa   We could do Halfords.

Neil   Halfords?

Melissa   I've got a forty-five-second piece contextualizing the economic downturn. Then we've got a three-minute VT from the team on the ground about the changing face of the high street.

Neil   We're not running that second.

Melissa   Why not?

Neil   People aren't going to want to sit and listen to a five-minute lecture on the economy while they're trying to eat their dinner. What else have we got?

Amy   What about Neil Heywood?

Neil   Yeah, alright, bump that up.

Julie   How long are we giving it? Two and a half?

Neil   Give it three minutes.

Julie   So a minute and a half lead-in?

Neil   Yeah, this happened back in April so we need to contextualize it.

Julie   That leaves us with a minute and a half for the piece itself.

Neil   Perfect.

Julie   Then Halfords?

Neil   Yeah, that works better.

Melissa   How long does that give us?

Julie   No more than three minutes.

Melissa   The VT's three minutes on its own.

Neil   Better get cutting then.

Julie   Then we're into the ad break.

Gavin   Facebook shares?

Neil   We can't do back-to-back financial stories, we'll lose them.

Julie   What about one of the international stories?

Melissa   So Vietnam landslide or Congo civil unrest?

Julie   We've got time to do both.

Neil   How many dead?

Gavin   Where?

Neil   Vietnam.

Gavin   Sixteen.

Melissa   No Brits.

Neil   Okay. Congo first, then Vietnam.

Amy   And then Afghanistan?

Julie   We've got time for a thirty-second update at the end.

Amy   Thirty seconds?

Neil   I'm sorry, Amy.

Amy   Three British Soldiers could be dead.

Neil   If we get any new information before the broadcast we'll bump it up. Until then, it's staying where it is.

Amy   I'm sorry, I disagree.

Neil   Okay, let's talk about this, then . . . What do we know?

Amy   There's been a major attack against ground forces in Afghanistan.

Gavin   Three soldiers from the Third Battalion Grenadier Guards are still unaccounted for.

Amy   They've been missing for nearly forty-eight hours . . .

Neil   Which throws up any number of situations; but we just don't know.

Julie   The MoD released a statement last night confirming the names of two of the three soldiers but they're making no further comment until the rescue operation is complete.

Neil   Exactly. We've got nothing.

Amy   Take a look at this.

Neil, **Julie**, **Melissa** *and* **Gavin** *crowd around* **Amy***'s iPad.*

Neil   What is it?

Amy   Hang on . . . there.

Gavin   Is that the Prince?

Julie   Who's he with?

Amy   Lance Corporal Andy Glover, one of the two names released last night.

Neil   Where's it come from?

Amy   His little brother posted it on Twitter.

Neil   When?

Amy   Just now.

Neil   How's he got hold of a photo of his brother with the Prince?

Amy   The kid's saying the Prince is serving with his brother in Helmand and that he's one of the missing soldiers.

Neil   Is there any confirmation on Reuters?

Julie   No, nothing.

Amy   It's trending on Twitter.

Neil   Gavin, get the Royal Press Office on the line, we need to get this verified as quickly as possible.

Gavin   I'm on it.

Neil   And have a word with Marcus at the MoD if you can?

Amy   There's no time.

Neil   I'm not sending this out until it's verified, Amy.

Amy   Verified?

Neil   The fact that it's on Twitter isn't enough.

Amy   They're brothers, Neil. As far as I'm concerned he's a pretty reliable source.

Neil   We need double confirmation on this before it goes anywhere near the broadcast.

Julie   Neil . . .

Neil   What?

Julie   Sky News.

Neil   What are they saying?

Julie   'Unconfirmed reports have emerged suggesting the Royal Prince may be one of the missing soldiers in Kabul.'

Amy   See!

Neil   Where's this?

Julie   Twitter.

Neil   What's their source?

Julie   I don't know.

Neil   You don't know?

Julie   They must know something we don't.

Neil   Right, everyone, back to their desks, talk to anyone you can find. Amy, can you try and get through to our man at Camp Bastion? I want official verification on the location of the Prince. Where is he? When was the last confirmed sighting? Is he even in Afghanistan? (*To* **Melissa**.) I think if he were out there we would know.

Julie   ITN have put it on Twitter as well.

Neil   Are they aggregating?

Julie   Looks like it, yeah.

Neil   So where's it coming from?

Gavin   Still nothing from the press office.

Neil   What about the MoD? Are they saying anything? Or Reuters?

Melissa   No nothing.

Neil   The Beeb?

Julie   They're not running it either.

Neil   Can somebody please tell me where the fucking Prince is?

Amy   The last confirmed sighting of the Royal Prince was at a public engagement in May.

Neil   Two months ago?

Amy   According to military sources, the Third Battalion have only been deployed for six weeks.

Neil   Jesus.

Amy   It all fits.

Neil   Yes, I can see that.

Amy   It's him.

Melissa   It could be anyone.

Julie   It's your call, Neil.

Amy   What are we waiting for?

Neil   We don't know anything until we get official verification.

Amy   If we don't broadcast it right now people will go elsewhere for this story.

Neil   I don't care. We're not putting it on air without verification from at least one reputable source.

Amy   Come on, Neil.

Neil   No. We'll go ahead when it's verified.

Amy   We can't wait that long.

Neil   There are lives at stake, Amy.

Amy   But –

Neil   We're following procedure.

Julie   Neil . . .

Neil   What?

Julie   It's us.

Neil   What do you mean 'it's us'?

Julie   We're the source. 'NSC News are reporting that the Royal Prince may be one of the missing soldiers in Kabul.'

Beat.

Neil   Amy?

Amy   I put a breaking news feature on the website.

Neil   You did what?

Amy   I put it on the website.

Neil   Why did you do that?

Amy   It's trending on Twitter.

Neil   What's that got to do with it?

Amy   There was nothing on any of the other news websites.

Melissa   For good reason I imagine.

Neil   You can't just post something like this on our website.

Amy   Why not?

Neil   Because you're not Julian-pissing-Assange.

Amy   Or because you haven't got the balls to break a story?

Neil   I'm sorry?

Amy   The Royal Prince might be one of the missing soldiers!

Neil   Elvis Presley might have faked his own death but it doesn't make it true.

Amy   But what if it is true? News stories break on Twitter all the time –

Neil   I know how Twitter works.

Amy   Arab Spring, Neil. Twitter users around the Arab world –

Neil   Are you done? It's just I need to clear up this enormous mess you've started.

Julie   Neil –

Neil   Have you got it up now?

Amy   What?

Neil   The website.

Amy   What about it?

Neil   How have you phrased it?

Amy   Phrased what?

Neil   I presume you didn't just upload the photograph on its own. What have you captioned it with?

Melissa   'An image which appears to show the Royal Prince with missing soldier Lance Corporal Andy Glover has appeared on Twitter. Missing British soldier Lance Corporal Andy Glover with the Royal Prince. Brothers in arms.'

Neil   What about the live blog?

Julie   'Missing British soldier Lance Corporal Andy Glover with the Royal Prince. Brothers in arms.'

Neil   'Brothers in arms'? Are you fucking kidding me?

1968.

The plane shakes with turbulence.

Red   You okay?

Mary   Yes. Fine. You're so calm.

Red   This is my downtime.

Mary   Ha! Is it? This is my 'about to be sick in a bag time'.

Red   Ha.

Mary   Bet you're glad you got stuck sitting next to me.

Red   I've got a sense of humour.

Mary   Thanks.

2012.

Gavin   Shit.

Neil   What?

Gavin   They've issued a statement.

Neil   Who?

Gavin   The royal press office.

Julie   On their website.

Neil   Saying?

Gavin   It's quite long . . .

Neil   Get on with it, then!

Gavin   'At the Queen's request, the following statement has been issued by the press secretary.'

Neil   Yeah, yeah, whatever . . .

Gavin   'It is with great regret that the Palace must confirm that the Royal Prince has been forced to return early from a six-month deployment in Afghanistan, where he has been serving with the Third Battalion Grenadier Guards.'

Neil   So he is out there.

Gavin   'Contrary to reports from NSC News, the Palace can confirm that the Royal Prince is safe and unharmed but – for the safety of the regiment – will be flown home immediately.'

Amy   Fuck.

Neil   Yeah, just a bit.

1968.

The plane shakes with turbulence.

2012.

Julie   We need to get the Palace back onside.

Neil   And how do you suppose we do that?

Julie   We could update the website for a start.

Neil   And say what? We're really sorry but one of our senior reporters was fucking gullible enough to believe a tweet from a sixteen-year-old boy?

Julie   We need to say something.

Gavin   I've got CNN, Al-Jazeera and ITN all on hold.

Neil   Just hang up.

Melissa   The Beeb are airing the Palace's statement. They're having a field day.

Gavin   It's for you, Neil . . .

Neil   I told you to hang up.

Gavin   It's upstairs.

Neil   What?

Gavin *hands the phone to* **Neil**.

Neil *exits.*

Melissa   Nice one, Amy.

Amy   Oh, fuck off.

Melissa   What did you think you'd achieve exactly?

Amy   Fuck off.

Melissa   Did you actually think you of all people would be the one to source a story of that magnitude?

Amy   I did source it.

Melissa   But you were wrong.

Amy   Still sourced it.

Melissa   You clicked copy and paste, Amy, anyone can do that.

Amy   What, like reading off an autocue?

Julie   That's enough.

Neil *enters.*

Neil   Kill it.

Julie   What?

Neil   Delete the content from the website. Bump the Olympics story back up.

Julie   What did they say, Neil?

Neil   We broke an MoD embargo on the Prince's whereabouts. Delete it from the live blog, Twitter, everywhere.

Melissa   Or you could just sack Amy.

Amy   What?

Melissa   She posted it. She should be held responsible.

Amy   Oh come on, it was just an image.

Neil   No, Amy, you posted a completely unverified photo. I'd say that's a pretty sackable offence, wouldn't you?

Amy   You can't just sack me.

Beat.

Please don't sack me.

Neil   I want you to resign.

Amy   Resign?

Neil   Somebody's got to own up to this mess.

Amy   It wasn't just me.

Neil   Who uploaded the photo?

Amy   I did.

Neil   Who posted it on the website?

Amy   Well, yeah –

Neil   There we go, then.

Amy   But –

Neil   No buts, Amy.

Julie   If she goes, you'd have to go too.

Neil   What?

Julie   Neil this has happened under your watch.

1968.

The plane shakes with turbulence; **Mary** *holds onto her seat.*

Red   Are you sure you're okay?

Mary   Yes. I'm fine. You 'calculate your risks'.

Red   I'm not a mathematician.

Mary   An economist then?

Red   God no. I don't trust economists. They were created to make weather forecasters look good.

Mary   Not a mathematician. Not an economist. Sort of – but not really – a young entrepreneur. What would you call yourself?

Red   I'm a storyteller.

2012.

Gavin   Why don't we make an apology?

Neil   An apology?

Amy   That would just draw even more attention to ourselves –

Julie   Well, we've made a mistake –

Neil   We haven't done anything.

Amy   Let's think of this as any other news story. Take tonight, for example. The Olympic Games. What's our peg again?

Gavin   The boy. The other boy. The eleven-year-old from Italy.

Amy   Our angle is security concerns, yeah? But we could just as easily have focused on public excitement, or public spending, or David Beckham.

Neil   Amy, we haven't got time for this.

Amy   I just think we're shooting ourselves in the foot. Everyone's looking at us so why don't we make them look elsewhere?

Neil   It's a big fuck-up, Amy. People aren't going to forget all about it just because of the Olympics.

Amy   Not the Olympics. The kid.

Neil   Who?

Amy   Jamie Glover. The brother of the missing soldier.

Neil   What about him?

Amy   Make him our story.

Neil   What?

Amy   Well, why not? He's the one who uploaded the photograph.

Neil   He's sixteen years old!

Amy If he was our peg how would we play it?

Julie Well, we wouldn't mention the ongoing operation in Afghanistan for a start.

Gavin Or the Prince.

Julie Or the statement from the Palace.

Amy Exactly. We don't mention any of that. We just talk about him.

Neil And say what?

Amy 'Sixteen-year-old Jamie Glover from Hertfordshire found himself at the centre' –

Neil How do you know that?

Amy Know what?

Neil Where he's from.

Amy It's on his Facebook profile. 'About me'.

Neil You found him on Facebook?

Amy There was a link on his Twitter.

Gavin Were there any pictures?

Amy I didn't look.

Gavin Can you link me?

1968.

Mary A storyteller who doesn't want to share his own story.

Beat.

You, sir, are an oxymoron.

Red I tell other people's stories.

Mary Are you a journalist!?

Red No.

Mary Tell me!

Red No. I'm not. Not so keen on the papers are you?

Mary No. I'm not.

Red A story told well can tell you more about the world than any fact or figure. It can capture the imagination.

Mary . . .

Red We're on a plane flying at 35,000 feet and we're not asking what's going on in the cockpit. Why would we? We're not dropping out the sky. We're cruising and all appears to be fine. You listen to that stewardess's announcement and you do what you're told. You buckle up, sit back and enjoy the ride. But what happens if this plane starts falling? 35,000 feet and suddenly, boom, you're hurtling towards the ground.

2012.

Gavin   If we want to run with this we need images for the package.

Amy   We'll need to avoid using the photo he posted on Twitter.

Neil   Sorry, but what is going on?

Julie   We don't want any more trouble with the Palace.

Gavin   What about of him and his brother?

Julie   We can't use any of his brother.

Amy   Why not?

Julie   We'd be drawing even more attention to the rescue operation.

Amy   And away from us.

Julie   It's hardly going to get the MoD back onside though is it?

Amy   Then we don't mention his brother.

Melissa   If we're not mentioning his brother, what's the point?

Amy   What do you mean?

Melissa   Why do you think he posted it in the first place?

Amy   Because he's an attention-seeking little shit probably.

Neil   Because he wants information.

Gavin   Information?

Amy   About what?

Neil   About his brother.

Amy   Then we give him information.

Neil   We don't have any.

Amy   He doesn't know that.

Neil   Lie to him?

Amy   He lied to us.

Gavin   We still need a sound bite. A statement from the kid. Otherwise we don't have a story.

1968.

Red   Thirty thousand feet. There's a pilot in that cockpit you're losing faith in. No one in the cabin knows what's ahead and you're beginning to think the pilot doesn't know either. Twenty thousand feet. This pilot is out of ideas. He's spent. The engines are down and you're holding on for dear life.

2012.

Amy   We can Facebook message him.

Neil   Facebook message him?

Amy   How else are we going to contact him?

Neil   No.

Amy   Why not?

Neil   We're not using a Facebook message as a fucking soundbite.

Gavin   We could add him as a friend.

Neil   We're not adding him as a friend.

Amy   That would allow us to talk to him more freely.

Neil   Talk to him how?

Amy   We can get his contact details. A phone number. We can draw up a list of questions. Record the call. There's our soundbite.

Beat.

Neil   We'd need his permission.

Amy   We'll get his permission.

Neil   How long have we got?

Julie   Just over an hour.

Neil   How long's all this going to take?

Amy   Five minutes?

Neil   Realistically.

Amy   Depends if he's online.

Neil   Okay, providing he's online, how long will it take to edit the material from the phone call?

Gavin   Fifteen, twenty minutes?

Julie   We don't have time, Neil. We still need to edit the VT for the Olympic story, set up the two-way, write the copy –

Amy   Why don't we set up a two-way with the kid?

Gavin   We need something from the horse's mouth otherwise we haven't got a story.

Neil   There's too many variables. Besides we wouldn't have time to get a team out to him and set up before the broadcast.

Amy   Then why don't we get him in?

1968.

Red   Ten thousand feet. It's time to take action. You charge down to the cockpit, tear the pilot off the controls and yell, 'Who can fly this bloody plane?' Everyone in the cabin is shouting and panicking when, all of a sudden, someone right up at the back stands up and says, 'I've got an idea. If you let me at those controls I'll give it a shot.'

2012.

Neil   What do you mean 'get him in'?

Amy   Get him to come here and do it on air.

Neil   Do what on air?

Melissa   I'll interview him.

Amy   Yes!

Melissa   I could interview him.

Amy   She can do it on air. Get him to fess up.

Neil   It's not a question of fessing up, Amy.

Amy   No.

Neil   He hasn't done anything wrong.

Amy   Well, no –

Melissa   But we could talk to him.

Neil   And say what?

Amy   Find out why he did it.

Neil   We know why he did it.

Amy   Well, exactly, he wants someone to listen to him.

Melissa   We can get him onside.

Amy   We'll do it all by the book.

Melissa   Draw up a list of questions.

Gavin   Pre-approved questions.

Amy   We'll run it all by compliance.

Neil   Who are we meant to have in the chair tonight?

Julie   We can cancel it.

Neil   We can't force him to do this. He has to consent.

Amy   In an ideal world –

Melissa   In an ideal world we wouldn't have to do it at all but it is in the public interest to talk to this kid on tonight's broadcast. Everyone wants to hear from him.

Gavin   If it was anyone else, we'd get them in.

Melissa   It's also in his interest. He clearly wants the coverage.

1968.

Red   Five thousand feet and you're thinking, 'the pilot's out of options, let's give this guy a shot'.

2012.

Neil   Okay. No bullshit. How do we play this?

1968.

Red   In desperation you decide to put your faith in a man who says he has an 'idea'. That's it. Before you know it, he's walked down the aisle and shut the cockpit door behind him. Three thousand feet. Two thousand feet. One thousand feet.

2012.

Melissa   'Sixteen-year-old Jamie Glover from . . .'

Amy   Hertfordshire.

Melissa   '. . . from Hertfordshire found himself at the centre of an international controversy today after he posted a photograph of the Royal Prince on the social networking site Twitter.'

Amy   'Broadcasters were plunged into near meltdown, when news agencies struggled to verify an incendiary tweet.'

Melissa   'It has since been ascribed to Jamie Glover. We're joined by Jamie in the studio now.' Gavin, can you?

Gavin *sits down opposite* **Melissa** *and answers as* **Jamie**.

Gavin   Alright.

Melissa   Good evening, Jamie. Perhaps you could begin by telling us, and viewers at home, what it was you were attempting to achieve by tweeting this particular photo?

Gavin   It was my intention to raise the profile of my brother who is currently missing in Afghanistan. Feared dead actually. Do you happen to have any information about him?

Melissa   Did you have any notion of the attention your tweet would receive when you decided to share it?

Neil   Yeah, nice.

Gavin   No I didn't realize how –

Amy   Or is it simply the case that social media afforded you the opportunity to throw a spanner in the works from a safe distance?

Melissa   There's loads in that.

1968.

Red   Eight hundred, five hundred, three hundred feet, nothing's changing. But still we sit, and we wait, with blind faith. One hundred feet. Why have we stopped asking questions? Why does he get to sit up front with the door closed? He feeds us just enough information to keep himself at the controls and we don't question it.

2012.

Julie   It's your call, Neil.

Neil   How long have we got?

Julie   We're live in an hour.

1968.

Red   A story told well can tell you more about the world than any fact or figure. Stories capture the imagination. The storytellers are taking charge. We're gonna break down the door.

2012.

Neil   Okay, Melissa, cover the interview questions. Gavin, can you write the copy for the story itself?

Gavin   Are we still running the Olympics story?

Neil   Bump it down to second. Julie, can you sort it? We need to polish the lead-in and check the VT. Amy contact the kid. Facebook message him. Whatever you have to do. I need him in my office, ready to be briefed in half an hour.

1968.

Red   The world is changing very fast. Big will not beat small anymore. It'll be the fast beating the slow.

The seat-belt sign pings on as the newsroom explodes into a frenzy of activity.

Tannoy   Ladies and gentlemen, the captain has switched on the seat-belt sign as we begin our descent into London Heathrow . . .

Mary   What brings you to London?

Red   The British people.

Mary   For a man who likes the sound of his own voice you don't give much away do you?

Red   Three questions. You've got three questions.

Mary   Where are you staying?

Red   The Savoy.

Mary   Do you have any plans Thursday evening?

Red   None.

Mary   Would you like a drink at eight?

Beat.

Red   Okay.

Mary   What are you doing in London?

Red *smiles.*

The plane lands.

Red   Taxi! Taxi!

A storm breaks.

Taxi!

He gets into a taxi.

Fleet Street.

Scene Ten

08:31, Friday 27 December 1968. Fleet Street, London.

The following has the physical and musical energy of a circus show; Creedence Clearwater Revival's 'Bad Moon Rising' plays.

Journalists   Mr Murdoch –

Journalist 1   Welcome to London, Mr Murdoch.

Journalist 4   How was the flight?

Journalist 3   Enjoying the weather?

Journalist 2   What you doing in London, Rupert?

Journalist 1   Are you here to take over the British press?

Red   Well –

Journalist 4   How's the empire in Australia?

Red   It's not quite an empire –

Journalists 1 & 3   Our press is working just fine.

Journalists   Why do we need you?

Red   I'm not saying it's broken, I'm saying it needs to be improved. We need to put some discipline into your industry.

Journalists 2 & 4   Give us a taste of what your *News of the World* would be.

Red   My paper will be more fair . . . more democratic than anything Britain has ever seen.

Journalists   Do you really think you've got what it takes?

A day passes.

Red *greets* **Drew** *on Fleet Street.*

Journalists –   Mr Murdoch –

Journalist 2   How was the first day?

Journalist 1   Did the panel seem receptive?

Journalists 4 & 2   How's the jetlag?

Journalist 3   Done any sightseeing, Mr Murdoch?

Journalists   What can you offer the people of Britain?

Red   I'm here with the money and the mind to make the *News of the World* valuable to the British public. If the press is powerful, it's good for everybody.

Journalist 1   If you win, what will be your first move?

Red   We'll discuss plans for the paper at my victory party on Friday night.

Journalists   Ha-ha-ha!

Journalists 3 & 2   Will you keep British staff?

Red   The essential values that Britain holds dear will not be forgotten. I have a great team of editors and journalists behind me.

Journalists   Mr Murdoch –

Red   I'll keep things as British as a beef roast with Yorkshire pudding.

A day passes.

Journalists   Mr Murdoch –

Journalist 4   Tomorrow's the big day.

Journalist 2   Nervous, Mr Murdoch?

Journalist 1   Do you think you can win the vote?

Journalist 4   What do you make of your rival?

Journalist 3   Mr Maxwell says you use 'the laws of the jungle'.

Journalists   We don't trust you.

Red   Look –

Journalists 1 & 2   You're a man who makes false promises aren't you, Mr Murdoch?

Red   Look –

Journalist 4   You've got the gift of the gab, Mr Murdoch, there's no denying that.

Journalist 2   We want facts.

Red   I'll double the *News of the World*'s circulation within the next two years. How's that? Look, facts are all well and good but what this industry needs is stories –

Journalist 1   Sleaze!

Journalist 4   If people want thrills, they can go to the picturehouse.

Red   Journalism isn't science; it's sport.

Journalists 1 & 2   Rubbish!

Journalist 4   So your *News of the World* will set out to agitate?

Red   I just don't believe that those in power should continue to mark their own homework.

Journalist 2   You'll make enemies.

Journalist 4   We don't want you here.

Journalist 3   Go home.

Journalist 1   You don't have the stomach for it –

Red   Well, we'll soon find out.

A day passes.

Mary   Did you think I wouldn't find out?

Red   Mary . . .

Mary   You thought I was some dumb blonde with an axe to grind you could lure onto your front page didn't you?

Red   I have no idea what –

Mary   Well you know what, Rupert . . . I'm smarter than you, I'm smarter than your bullshit –

Red   Look, you either get out now or I'm calling the front desk.

Mary   Oh, that would suit you wouldn't it? More scandal for your 'first edition'.

Red   What are you talking about, Mary?

Silence.

Mary   My story. That's what you're after isn't it?

Red   . . .

Mary   I saw your photo in the Standard. Heard that you're buying the *News of the World*.

Red   Bidding for it –

Mary   Bidding . . . buying . . . And you made that great speech on the plane about 'taking charge'. And I put two and two together . . .

Red   . . .

Mary   You really don't know do you?

Red   Know what?

Beat.

Mary   I have a 'history' with the press. To tell you the truth, I've been ridiculed for two years straight. All because I slept with a man with a big wallet and a membership at a very nice Westminster bar. When it came out, I was the easy target. I went to Hong Kong to escape from it so to meet you and discover that you're a . . . I just assumed . . .

Red   . . .

Mary   I'm sorry.

Mary *goes to leave.*

Red   Still fancy that drink?

Mary   . . .

Red   Come on. One drink never hurt anyone . . .

Mary   From experience, Mr Murdoch, that is completely untrue.

A day passes.

Red *wins the shareholder vote.*

A swanky Fleet Street bar.

Drew *reads from a copy of the* Daily Mail.

Drew   '. . . and earlier today secured the shareholder vote with his Aussie charm and "the laws of the jungle" according to opponent Robert Maxwell'.

Red   The sorest of losers.

Drew   'Murdoch didn't lower himself to Maxwell's poke, stating that he had simply made a "more fair and bona fide offer".' Nicely put, mate.

Red   Maybe I was too hard on him. I could have been more humble.

Drew   It's your victory.

Red   It's the people's victory, Drew. I truly believe that. We haven't just unlocked a door here, we've kicked the bloody thing down. We're changing things.

Drew   I'm proud to be alongside you, mate.

He raises his glass.

Here's to you, you bloody 'moth-eaten kangaroo'!

Red *and* **Drew** *cheers.*

Red   Listen, there's someone I want you to meet.

Drew   Yeah?

Red   We met on the flight over.

Drew   Right.

Red   She has a story.

Drew   You don't hang about.

Red   We need to make our mark early. Set our stall. This person. Her story. It's of particular interest to the British public and I know she's keen to tell it.

Drew   You thinking a feature?

Red   A series of interviews.

Drew   Right. You wanna give this girl a voice.

Red   We've got a point to make, Drew. I want to give this girl a megaphone.

Drew   Yes, sir.

Mary *enters.*

Drew *exits.*

Mary   Congratulations on the win.

Red   I have an offer for you.

Mary   Do you?

Red   You know why I came here –

Mary   I think so, though I'm not sure all these shareholders heard the same speech you gave me last night.

Red   Rome wasn't built in a day.

Mary   We're not in Italy, Mr Murdoch.

Red   I've come here to change things, yes, but you of all people should appreciate that.

Mary   How so?

Red   I've come to fight for you.

Mary   I can fight my own battles.

Red *hands* **Mary** *a note.*

Red   I want to buy your story.

Mary   You're in the news business, Mr Murdoch, and my story isn't new, it's already been told. At length.

Red   You were the victim of an inequitable case and the world needs to hear your side of the story.

Mary   . . .

Red   All I'm asking is that you consider my offer. Okay?

Mary *concedes.*

Red   Drew! Get yourself over here.

Mary *and* **Red** *down their drinks as the music swells and they dance.*

Scene Eleven

18:03, Friday 27 July 2012. NSC News, London.

An image release form sits on the desk.

Neil, **Amy** *and* **Jamie** *enter.*

Neil   Would you like something to drink?

Jamie   I'm not thirsty.

Neil   Well, I'm gasping. Amy, can you grab me a coffee? Black. Four sugars. You sure you don't . . .

Jamie   I don't drink coffee.

Neil   That's good. Good for you. Me? I go through the stuff like it's going out of fashion. Amy's got skinny latte pouring out of her ears. Bad for you really, but that's life, isn't it?

Jamie   Is it?

Amy   We have Fanta?

Jamie   Fanta?

Amy   Or there's Coke? Diet Coke? 7 Up, Dr Pepper –

Jamie   Tizer.

Amy   Tizer?

Neil   Tizer? Is that still a thing?

Jamie   I'll have one of those.

Amy   I don't think we do Tizer.

Jamie   Don't bother then.

Amy   We do the Fanta Fruit Twist Flavour?

Jamie   I said I'm alright.

Neil   I think we're done here, Amy.

Amy   Right.

She exits.

Thanks for coming in. Please, sit down.

Jamie   Is she your PA?

Neil   Amy? No. She's our Online Editor.

Jamie   Does she have to do whatever you say?

Neil   Within reason. Take a seat.

Jamie   If you told her to punch herself in the face, would she do it? I bet you could make her cry. If you really wanted to.

Neil   Possibly.

Jamie   I bet you could scream in her face and she'd just stand there cause you're the boss. Could you do that? Andy told me about a drill sergeant who made the lads scrub their teeth with boot brushes. He'd stand over them and watch until their gums went septic and started bleeding. One time this boy's tooth came loose and he accidently swallowed it. Shat out one of his molars a week later. Now he's got a gold filling instead. But that's life, isn't it?

Neil (*offering his hand*)   My name's Neil.

Jamie   Is this your office?

Beat.

Horrible. Feels like being inside a fish-tank. People looking in. Prying eyes. Not very . . .

Neil   . . . private?

Jamie   Yeah.

Neil   That's the general idea. Maximum transparency for enhanced efficiency. All the offices are like this now. Everyone keeps an eye on each other. It's supposed to drive up productivity.

Jamie (*gesturing to the form on the desk*)   Someone tried to make me sign that piece of paper on the way over here.

Neil   That'd be Gavin –

Jamie   I told him to fuck off and shove it up his ass. Said I'd stick a biro in his eye-socket.

Neil   Did you?

Jamie   I did, yeah. He was shocked.

Neil   Well, he would be. Bit of a delicate flower our Gavin. He can be a bit . . . Did he explain?

Jamie   Not really . . .

Neil   Right.

Jamie   He said some stuff. I could see his mouth moving. There were words coming out, but the truth is, I wasn't really listening.

Neil   I see.

Jamie   I do that sometimes. I have this fantastic social antennae for filtering out bullshit. So whenever anyone is talking bullshit, I just zone out. Switch off. Then, when they're done, I come back online.

Neil   That sounds incredibly useful.

Jamie   It is. You should try it.

Neil   I will. Thanks.

Jamie   So? Why am I here?

Neil   We need to discuss the recent circumstances.

Jamie   Has something happened to my brother?

Neil   There's been no further developments.

Jamie   I don't believe you.

Neil   We're not in the business of keeping secrets, Jamie.

Jamie   You know something.

Neil   We don't.

Jamie   You have reporters out there, they must know –

Neil   The fact is, we're in the dark. Now, I know that must be difficult to accept, I really do, but it's the truth.

Jamie   It's your job to bring it to light.

Neil   Our job is to report the news, not to make it. Right now, at this moment, there are professionals working around the clock to find Andrew. We have to rely on them to do their job.

Jamie   That's not good enough.

Neil   We can't start playing guessing games, Jamie. That's not how it works.

Jamie   So how does it work? Tell me, cos I'm fucked if I know.

Neil   We abide by the rules. We let the professionals do their job. We don't interfere. We don't speculate. We don't do anything that could make a bad situation even worse than it already is. Most of all, we don't throw a spanner in the works by circulating an incendiary photograph via Twitter.

Jamie   So this is my fault?

Neil   I understand that this is distressing –

Jamie   You don't even know him.

Neil   That doesn't mean –

Jamie   I saw your report. His face plastered all over the telly. What was it again? Honourable. Dedicated. Brave. A model soldier. Patronizing shit. Why do you do that? Build up a nice friendly picture, bit by bit, and hope people watching will care?

Neil   People do care.

Jamie   By the end of yesterday it was headlines about pensioners running marathons. That's how much people care.

Neil   Is that why you tweeted the photo? To make a point?

Jamie   Who gives a shit about a couple of dead squaddies?

Neil   Because you wanted to get people asking questions? Is that why?

Jamie   Except my brother isn't dead. He's alive. And you won't even talk about it.

Neil   Answer the question, Jamie.

Jamie   You forgot about him. I was just reminding you.

Neil   Look, I get it. I do. You're scared. I can see that. You feel desperate. Helpless. So, you see an opportunity and you take it. No one's going to stand here and point the finger. No one can blame you, in the circumstances. But surely, surely you can see that we're a little bit stuck here.

Jamie   How's that then?

Neil   The photo you tweeted.

Jamie   I didn't do nothing wrong.

Neil   That's debatable.

Jamie   Last time I checked it wasn't a crime to tweet a photo.

Neil   What you need to understand, Jamie, what you need to realize is that I'm just the messenger. Well, you shot the messenger. That's hardly fair now is it?

Jamie   Shouldn't there be someone else in here with me?

Neil   Did you know for certain the Prince was serving?

Jamie   What?

Neil   It's not a trick question, Jamie.

Jamie   I guessed.

Neil   A hunch?

Jamie   Sort of.

Neil   Pretty fucking good hunch. One in a million, if you ask me. And the photo?

Jamie   What about it?

Neil   Where did you get it?

Jamie   What do you want?

Neil   To give you an opportunity.

Jamie   What opportunity?

Neil   We're offering you the opportunity to make a statement. Live on air. On tonight's broadcast.

Jamie   Are you being serious?

Neil   Absolutely.

Jamie   What sort of statement?

Neil   That's entirely up to you, Jamie.

Jamie   So, what, you're just going to let me talk, on TV. I can literally go on TV and say anything I want?

Neil   Anything within reason. There will have to be some framework, some questions. You've seen how it works. But. Yes. That's exactly what we're offering.

Jamie   What's in it for you?

Neil   For us?

Jamie   I'm not a dickhead. There's no fucking way you'd just let me waltz onto TV unless you had something to gain from it. So? Come on. What is it?

Neil   We want you onside.

Jamie   . . . and?

Neil   And? That's it.

Beat.

Look at it this way. We reported your Twitter stunt. We turned a spotlight onto it. The fact is we fell for it. Hook, line and sinker. But you, you, you pressed the button, Jamie. Didn't you? Now, you have the opportunity to, yes, accept responsibility, but also to communicate. To say something. To participate. The viewers want to know. They want to know who this person is. That's you. So why not reveal yourself?

Jamie   And in return, you don't look like such a bunch of dickheads.

Neil   If you like.

Jamie   So this is damage control for you lot?

Neil   It's also a perfect opportunity for you to communicate nationwide. We're willing to give you that. A platform. We've arranged for you to go live on tonight's programme. You'll have five minutes. All you need to do is get up there, answer some questions, say your piece and then you can go home.

Jamie   But you can't actually make me do it. Can you?

Neil   That's true.

Jamie   I refuse.

He goes to leave.

Neil   Jamie, think about –

Jamie   Fuck it. Seriously. All you want is for me to jump through your little hoops so you can, what? Pat yourself on the back? Tell yourself you've done a good job? Hope the ratings improve? Fuck that. I'm not performing on your say-so.

He goes to leave.

Neil   That's your prerogative. But if you fail to see this as an opportunity, a platform to –

Jamie   Go fuck yourself!

He goes to leave.

Neil   We'll say that you declined our offer to make a statement on your brother's behalf. Is there any particular reason you'd like us to relay? No? Suit yourself. We'll say that you refused to comment. Perhaps refused is a bit strong? Declined? Yes, that's better. We'll say you declined to comment. You can go home. I really don't have all day, Jamie.

Jamie *sits.*

Neil   We'll brief you on the questions. There won't be any surprises. You're doing the right thing. I'm sure Andrew would agree.

Jamie   Don't fucking use his name.

Neil   Fair enough.

He slides the form to **Jamie**.

Jamie *signs the form.*

Amy *and* **Gavin** *enter.*

Neil   Amy'll brief you on the questions. Gavin'll escort you down to the studio shortly.

Scene Twelve

18:29, Friday 27 July 2012. The studio at NSC News, London.

Julie   Five minutes, everybody.

Neil   How're we doing?

Melissa   What is it we're dealing with here? Really?

Neil   We're dealing with a volatile sixteen-year-old whose brother is missing. That means kid gloves. Stick to the questions we've agreed.

Melissa   What's he like? Jamie?

Neil   He's smart. Melissa, don't overthink this. Just stay away from Afghanistan. Don't let him draw you into foreign affairs.

Melissa   Foreign affairs? He's sixteen! What if he, I don't know, kicks off or something? I'm not a bloody social worker, Neil.

Neil   I'll be listening from the gallery.

Melissa   I can feel a migraine coming on.

Neil   You'll do fine. You always do.

Melissa   Right.

Neil   Tell you what, we pull this off and I'll have a large Shiraz waiting for you afterwards.

Melissa   Yeah, yeah, all right.

Beat.

Go away.

Gavin *puts* **Jamie** *in a seat opposite* **Melissa**.

Gavin   Jamie, this is Melissa. She's going to ask you some questions. All you have to do is answer them.

Melissa   It's very straightforward.

Gavin   Ignore the cameras. All you need to think about is giving clear answers. You'll need to wear this microphone.

Jamie   . . .

Melissa & Gavin   Jamie?

Melissa   Is it okay if Gavin attaches the microphone?

Jamie   Fine.

Gavin *attaches a microphone to* **Jamie**.

Gavin   Do you have any questions before we begin?

Jamie   Can I go to the toilet?

Gavin   It's too late for that now.

Jamie   I'm bursting.

Gavin   There's not enough time.

Melissa   It's only five minutes, sweetheart. Do you think you can hold it in for five minutes?

Jamie   Fuck off!

Gallery.

Julie   Twenty seconds.

Studio.

Gavin   Let's just calm down, shall we? Jamie, you'll need to wait.

He heads to the gallery.

Gallery.

Julie   We're live in five . . . four . . . three . . . two . . .

Studio.

Melissa   Good evening and welcome to NSC Newhour. On tonight's programme . . . News of an embarrassing breach of security just hours before the start of London 2012. We've got the latest from China where Gu Kailai has been charged with the murder of British businessman Neil Heywood. / And with Halfords becoming the latest business to fall into administration, we ask what's next for the British high street?

Gallery.

Gavin *enters*.

Neil   How's it all looking down there?

Gavin   . . .

Neil   Gavin?

Gavin   Good. We're good.

Julie   Still no word from Amy?

Neil   Probably updating her Facebook.

Julie   Camera two.

Studio.

Melissa   But first, we turn our attention to NSC News itself. Broadcasters were plunged into near meltdown earlier today, when news agencies struggled to verify an incendiary tweet. The tweet appeared to show the Royal Prince with Lance Corporal Andy Glover . . .

Gallery.

Julie   Cue graphic.

Studio.

Melissa   . . . one of the three missing soldiers in Afghanistan. It has since been ascribed to Jamie Glover, brother of the missing soldier. Jamie joins us in the studio.

Gallery.

Julie   Camera three.

Studio.

Melissa   Good evening, Jamie.

Jamie   . . .

Melissa   It's good to finally have you with us.

Gallery.

Gavin   What's the matter with him?

Neil   Just nervous I expect.

Julie   Let's get a close-up of Jamie with camera four.

Neil   Melissa get straight into it.

Studio.

Melissa   Perhaps you could begin by telling us, and viewers at home, what it was you were attempting to achieve by tweeting this particular photo?

Jamie   . . .

Gallery.

Neil   He's totally frozen.

Julie   Cut to Melissa.

Neil   Go to the next question, Mel.

Studio.

Melissa   I appreciate that this must be a delicate subject for you at this time but did you have any notion of the attention your tweet would receive when you posted it?

Jamie   No. I mean. Yeah?

Gallery.

Julie   He's back in the room.

Neil   Okay, now focus on intentions.

Studio.

Melissa   To clarify did you anticipate this level of response to the photo?

Jamie   You mean did I think you lot would go mental?

Gallery.

Neil   Melissa, keep it simple. Ask him if he planned to cause a fuss.

Studio.

Melissa   Was it your intention to cause panic?

Jamie   No.

Melissa   But you accept that that is what happened as a result?

Jamie   That's your opinion.

Melissa   Well, that opinion happens to be shared by other broadcasters and the vast majority of our viewers.

Gallery.

Neil   That's good, Melissa. Keep pressing him.

Gavin   Is he okay?

Studio.

Jamie   Isn't that what you lot call supply and demand?

Melissa   I beg your pardon?

Gallery.

Julie   We're a minute in.

Studio.

Jamie   I only tweeted it. It was you lot who ran with it.

Melissa   Presumably, this is what you wanted? A platform to be –

Jamie   I never asked to be here.

Melissa   Or is it simply the case that social media afforded you the opportunity to throw a spanner in the works from a safe distance?

Jamie   What am I supposed to have done wrong?

Melissa   In choosing to tweet a photo of your brother with the Royal Prince you knowingly attempted to create widespread speculation and panic.

Jamie   That's not true –

Gallery.

Neil   Keep pressing, Mel.

Studio.

Melissa   You attempted to implicate a royal subject in a case of grave national concern, a case I might add that was at risk of being further destabilized by your actions.

Gallery.

Julie   Melissa, put the brakes on.

Amy *bursts in.*

Neil   Where have you been?

Amy   There's a problem.

Neil   What is it?

Amy   There are reports of casualties in Afghanistan. It's the rescue operation. It's just broken.

Studio.

Jamie   So a prince's life is more important than my brother's?

Melissa   That's not at all what I was implying –

Jamie   Not quite as exciting is it? Squaddie's getting shot, trying to stay alive. A few of 'em go missing and the first thing you think about is how to sex it up. Otherwise, you don't give a shit.

Gallery.

Gavin   The rescue team moved early.

Amy   The *Guardian* live blog are reporting a botched hostage rescue. Reuters says there's casualties.

Gavin   The Beeb are still quiet but it's only a matter of time.

Neil   What went wrong?

Studio.

Melissa   Let's try and stick to the topic at hand, shall we?

Jamie   What topic is that? Ignoring my brother or forcing me to apologize live on TV?

Melissa   No one is forcing you to . . . We're trying to establish –

Jamie   I need the toilet. Why won't you let me go to the toilet?

Gallery.

Julie   Neil . . .

Neil   Not now, Julie.

Julie   Melissa's in trouble.

Neil   So deal with it!

Julie   Melissa, you need to stall for time.

Neil   Talk to me, Amy.

Amy   Well, nothing's certain, so we can't confirm, but –

Neil   Come on, Amy!

Amy   Initial reports involving the Royal Prince spooked the rescue team. They moved early and the insurgents responded in kind.

Studio.

Melissa   Why don't you tell us what it is you want from all this?

Jamie   Are you even listening to me? I want my brother back. I want to go the toilet. I want to go home.

Melissa   I understand but . . . Neil?

Gallery.

Julie   Neil?

Neil   I need more time.

Julie   Melissa, we're receiving reports about the rescue attempt in Afghanistan. Throw to the VT.

Studio.

Melissa   Let's take a quick break before we come back to you, then, Jamie and look at the day's events in this report from our online correspondent, Martin Donahue.

Gallery.

Julie   Thirty seconds.

Studio.

Melissa   Can someone tell me what the fuck is going on?

Gallery.

Julie   We don't know, Mel.

Gavin   We need to get him off the air.

Neil   Not yet.

Studio.

Jamie   Do you know something about my brother?

Melissa   We're back on air in twenty seconds, Jamie. Just stay with us a few more minutes.

Gallery.

Neil   Have the casualties been confirmed by the MoD?

Studio.

Melissa   We've got a few technical issues.

Jamie   You mean voices in your head?

Gallery.

Amy   No word yet.

Gavin   I think we should take them off air.

Neil   No one do anything.

Julie   Fifteen seconds.

Gavin   Fuck this.

He pulls his headset off and exits.

Neil   Gavin!

Amy   I'm getting confirmation.

Studio.

Melissa   We'll be back on air momentarily.

Jamie   We'll be back on air momentarily.

Melissa   That doesn't help matters.

Jamie   That doesn't help matters.

Melissa   Stop it.

Jamie   Stop it.

Gallery.

Amy   'Three soldiers are confirmed dead in a failed rescue attempt in Helmand Province.'

Neil   Do we know for sure that it's the hostages?

Amy   It's confirmed, Neil.

Julie   Get him off air.

Studio/gallery.

Melissa   Can someone tell me what's going on?

Jamie   Can someone tell me what's going on?

Julie   Five seconds.

Amy   Andy Glover has been killed in action. All three soldiers are dead.

Julie   Four.

Melissa   All three soldiers are dead?

Julie   Three.

Jamie   All three soldiers are dead.

Julie   Two.

Melissa   Am I reporting it?

Julie   We're live.

Silence.

Gavin *enters the studio and stops.*

Silence.

Jamie *pisses himself.*

Silence.

Neil?

Amy   Neil?

Neil   . . .

Melissa   We apologize but we, er . . .

Jamie *cries.*

Melissa   We've just received some very sad news in the studio.

1969.

Red   Good evening, everyone. Some of you know me, others of you know of me, but all of you will be getting to know me very well.

2012.

Neil Throw to the break. Get her to say it's a technical problem.

Julie I don't think we can say that, Neil.

1969.

Red There were some shareholders in the room earlier this evening that weren't so keen on a foreigner taking over this paper. If there's anybody in this room who thinks they know how things are going to run around here. Leave now.

2012.

Neil Any better suggestions? Cut to the break.

1969.

Red If there's anybody here who sees this job as a stopgap and would rather be elsewhere. Leave now.

2012.

Neil Cue us out.

1969.

Red If anybody has a problem with either of my last two statements. Leave now.

2012.

Melissa We have just received confirmation that the three missing soldiers from the Third Battalion Grenadier Guards have been killed in action following a botched rescue attempt in Helmand Province. BBC News has named the soldiers as . . . as Corporal Mark Williams, Officer Alex Astin and Lance Corporal Andy Glover. Their families have been informed.

Beat.

We'll take a break. We hope to return shortly with the latest from the Olympic Park.

Amy Julie?

Julie Roll VT.

1969.

Red I'm going to be making some changes around here and they're not all going to be comfortable. Particularly for those at the top. To our ministers, celebrities and high-flyers I say this . . .

You're not above us and you're not above the law. You are people. Just as fallible as the rest of us. Our business is the everyday man and they want their news fast. And they want it now. And they deserve it. We publish news for the British public. Mark this day. Because it's the start of a revolution.

The crowd cheers.

Epilogue

12:20, Tuesday 1 September 2015. A yacht moored at St Katharine's Docks, London.

Jamie *dries himself with a towel while* **Neil** *takes in the room.*

Jamie   Can I get you a drink? I'm having this tomato stuff.

Neil   One of those for me is fine.

Jamie   I've got to work later but you could have a drink?

Neil   I'm fine. Nice place.

Jamie   Thanks. You sure you don't . . .?

Neil   Yeah. I'm working too. Only got a half-day off.

Jamie   Kingsford Community College isn't it?

Neil   How do you –

Jamie   Facebook.

Neil   Right.

Beat.

Yeah, it's good. Never thought teaching was my thing but these kids . . . I don't know . . . it's amazing when you make a difference.

James *hands* **Neil** *a tomato juice.*

Jamie   Wish I'd had some decent teachers at my old school. They were more interested in fucking each other than teaching us. We had this deputy head teacher that'd fucked every PE teacher since 1973. We called her Deputy Head.

Beat.

Deputy *Head.*

He makes a gagging blowjob gesture as he says 'head'.

Anyway. It's been three years, Neil.

Neil   I know.

Jamie   And I guess, after seeing so much of each other, I miss you.

Neil   You miss me?

Jamie   Well, time passes and I've started to leave what happened that day behind me. I've started to understand the pressures of work. The pressures of our world. And I've started to . . . sympathize.

Neil   . . .

Jamie   You're only human.

Neil   Right . . .

Jamie   I'm glad you came.

He offers his glass to **Neil**.

Neil *and* **Jamie** *cheers.*

Jamie   Fucking hell, we couldn't have been stood here like this a little while back, could we? Apart from anything else it wouldn't have been legal, would it?

Neil   I don't know . . .

Jamie   My lawyer told me to stay well clear of you. He said any contact while the inquiry was going on would have been totally unacceptable to the Lord Justice. Would have weakened my case.

Neil   My lawyer said the same.

Jamie   Mind you, my case was backed up by a YouTube video with a hundred million hits worldwide. I still haven't been able to beat that by the way.

Neil   How is the blog?

Jamie   Blogosphere. It's called a blogosphere. A network of blogs that feed into one enterprise or come under one single umbrella. That's what we are now. And it's very lucrative. Thanks. Your friend Amy works for me. And the other one . . . argh . . . what's their name . . .?

Neil   Gavin?

Jamie   Melissa. Anyone can join in but your hits and previous posts determine your placement on the main page. And trends come into it of course. It's location and taste based, so the public get the news they give a shit about.

Neil   Simple.

Jamie   Beautiful.

Neil   Perhaps.

Jamie   No need for editors here, Neil.

Neil   You've given the public what they want.

Jamie   Yes I have.

Neil   But sometimes the public don't know what they need.

Jamie   You know best?

Neil   Henry Ford said, 'If I'd asked people what they wanted, they would have said faster horses'.

Jamie   You've got some nerve.

Beat.

Neil   Jamie, I'm not sure why I'm here.

Jamie   It's twelve-thirty . . .

He switches on the television and flicks to where the NSC News bulletin used to be; the theme tune for a hideous soap opera plays.

Oops. No more lunchtime bulletin.

He switches off the television.

Neil *goes to leave.*

Jamie   I wanted to see you, Neil. Because I wanted to tell you something I never got to tell you in that inquiry room. (*Whispering.*) Too many microphones.

You inspired me. Or rather that little film we made together did. I was an unwilling participant but your vision made me a box-office smash so . . . thank you.

Do you know more people watched that video of me finding out my brother's brain had been blown to pieces live on air than the sum of your programme's audience in 2012?

Neil   No I didn't.

Jamie   Can you believe that? I can. Because it was news happening right in front of them. Nobody cutting and shaping and deciding what's in and what's out. You pointed a camera at a war zone and you let it roll and people love that shit. It's *Big Brother*. *I'm A Celebrity*. It's fucking juicy shit going on right in front of you. For real. And – here's the reason I invited you over today – throughout our time together sitting in that inquiry room hearing witness after witness make their testimonies about how dreadful it is that you let a sixteen-year-old kid go through something like that on live national television, I never once heard you say that you regret your actions. So I was wondering if maybe you agree with my theory? People will always want what we gave them . . .

Neil   No.

Jamie   . . .

Neil   No, I don't agree. I knew we were heading into a storm the moment Amy published your tweet. And where we ended up – with you in that studio, Melissa asking you those questions completely unprepared – it goes against every reason I became a journalist. If you're asking me whether I regret what happened to you . . . Well, when I was sitting in front of the Lord Justice I was representing a broadcaster – an organization I was committed to – so 'no regrets'. But privately . . . Standing here . . . Of course I regret what happened. It was disgusting. And I'm ashamed. I think about it every day. And I'm sorry.

He reaches into his pocket and takes out his phone.

Jamie?

Jamie   Got this place fitted with a two-camera set-up. (*Pointing to the corners of the room.*) One there. One there. Both feeding via Bluetooth into my phone, which has a built-in microphone. You're about to go viral, Neil.

Neil   You filmed that?

Jamie   It's actually a live stream. Goes straight onto the blog.

Neil   . . .

Jamie   It's a good story, Neil.

Neil   It's not a story, Jamie. It's show and tell.

Jamie   And millions watch. Over eighty per cent of people under the age of thirty use my website as their primary news source. Three years ago eighty per cent of people under the age of thirty didn't even watch the fucking news so don't tell me how to do my job.

Neil   Ten thousand people died in a massacre in Sudan last week, it was placed seventieth on your website.

Jamie   Thanks for the hit.

Neil   You couldn't point to Sudan on a map.

Jamie   Try me.

Neil   You're simplifying the unsimplifiable.

Jamie   Hey – you said it, Neil – people are getting what they want. If enough people mention something, it trends, and it'll be right up there on the homepage. It's an information democracy –

Neil   And it's turning us into dunces.

Jamie   It's not my problem if half the population of this country don't know the capital of Switzerland, let alone fucking Sudan.

Neil   You're irresponsible.

Jamie   Pot. Kettle. Black. Cunt.

Silence.

I've got to go now. Don't know what plans you've got but I have a live blog to chair tonight. So yeah, would you mind –?

The **Tweeters** *enter.*

Tweeter 7   Do you feel like a big man?

Tweeter 6   Call yourself a journalist?

Tweeter 2   How much did they pay you?

Tweeter 7   Did it make you feel good?

Tweeters 4 & 5   You'll never live this down

Tweeter 3   How do you sleep at night?

Tweeter 6   Hashtag cringe –

Tweeter 5   Scum of the earth –

Tweeter 7   Watched it eighty, ninety times.

Tweeter 3   LOL.

Tweeter 3   It's disgusting –

Tweeter 6   Hashtag prick –

Tweeter 2   Cunt –

Tweeter 3   Monster –

Tweeters 4 & 5   P45 –

Tweeters   Most hated man in Britain.

Tweeter 2   Hashtag –

Tweeters   Justice for Jamie.

Blackout.

Molly

This play was first performed publicly at Pleasance Courtyard, Edinburgh in August 2015.

Created by Lee Anderson, Adam Foster and Andrew Whyment
Text by Lee Anderson, Adam Foster and Andrew Whyment

Molly | Lizzie Clarke
Actor 1/Mum/Miss Woods/Kim/Amy/Angela | Louise Roberts
Actor 2/Laura/Jessica | Fran Regis
Actor 3/Dad/Liam/Nathan/Duncan | Geoff Arnold
Actor 4/Kieran/Dan/James | Rhys Isaac-Jones

Director | Andrew Whyment
Writers | Lee Anderson, Adam Foster
Designer | Adrian Gee
Lighting Designer | Aaron J. Dootson
Composer | Rhys Lewis
Video Designer | Ash J. Woodward
Movement Director | Kane Husbands

Producers | Lucy Hollis, Ruth Milne
Assistant Producer | Fiona Steed
Production Manager | Jordan Whitwell
Stage Manager | Kirsten Buckmaster

Characters

Molly
Actor 1
Actor 2
Actor 3
Actor 4
Mum
Dad
Dan
Laura
Kieran
Liam
Miss Woods
Nathan
Kim
Jessica
Amy
Duncan
James
Angela

Notes

The action takes place in multiple locations from the day of **Molly***'s birth through to the day of her arrest at twenty-six years old.*

The design should embrace the non-literal and lean into the fact that **Molly***'s story is being presented as an investigative live performance. There should be a showbiz* **Molly** *sign and a clock displaying years, months, days, hours, minutes and seconds (YY:MM:DD:HH:MM:SS) at the rear of the space.*

The characters can be distributed amongst the cast in any way and genders can be changed but the actor playing **Molly** *should only play that role.*

Pre-Show

As the audience arrive, final preparations are being made for the show; the **Actors** *welcome the audience, warm up, get into costume and study scripts.*

Molly *enters, escorted by the* **Actors***; she wears prison clothes.*

Molly *(to the audience)*   Hello, hi. Thank you all so much for being here.

I see some familiar faces . . .

Laura . . .

She smiles at **Laura** *in the audience.*

Molly   They said I can make a statement so . . .

I'm not here to seek forgiveness. I won't be talking about recent events. I'm offering an honest account of my childhood in the hope that you'll glean some understanding of who I am.

She laughs.

I'm actually very nervous.

How do you sum up a life in sixty minutes?

I'm hoping we can find some answers and, with these people's help, we can discover what led to such tragic events so we can prevent more of the same.

She looks at **Actor 1** *for what happens next.*

Molly   That's it . . . Do I . . .?

The **Actors** *escort* **Molly** *to a costume rail where she gets changed.*

Actor 1   Standby everyone.

Molly *sits on a chair in the centre of the stage.*

Actor 3   Three, two, one . . .

Prologue

The clock lights up at 00:00:00:00:00:00.

Actor 1   Molly Chambers. Twenty-six years old.

The clock rewinds and lands at 26:00:01:00:04:31.

Actor 3   You were born in Bedford Hospital. A town in which you lived for eight years before you moved – with your mother – to Berkshire, where you spent the remainder of your childhood.

Molly   . . .

Actor 1   Well, that's where it all began –

Actor 3   And now you're here today.

Actor 1   But Molly –

Actor 4   Molly –

Actor 3   Molly.

Actor 1   Will you tell us –

Actor 4   Them –

Actor 3   All of us.

Actors   *Your story.*

Beat.

Molly   I need a drink.

Actor 4   Of course.

Actor 4 *fetches* **Molly** *a drink.*

Actor 3   They're here to help you.

Actor 2   We are too.

Actor 1   We want to know what made Molly, Molly . . .

Actor 3 *gestures and the clock starts ticking.*

Molly *is one minute old.*

The muffled sound of a hospital.

Actor 2   Where are we Molly?

Molly   Bedford Hospital.

The clock fast-forwards and lands.

Molly *is three years old.*

The sound of the sea.

Actor 2   And now?

Molly   Frinton Beach.

The clock fast-forwards and lands.

Molly *is five years old.*

The sound of a school playground.

Actor 2   And now?

Molly *(smiling)*   Nursery school.

The clock fast-forwards and lands.

Mum   Have you seen my jacket?

Dad   What jacket?

Mum   My blazer, my blazer jacket.

Dad   Why are you putting that on now?

Actor 2   And now?

Molly   Home.

Actor 1   How old are you Molly?

Molly   Twenty-six.

Actor 2 *hands* **Molly** *a teddy bear.*

Actor 1   How old were you nineteen years ago?

Molly   Seven.

Scene One

Molly *is seven years old. Home. Evening.*

Mum   She's running late.

Dad   What?

Mum   The babysitter. She's running late.

Dad   Well, we'll have to wait then won't we?

Mum   What do you mean wait?

Dad   Until she gets here . . .

Mum   I'll be late.

Dad   I know, darling, but –

Mum   I'm not turning up for this late.

Dad   You're nervous, I know you're nervous –

Mum   Have you seen my jacket?

Dad   What jacket?

Mum   My blazer, my blazer jacket.

Dad   Why are you putting that on now?

Mum   We need to go.

Dad   Shall I stay here then?

Mum   What?

Dad   I'll stay here and join you when Kirsty turns up.

Mum   Oh, that would suit you wouldn't it?

Dad   No I'm just saying –

Mum   You don't want to come.

Dad   I do want to come but –

Mum   How will I get there if you don't drive?

Dad   You could –

Mum   We're late. We're already late. We need to leave now.

Dad   But what about Molly?

Mum   . . .

Dad   Are we taking her with us?

Mum   We can't take her with us.

Dad   Well, we can't leave her here.

Mum   . . .

Dad   She's seven years old for God's sake!

Mum   . . .

Dad   No!

Mum   It's only half an hour . . .

Dad   I'm not leaving her here on her own!

Mum   Kirsty's on her way.

Dad   That's not happening. I'm sorry.

Mum (*to* **Molly**)   Shall we choose a book, Molly?

Dad   What are you doing?

Mum (*giving* **Molly** *a book*)   Read your book, Molly, there's a good girl –

Dad   What do you think you're doing?

Mum   I'm giving Molly her book to read.

Dad   No. This isn't happening. No.

Mum   Have you got any better ideas?

Dad   Why can't you just be half an hour late?

Mum   Because I'm addressing the shareholders at seven o'clock.

Dad   . . .

Mum   And it's important.

Dad   I know . . .

Mum   She'll be fine. She likes her own company.

Dad   . . .

Mum   You'll be fine won't you, Molly?

Molly *smiles.*

Mum   There's a good girl. If someone rings the doorbell you won't answer will you?

Molly *shakes her head.*

Mum   And what happens if someone rings the house phone?

Molly   . . .

Mum   You'll just ignore it won't you?

Molly *nods.*

Mum *looks at* **Dad**.

Dad   Just . . . Be good, okay, darling?

Mum   She'll be good as gold.

Dad   Okay.

Mum   Okay, have you got everything?

Dad   What?

Mum   Keys? Wallet?

Dad   Yes, yes.

Mum   Okay.

Mum *and* **Dad** *go to leave.*

Molly   Love you Mummy.

Mum *and* **Dad** *turn back to* **Molly**.

Mum   Be good.

Mum *and* **Dad** *exit.*

Actor 4   Mum and Dad went out one day,

Actor 2   And left young Molly alone at play;

An **Actor** *places a box of matches close to* **Molly**.

Actor 1   On the table close at hand,

Actor 3   A box of matches chanced to stand,

Actor 3   And kind Mamma and Pa had told her,

Actor 2   That if she touched them they would scold her;

Actor 4   But Molly said –

Molly   'Oh, what a pity! For, when they burn, it is so pretty;

Actor 3   They crackle so –

Actor 1   – and spit –

Actor 2   – and flame;

Actor 1   And Mamma often burns the same.

Molly   I'll just light a match or two as I have often seen my mother do.'

She strikes a match.

Actor 4   And all the world –

Actor 2   – they saw this,

Actor 3   They said –

Actors   'Oh, naughty, naughty miss!',

Actor 1   And stretched their claws,

Actor 2   And raised their hands;

Actors   'Tis very wrong, you understand',

Molly *raises the match.*

No. No.

Actor 4   You will burn if you do so.

Molly *blows out the match.*

The clock fast-forwards and lands.

Scene Two

One year later. **Molly** *is eight years old. A school playground.*

Molly *and* **Dan** *are swinging a skipping rope for* **Laura**.

Molly & Dan   Apples, peaches, pears and plums

Tell me when your birthday comes.

Laura   January, February, March, April, May, June, July –

She jumps out the rope.

Molly *and* **Dan** *cheer.*

Kieran   Right, who's next then?

Molly   Can I have a go?

Kieran   Anyone?

Molly   Yeah, me!

Kieran   No? Oh well. Do you want another go, Laura?

Molly   Can I have a go?

Kieran   It's Laura's turn. Laura's having a go now.

Molly   But that's not fair, she's already had a go.

Kieran   It's my game.

Molly   But it's my birthday . . .

Beat.

Kieran   Well, if we'd known that!

Kieran & Laura   Happy birthday, Molly!

Kieran (*singing*)   Happy birthday to you, / stick your head down the loo!

Laura   Stick your head down the loo!

Kieran   Well, birthday girl . . . ready when you are.

Molly *steps onto the rope.*

Kieran   Ready?

Dan & Laura   Apples, peaches, pears and plums

Tell me when your birthday comes.

Molly   Janu –

Dan *and* **Laura** *stop swinging the rope.*

Kieran   Oh, silly Molly.

Laura   Your birthday's not in January!

Kieran   Sorry, my fault.

Laura   His fault.

Kieran   Accident.

Laura   Just a bit of an accident.

Kieran   Shall we try again?

Laura   Let's try again.

Molly *steps onto the rope.*

Dan & Laura   Apples, peaches, pears and plums

Tell me when your birthday comes.

Molly   January, February, Mar –

Dan *and* **Laura** *stop swinging the rope.*

Kieran   Joking!

Molly   Stop doing that!

Kieran   We're just joking.

Laura   Stop doing that now, you're winding her up.

Kerian   Okay I will, I'll stop. Ready?

Molly *steps onto the rope.*

Dan & Laura   Apples, peaches, pears and plums

Tell me when your birthday comes.

Molly   January, February, Mar –

Dan *and* **Laura** *stop swinging the rope.*

Kieran *laughs hysterically.*

Molly *takes out a pair of scissors and cuts the rope.*

Kieran   What did you –? I'm telling!

The clock fast-forwards and lands.

Scene Three

One year later. **Molly** *is nine years old. A clothes shop.*

Molly *is holding a bracelet as* **Liam** *approaches.*

Liam   You're going to pay for that I hope?

Molly   I'm here about the job.

Liam   I'm sorry?

Molly   My name is Molly. I'm looking for a job.

Liam   What?

Molly   You do have a job going at the moment don't you?

Liam   I don't think so . . .

Molly   There's a sign.

Liam   Is there?

Molly (*pointing*)   Out there. In the window. I saw a sign.

Liam *looks and* **Molly** *pockets the bracelet.*

Liam   Right. Okay. I wasn't aware of that. Shouldn't you be at school?

Molly   I don't go to school.

Liam   You don't go to school?

Molly   I'm home schooled.

Liam   Why are you in school uniform then?

Molly   My parents make me wear it.

Liam   Right.

Beat.

Are your parents here?

Molly   What?

Liam   Your parents. Are they with you or –

Molly   No, they're at work. Well my mum is. My daddy's away. He's in the navy.

Liam   How old are you?

Molly   What?

Liam   It's a simple question.

Molly   Nine.

Liam   Nine?

Molly   Yes.

Liam   You're nine years old?

Molly *smiles.*

(*Shouting off.*) Is this a joke, Sinead? This is a joke, right? Hidden camera show or something?

Molly   It's not a joke.

Liam   What are you doing here on your own then?

Molly   The job, I told you.

Liam   But you're nine . . .

Molly   Yeah.

Liam   What's wrong with you?

Molly   Thought it might be fun.

Beat.

So when can I start?

Liam   Start what?

Molly   The job.

Liam   I'm afraid that's not really how it works.

Molly   Isn't it?

Liam   Well, no, we can't just give you the job.

Molly   Why not?

Liam   Because you're a snotty little brat that's why.

Molly   How does it work then?

Liam   Well, first of all you'd need to send in a CV.

Molly   What's that?

Liam   It's like a record of all your previous employment.

Molly   I haven't had a job before.

Liam   Okay, so then you'd have to just – I don't know – put down what qualifications you have.

Molly   I'm nine years old . . .

Liam   Can you see why we might struggle to employ you? If you don't have any qualifications or previous experience?

Molly   I'm a fast learner.

Liam   I'm sure.

Molly   I know all my times tables.

Liam   Look, it's great that you're so keen to get a job. I mean, good for you. Really.

Beat.

Look, why don't I have a word with my supervisor? You could give us a hand with the stock or something?

Molly   Okay.

Liam   Yeah?

Molly   Yeah. Okay.

Liam   I'll be back in a minute, alright? Wait there.

Molly *takes the bracelet out, puts it on and admires it.*

The clock fast-forwards and lands.

Scene Four

One year later. **Molly** *is ten years old. A school playground.*

Molly *and* **Laura** *stand at their makeshift stall.*

Kieran *enters.*

Kieran   Can I get two packets of the Magic Stars please?

Molly   That'll be one pound please.

Kieran   A pound?

Laura   Yep.

Kieran   Thought they were forty p?

Laura & Molly   They've gone up.

Kieran   But I – I haven't got enough then.

Laura   Sorry.

Kieran   Can I pay you tomorrow? Left my wallet at home, didn't I?

Laura   Mr Forgetful.

Kieran   Promise I'll bring it in tomorrow.

Laura   You better.

Kieran   I will. I promise.

Laura   It's fine. I'm joking. Don't worry about it.

Kieran   You're a star. A magic star.

Laura   I know.

Kieran   I know you know.

The school bell rings.

I'm gonna go now. See you later, yeah?

Laura   Yeah, see you Kieran!

Kieran *exits.*

Laura   Great sale!

Molly   What did you just do?

Laura   Two packets!

Molly   How does it work when you go to a shop?

Laura   How does what work?

Molly   When you go to a shop, what happens?

Laura   What do you mean?

Molly   You go into the shop . . .

Laura   Yeah . . .

Molly   .. wanting something . . .

Laura   Yeah . . .

Molly   .. and you come out . . .

Laura   .. you come out . . .

Molly   .. with that something?

Laura   Yeah. Exactly.

Molly   So you . . .

Laura   You . . .

Molly   How do you get that something?

Laura   You . . . buy it?

Molly   Yes!

Laura   You pay for it.

Molly   There we go.

Laura   You go in with some money and you pay for it.

Molly   So where's the money?

Laura   What money?

Molly   You gave Kieran some sweets . . .

Laura   Two packets!

Molly   So where's the money?

Laura   He'll bring it in –

Molly   Thanks for your help, Laura.

Laura   Um, you're welcome?

Molly   It's been great but this isn't working.

Laura   What isn't?

Molly   This. You.

Laura   Funny!

Molly   I'm not joking.

Laura   But, Molly –

Molly   Sorry Laura.

Laura   We were just playing.

Molly   Playing?

Laura   We were just playing shop. We were just selling sweets!

Molly   Selling. Exactly. We're supposed to be selling.

Laura   I did sell. I sold two packets.

Molly   That wasn't selling.

Laura   He'll bring it in tomorrow, alright!

Molly   We're not a charity, we're a business.

Laura   'Business'?

Molly   The stock exchange will plummet if I let our market slip.

Laura   It was just Kieran . . .

Molly   Why should we treat Kieran differently?

Laura   I'm not saying that.

Molly   You fancy him!

Laura   I don't fancy Kieran.

Molly   Do too.

Laura   I do not!

Molly   Shall I go and tell him?

Laura   No!

Molly   Kieran!

Laura   No, Molly, shut up!

Molly   Kieran!

Laura   Molly!

Molly   Kieran! Laura fancies you!

Laura   Molly!

Molly   She loves you forever and ever –

Laura   Shut up!

Molly   She wants to kiss you and cuddle you and marry you and have your babies and –

Laura   Please, Molly, just –

She starts having an asthma attack.

Molly *is fascinated as* **Laura***'s face turns red.*

Laura *looks pleadingly at* **Molly** *for help but she remains still.*

Molly *goes to help* **Laura***.*

Actor 1   Not yet, Molly. That's not how it happened.

Actor 3   Fifteen seconds more . . .

Laura *begins losing consciousness.*

Molly *retrieves* **Laura***'s inhaler and gives it to her.*

Laura *inhales and coughs loudly.*

She looks at **Molly***.*

Laura   Th-th-thank you.

Molly   You're welcome. (*To the* **Actors***.*) Can we take a moment please?

The clock fast-forwards.

Actor 3   Not now, Molly.

Actor 1   You're going on report.

The clock lands.

Scene Five

A few months later. **Molly** *is ten years old. A classroom. After school.*

Miss Woods   Report, Molly. We're putting you on report.

Molly   What have I done wrong?

Miss Woods   This has to stop.

Molly   What has to stop?

Miss Woods   You know exactly what I'm talking about.

Molly   You haven't even told me why I'm here . . .

Miss Woods   You're a clever girl.

Molly   Thank you.

Miss Woods   So you don't need me to tell you. You're quite capable of working it out for yourself.

Molly   I don't know what you're talking about, miss.

Miss Woods   Do you really need me to spell it out for you?

Molly   No –

Miss Woods   How long have you been selling things in the playground? Molly?

Beat.

Come on, Molly, I would like to go home at some point.

Molly   What did you want to be, miss?

Miss Woods   What?

Molly   When you were eleven. Did you always want to be a teacher? My mummy says those who can, do; those who can't, teach.

Miss Woods   Does she?

Molly   Where do you live, miss?

Miss Woods   I'm not telling you where I live.

Molly   Do you live in a big house? Do you have a big TV and a swimming pool and lots of flashy cars?

Miss Woods   That's enough.

Molly   Do you earn lots of money, miss? My dad does. What do your parents do?

Miss Woods   Enough, Molly.

Molly   But –

Miss Woods   That's enough.

Molly   Why are you allowed to ask questions and I'm not?

Miss Woods   Because . . . because we're not here to discuss how much money I make.

Molly   We're here to discuss how much money I make.

Beat.

Miss Woods   Yes.

Molly   Twelve thousand.

Miss Woods   What?

Molly   I make twelve thousand pounds.

Miss Woods   . . .

Molly   Sixty to seventy pounds a day. Multiply that by five and you've got three hundred. Multiply that by the four weeks in a month and you get one thousand two hundred. One thousand two hundred a month. Multiplied by the twelve months of the year makes fourteen thousand four hundred take away two thousand four hundred for school holidays and wages and stock and you're left with twelve thousand pounds.

Miss Woods   Is that overall or –

Molly   A year. Twelve thousand pounds a year for the last two years.

Miss Woods   That's –

Molly   Twenty-four thousand pounds.

Miss Woods   Right.

Molly   Can I go home now?

Miss Woods   Do you get on well with your dad, Molly?

Molly   What? I don't know.

Miss Woods   Do you tell him everything that goes on at school?

Molly   Not everything.

Miss Woods   But this. He knows about this?

Molly   He buys me the stock.

Miss Woods   So I don't need to phone him then?

Molly   . . .

Miss Woods   Your dad, Molly. I don't need to phone your dad and tell him what's been going on?

Beat.

Look, what you've done – what you've been doing – it's a great idea.

Molly (*standing up*)   Well, then, there's no problem.

Miss Woods   Sit down, Molly.

Molly   But you just said –

Actors   Sit down.

Molly *sits.*

Miss Woods   You need to listen. It's important. It's really important. I really can't . stress how important it is that you listen to what I'm about to say to you.

The clock pauses.

Actor 3   What did she say, Molly?

Actor 2   Do you remember what she said?

Molly   That I . . .

Actor 3   Yes . . .

Actor 4   That you . . . needed to . . .

Molly   That I need to be like everyone else.

Actors   Yes.

Actor 1 (*referring to notes*)   That's what I've got here. 'Like everyone else.'

Actor 3   So even now, even exactly now –

Actor 4   Something's not quite right.

Actor 2   She's different.

Actor 4   Already different.

Actor 3   So this moment was . . .?

Actor 4   Formative? Is formative too strong?

Actor 1   No, formative's right.

Actor 3   This is a formative moment then.

The clock resumes.

Miss Woods   You're not a bad person, Molly. I know you're not a bad person. But some of the things you do, Molly. Some of the – They're not normal.

Molly   Normal?

Miss Woods   I've seen you. You don't – The way you interact with some of your classmates. You're very different.

Molly   No I'm not.

Miss Woods   You are, Molly. You've got away with it here. We've let you get away with it. But you can't behave like this when you go to secondary school in September.

Molly   Why not?

Miss Woods   Because they won't tolerate it. I'm telling you now they won't stand for this. They won't. People won't be as tolerant and as accepting as we are for the rest of your life.

Molly   Why not?

Miss Woods   Because you're not a child anymore.

Beat.

If you behave like you do now in secondary school you're fucked.

Molly   Miss!

Miss Woods   You are, Molly. You're fucked. You won't last a week.

Molly   Stop swearing, miss.

Actor   You push people too far.

Actor   You make people very angry.

Miss Woods   But because you're only little it gets overlooked.

Actor   It won't be like that forever.

Molly   Stop it.

Miss Woods   You'll find – if you keep behaving like this – you'll very quickly find that people won't like you.

Molly   . . .

Miss Woods   Look, let's be clear. You can do whatever you want. You're extraordinary. You're an extraordinary little girl. Everyone can see that. You can change the world if you want to. But the rules are about to change and you've got to fit in.

Actors   You've got to be like everyone else.

Miss Woods   You'll never achieve anything, Molly, unless you learn how to be like everyone else.

Molly   How?

Miss Woods   What?

Molly   How, miss? How do I do that? How do I be like everyone else?

Miss Woods   . . .

Molly   Miss?

Miss Woods   . . .

Molly   Where are you going, miss?

Miss Woods *exits.*

The clock fast-forwards.

Actor 2   What happened after that day in primary school, Molly?

Molly   I started secondary school.

Actor 3   And then?

Molly   I chaired the junior debating society.

Actor 2   And then?

Molly   I captained the girls' hockey team.

Actors   And then?

Molly   I became a prefect.

Actors   And then?

The clock lands.

Scene Six

Four years later. **Molly** *is fourteen years old. A school canteen.*

Molly   They've asked me to run for head girl.

Nathan   No way!

Kim   Oh my God!

Nathan   That's amazing, Molly, well done!

Kim   Aw, you must be well chuffed! Say well done, Laura.

Laura   Sorry, yeah, completely zoned out for a second there.

Nathan   Well, say it then!

Laura   Well done, Molly.

Molly   Thanks, Lau.

Nathan   Have you told your dad?

Molly   Um, no not yet.

Nathan   You should.

Kim   He'll be well proud.

Nathan   When did they tell you?

Molly   This morning. I had a meeting.

Nathan   Ohhh, official.

Molly   I know right.

Kim   Was it scary?

Molly   Not really.

Nathan   She's born for this sort of stuff aren't you, Molly?

Kim   Do you have to, like, do a speech and stuff?

Molly   Think so, yeah.

Nathan   Oh my God, you're so gonna get it.

Molly   Do you think so?

Nathan   Are you joking?

Kim   Who else is going for it?

Molly   I know Faith Williams got asked.

Kim   Pfft.

Nathan   Whatever.

Molly   And Natalie. I think Natalie got asked as well.

Kim   Natalie Farrell?

Nathan   Interesting.

Molly   Yeah.

Kim   Oh my God.

Molly   What?

Kim   We should make posters with your face on them.

Nathan   Oh my God, yeah!

Kim   And Molly in big capital letters –

Nathan   Love it!

Kim   And stickers! We should get stickers!

Nathan   Doesn't your brother work in a sticker shop, Laura?

Laura   It's a stationery shop –

Kim   Same thing.

Nathan   Do you think he could get some printed for us?

Laura   Well –

Nathan   I bet he would if you asked him.

Kim   Say I'll get with him if he does.

Nathan   Slut.

Kim   What? He's well fit.

Nathan   Such a slut.

Laura   I've actually been asked to run as well.

Beat.

Molly   What?

Kim   Amazing!

Nathan   Congrats!

Beat.

Molly   Why didn't you say anything before?

Laura   I don't know.

Nathan   Oh my God, competitive.

Kim   I know, right!

Nathan   Claws are coming out.

Laura   No.

Molly   When did they ask you?

Laura   This morning as well. I had a meeting.

Kim   Oh my God . . .

Nathan   Two besties.

Laura   No, it's not like that.

Kim   Yeah, yeah.

Laura   It won't be like that. Will it, Molly?

Beat.

Molly?

Actor 1   There. Look at that. Is this the moment?

The clock rewinds and the moment replays.

Kim   Yeah, yeah.

Laura   It won't be like that. Will it, Molly?

Beat.

Molly?

Actor 1   There. That flicker in her eye.

The clock rewinds and the moment replays.

Laura   It won't be like that. Will it, Molly?

Beat.

Molly?

Actor 1   There.

The clock fast-forwards and lands.

Scene Seven

A few weeks later. **Molly** *is fourteen years old. A playing field. Night.*

Molly Why are you smiling?

Laura No reason.

Molly You can tell me.

Laura It's nothing. It's stupid.

Molly Do you want to make a bet to see who can get with him first?

Laura What?

Molly You've been all over each other all day.

Laura Have not.

Molly Have too.

Laura We were not all over each other!

Molly I swear you were holding hands at one point.

Laura So?

Molly Are you twelve?

Laura What?

Molly *Holding hands?*

Laura So what?

Molly Who holds hands?

Laura It was cold.

Molly It was not cold.

Laura I had cold hands. Anyway, we're just really good friends

Molly Oh.

Laura We are!

Molly So you don't want to . . .

Laura Want to what?

Molly Make a bet.

Laura No. We're just friends. No.

Molly Shame.

Laura Why shame?

Molly I'll just have to get with him myself then.

Laura   What?

Molly   . . .

Laura   He wouldn't get with you.

Molly   What makes you say that?

Laura   No I didn't mean –

Molly   You saying I'm not good enough for him or –

Laura   I don't mean that just –

Molly   What then? Why wouldn't he get with me?

Laura   It's just – Well, you know he's really religious?

Molly   So?

Laura   So . . . he can only get with . . . kiss . . . he can only kiss other religious people.

Molly   Well, you're not religious.

Laura   Exactly. We can't get with each other so we're just friends. We have to be just friends.

Molly   Tragic.

Laura   I know, right?

Molly   And you're saying – what? – he can't get with someone who isn't religious?

Laura   No. And he's married to them.

Molly   He has to be married to them?

Laura   Yup.

Molly   Well, then.

Laura   What?

Molly   We'll see about that.

Dan *enters.*

Silence; **Laura**'*s uncomfortable,* **Molly**'*s not.*

Dan   Hi . . .

Beat.

This is weird. . . Why aren't you talking?

Molly   Laura was just talking. About you.

Laura   I was not! Molly!

Molly   What took you so long?

Laura   Yeah, we've been waiting for you.

Molly   All right, Laura, jeez, don't make him feel bad about it.

Laura   No, I didn't mean – You look nice.

Dan   Do I? Thanks.

Molly   Vom. Do you want some of this, Dan?

Dan   What is it?

Molly   Skittle vodka. I made it myself.

Dan   Oh, no, sorry, I can't.

Molly   You *can't*?

Dan   No it's just I'm –

Molly   – what. . .? You're just what?

Beat.

Dan   Well, I guess one drink won't hurt, right?

Molly   That's the spirit.

Laura   Dan.

Dan   What?

Laura   I thought –

Molly   You're not his mum, Laura, jeez.

Laura   I know but – You don't have to if you don't want to, Dan.

Dan   I know.

Laura   No I just mean –

Dan   I'm not twelve.

He has a sip of Skittle vodka and grimaces.

It's nice!

Molly   It's repugnant but it'll get you drunk.

Laura   Can I have some?

Molly   What?

Laura   Of the vodka. The Skittle vodka. Can I have some?

Molly   Did you not bring anything to drink?

Laura   You said *you* were bringing stuff to drink.

Molly   Yeah, for me.

Laura   But you just let Dan have some . . .

Molly   Yeah.

Laura   So can I try some too or . . .

Molly (*the bottle is practically full*)   Well, there's not much left now.

Laura   But there's –

Molly   Sorry, Laura.

Beat.

So – Dan – what's it like being religious?

Dan   What?

Molly   Laura told me you were really religious.

Laura   I didn't! Molly!

Dan   Did you?

Laura   No I just –

Dan   That's really out of order, Laura.

Molly   I did tell her this.

Laura   Will you fuck off?

Molly   I beg your pardon?

Laura   I'll tell him about the bet.

Molly   What bet?

Laura   The bet you wanted to make.

Molly   Er, what bet?

Laura   Funny.

Molly   No – really – what bet?

Laura   You really want me to tell him?

Molly   Tell him what?

Laura   You think you're so clever don't you?

Molly   I don't know what you're going on about, Laura.

Laura   I'm going.

Molly   What? Going where?

Laura   You clearly don't want me here.

She exits.

Molly   Where are you going? Wait, Laura! Oops.

Dan   A bet?

Molly   What?

Dan   What kind of bet?

Molly   Oh, we were gonna make a bet to see who could kiss you first.

Dan   Right.

Beat.

What?! Why?

Molly   Why do you think?

Dan   I don't know, that's why I'm asking.

Molly   Do you fancy Laura?

Dan   What? No.

Molly   You don't?

Dan   No.

Molly   But what about today?

Dan   We were just – We were walking around together that's all.

Molly   Holding hands.

Dan   I know holding hands but –

Molly   Why were you holding hands with Laura if you don't fancy her?

Dan   Just – I don't know, just . . .

Molly   For attention, right?

Dan   What?

Molly   You were doing it to get my attention.

Dan   *Your* attention?

Molly   Yeah.

Dan   Why would I be trying to get your attention?

Molly   To make me jealous.

Dan   I couldn't make you jealous.

Molly   You could. You did.

Dan   *You*?

Molly   Yes, Dan, me.

Dan You're telling me I made *you* jealous.

Molly Yes.

Dan Right.

Molly How do you think that made me feel?

Dan What?

Molly Seeing you with her like that.

Dan I didn't realize you . . . I mean are you saying you –

Molly I like you. Yeah.

Dan Really?

Molly Why, do you not like me?

Dan No I do. I do like you.

Molly Prove it.

Dan What?

Molly . . .

Dan You mean –

Molly Yes.

Dan Now?

Molly Yes, now.

Dan Do you not want to – I mean should we not go somewhere more private?

Molly Private?

Dan Yeah, somewhere more –

Molly I want to do it here.

Dan Why here?

Molly It's romantic. I want the whole world to see. I want everyone to know that you're mine.

Dan Do you? Really?

Molly Really.

She and **Dan** *kiss.*

Molly *goes to put her hand down* **Dan**'*s trousers.*

Dan No

Molly *No?*

Dan   Go slow. I've never –

Molly   Hah. Okay.

She and **Dan** *kiss.*

Laura *enters and sees* **Molly** *and* **Dan** *kissing.*

Molly *sees* **Laura** *and continues kissing* **Dan**.

Molly *and* **Dan** *finish kissing.*

Dan   That was amazing.

Molly *grins wildly.*

The clock fast-forwards and lands.

Scene Eight

Two weeks later. **Molly** *is fourteen years old. Outside the school hall. Afternoon.*

Dan   Screw this, I'm going.

Molly   Where are you going?

Dan   Home.

Molly   Why?

Dan   There's no point me being here.

Molly   You don't *need* a calculator.

Dan   What?

Molly   Not for every question.

Dan   It's advanced maths . . .

Molly   Yeah, so you'll just be at a very severe disadvantage.

Dan   Yeah. I'm going home.

He goes to leave.

Molly   No, Dan, hang on.

Dan   What?

Molly   I've got a spare.

Dan   What?

Molly *takes a calculator out of her bag.*

Molly   Hope for the best, prepare for the worst.

Dan   You were just gonna let me –

Molly   I wasn't.

Dan   Yeah you were.

Molly   Stopped you didn't I? Could have just let you leave. Here you go.

She holds out the calculator.

Dan *goes to take the calculator but* **Molly** *withdraws it.*

Molly   Have you got money on you?

Dan   What?

Molly   You didn't think I'd just give it to you did you?

Dan   Money?

Molly   How much money have you got on you, Dan?

Dan   I'll give it back.

Molly   I'm not suggesting you wouldn't.

Dan   I will. I'll give it back. I promise.

Molly   I know but I want some money for it.

Dan   You've got two. Why do you want money for it?

Molly   You're forgetting, aren't you?

Dan   Forgetting what?

Molly   This isn't a game. We're not doing this for fun, are we? This is an exam. We're here to sit an exam. In your strongest subject, I might add.

Dan   So . . .?

Molly   So why would I want to help you?

Dan   Because you're supposed to be my friend.

Molly   I am your friend.

Dan   And, and, and you have a spare. You have a spare and I need one.

Molly   Exactly. Supply and demand, Dan. It's basic economics.

Dan   I know supply and demand.

Molly   I have a spare calculator and you don't. I have the supply, you're in demand.

Dan   Great.

Molly   Now if demand increases – which given your lack of calculator it has – and supply remains unchanged, a shortage occurs, leading to a higher equilibrium price.

Dan   But supply has changed.

Molly   No it hasn't.

Dan   You had one calculator, now you have two.

Molly   Ah.

Dan   You don't need two so supply outweighs demand and the price goes down. Give me the calculator.

Molly   But I've always had two, I just didn't tell you.

Dan   Look, Molly, just give me the calculator.

Molly   *My* calculator.

Dan   Your spare calculator.

Molly   . . .

Dan   Please.

Molly   Alright.

Dan   Yeah?

Molly   Yeah alright then.

Dan   Thank you.

Molly   Once you pay me you can have it.

Dan   I'm not paying you!

Molly   Suit yourself.

She goes to leave.

Dan   I've got six pounds.

Molly *stops and laughs.*

Dan   Why is that funny?

Molly   Six pounds?

Dan   I'm not asking to buy it. Just borrow it. Please.

Molly   What am I going to do with six pounds?

She goes to leave.

Dan *punches a chair.*

Molly   There is one thing I like to do before an exam.

Dan   What?

Molly   Before an exam. There's something I quite like to do.

Dan   Yeah?

Molly   Yeah.

Dan   What's that then?

Molly   I like to wank.

Beat.

Dan   What?

Molly   Before an exam I like to have a wank. Relieves tension.

Dan   Good for you.

Molly   Yeah, usually I have a quick wank in one of the cubicles but seeing as you're here I thought maybe you'd . . .

Dan   . . .

Molly   I thought maybe you could provide some stimulus.

Dan   Hah.

Molly   No?

Dan   No. No. I'm not . . . I don't . . .

Molly   Suit yourself.

She goes to leave.

Dan   You're joking aren't you?

Molly   No.

Dan   You want me to –

Molly   Show me your cock, yeah. I want you to get your cock out.

She takes the calculator out of her pocket and holds it out to **Dan**.

Dan   What's wrong with you?

Molly   Think about your future, Dan.

Dan   You're joking aren't you? This is a joke.

Molly   No. I'm not.

Dan   . . .

Molly   A cock flash for a calculator. It's as simple as that.

Silence.

Dan   Okay.

Molly   . . .

Dan   I'll do it.

Molly   What?

Dan   If you want me to.

Molly   I –

Dan   Or are you too scared?

Molly   No I do. I do want you to.

Dan   Where?

Molly   Over here.

Dan   Quickly though. It's nearly one o'clock.

Molly   I'll be quick, don't worry.

Dan   Won't someone see us?

Molly   There's no one here.

Dan *gets his cock out.*

Silence.

Dan   Come on then.

Molly   Come over here.

Dan   What?

Molly   Quickly. Come on.

Dan *moves towards* **Molly** *but she walks towards the exam hall.*

Dan   Where are you going?

Molly   Changed my mind.

Dan   No hang on, what about the calculator?

Molly   You won't be needing that.

Dan   Give me the calculator.

Molly   You don't need it.

Dan   What?

Molly   They provide all the necessary equipment.

Dan   You –

Molly   People who experience intense stress immediately before taking a test find it has a significant effect on their performance.

Dan   You're a –

Molly   Oh, don't mention this to anyone. There's a camera up there.

Dan   . . .

Molly   Anyway, good luck.

The clock fast-forwards and lands.

Scene Nine

Three months later. **Molly** *is fifteen years old. The woods. Evening.*

Molly *drinks.*

Dan *and* **Laura** *enter.*

Dan   There she is.

Laura   Molly?

Dan   Go on. Tell her.

Laura   . . .

Dan   Quickly.

Molly   Just say whatever it is you've come here to say, Laura.

Laura   I won.

Molly   What?

Laura   I won Head Girl.

Molly   Oh.

Dan   Now tell her to her face what everyone thinks of her.

Laura   We don't want to be your friend anymore, Molly.

Dan   We. Don't. Like. You. Nobody likes you. Don't expect us to feel sorry for you just because you're a billy-no-mates. It's what you deserve.

Laura   That's enough, Dan.

Dan   Everybody hates you. Do you know why? Because you're a nasty little liar who does horrible things to people for no reason. You walk around like you're better than everyone. But you're not. You're a weirdo. You're a mistake. You're –

Molly *gets up.*

Dan *flinches.*

Molly   Congratulations.

Laura   What?

Molly   For winning Head Girl. You deserve it. You'll be brilliant.

She offers the vodka bottle to **Laura**.

Laura   Thanks?

She goes to take the bottle.

Dan   Laura doesn't drink anymore.

Laura   I . . .

Dan   She doesn't want it. Do you, Lau?

Laura *shakes her head at* **Molly**'*s offer.*

Laura   Let's go, Dan.

She goes to leave.

Dan?

Dan (*to* **Molly**)   Freak.

Dan *joins* **Laura** *and they go to leave.*

Molly   Wait.

Laura *stops.*

Molly   There's something I need to say.

Dan   Don't listen to her, Lau.

Molly   I want to apologize. I'm sorry, Laura. I'm sorry for all the horrible things I did to you.

Dan   She's making it up as she goes along. Come on.

Molly   There's something else.

Dan   No one cares, Molly.

Molly   I tried to tell you. But I thought it was my fault.

Laura   What are you talking about?

Molly   It only happened one time. It wasn't serious. We didn't go all the way. I didn't let it get that far. I didn't even want to do it in the first place. (*To* **Dan**.) I told you I didn't want to.

Laura (*to* **Molly**)   What are you saying?

Molly   Dan tried to do stuff with me.

Dan   What?

Molly   He said he wanted practice.

Dan   I didn't.

Molly   He said he wanted to do it on me before he did it on you.

Dan   That's not how it happened.

Laura   How what happened, Dan?

Dan   She's twisting it.

Molly   He tried to make me touch it.

Dan   Shut up.

Laura   When?

Molly   Summer term.

Dan   Stop.

Molly   He told me that if I told anyone they wouldn't believe me.

Dan   Just shut up.

Molly   I didn't know what to do.

Dan   Shut your mouth right now.

Molly   That's why I had to lie to you.

Dan   Shut up shut up shut up SHUT UP SHUT UP SHUT YOUR FUCKING FILTHY MOUTH YOU UGLY LYING FUCKING – I SWEAR I'LL FUCKING KILL YOU I WILL FUCKING –

He goes to hit **Molly**.

Laura *intervenes and* **Dan** *accidentally hits her.*

Dan   I'm sorry, I –

Laura   Get off.

Dan   It was an accident –

Molly   Her lip is bleeding.

Dan   I didn't mean to –

Molly   It might need stitches.

Dan   It was an accident.

Laura   Leave me alone, Dan.

Dan (*to* **Molly**)   Tell her the truth, Molly. Tell her that it was all a lie. Tell her.

Molly   You shouldn't hit girls, Dan.

Dan   It was an accident.

Molly   Laura's lip is bleeding because of you. You can't just hit my best friend and get away with it. Say you're sorry.

Dan   I'm sorry for accidentally hitting you, Laura.

Molly   Say it like you mean it.

Dan   I'm sorry, Laura.

Molly   Again.

Dan   Screw this –

He goes to leave but **Molly** *swipes his backpack.*

Dan   Give it back.

Molly   Laura. Catch.

She throws the backpack to **Laura**, *and she catches it.*

Laura *gives the backpack to* **Dan**.

Dan *goes to leave but* **Molly** *snatches the backpack again and throws it to* **Laura**.

Dan *tries to take the backpack, but* **Laura** *throws it to* **Molly**.

Molly *offers the backpack to* **Dan**.

Dan *goes to take the backpack, but* **Molly** *throws it to* **Laura**.

Laura *offers the backpack to* **Dan**.

Dan *goes to take the backpack, but* **Laura** *throws it to* **Molly**.

Molly *and* **Laura** *repeat this routine several times.*

Molly *offers the backpack to* **Dan**, *but he doesn't rise to the bait.*

Laura *takes the backpack from* **Molly** *and hands it to* **Dan**.

Dan *goes to leave but* **Molly** *snatches the backpack from him, unzips it and empties it onto the ground.*

Laura *giggles until it hurts.*

Molly   I could kill him if you like.

Laura   He's not worth it.

Molly   I mean it. I could do that for you. If you asked me to.

Laura   You're mental.

Molly   All you have to do is say the word. No one would ever know. It's quiet out here. It could be our secret.

Laura   How?

Molly   We could make it look like an accident. It would be easy. Make it look like he was hit by a car or crushed by a tree.

Laura   Murdered by a stranger.

Molly   Happens all the time. Stabbed.

Laura   Strangled.

Molly   Abducted.

Laura   Drowned.

Molly   Beaten.

Laura   Burned.

Molly   That's a good one. Burned alive. Do you want me to?

Laura   We could do it together.

Dan   Stop messing about, Lau.

Laura   Don't call me that.

Dan   What?

Laura   My name's Laura.

Dan   All right, fine. Can we go now, Laura?

Laura   I'm not going anywhere with you ever again.

Dan   Are you dumping me?

Laura   What do you think?

Dan   You can't dump me.

Molly   She just did.

Dan   This isn't funny anymore, Laura.

Laura   I'm not joking.

Dan   We need to go. It's getting cold.

Molly   Tell Dan to give you his jacket, Laura.

Laura   What?

Molly   He said it himself. It's getting cold. (*To* **Dan**.) Be a gentleman and give Laura your jacket, Dan.

Laura   Yeah, Dan, be a gentleman. Give me your jacket.

Dan *goes to leave but* **Laura** *trips him up and he hurts his arm.*

Laura *looks to* **Molly** *for approval.*

Molly *laughs.*

Dan   What was that for?

Molly (*to* **Laura**)   Go on.

Laura *tries to take* **Dan***'s jacket off, but he holds onto it.*

Molly *kicks* **Dan** *and he lets go of the jacket.*

Laura *puts the jacket on.*

Dan   Stop it.

Molly (*imitating*)   Stop it.

She pours vodka over **Dan**.

Molly *kicks* **Dan**.

Dan   Don't.

Molly   'Don't'.

Laura *laughs.*

Molly *hands the vodka to* **Laura**.

Laura *pours the vodka over* **Dan**.

Dan   Laura, stop.

Laura   'Laura, stop'.

Molly *and* **Laura** *kick and pour vodka over* **Dan** *until the bottle's empty and he's crying.*

Molly   Now build a fire.

Dan   What?

Molly   Come on, Dan, where's your sense of adventure? Make a campfire for Laura.

Dan   Please, let me go home.

Molly   Take off your clothes. We need something to burn.

Dan   I want my mum.

Molly   Aw, didums.

Dan   Please don't make me.

Laura (*to* **Molly**)   That's enough, Molly.

Molly   But we're not finished yet.

Laura   We've made our point.

Molly   I'm just getting started.

Laura   . . .

Molly   I thought we were doing this together.

Laura   . . .

Molly   I thought we were friends.

Laura   We are.

Molly   Best friends.

Laura   We are, Molly.

Molly   Well, then. Go on. Tell him.

Laura   . . .

Molly   Tell him to take off his clothes.

Laura (*to* **Dan**)   Take off your clothes, Dan.

Dan   Please . . .

Molly (*to* **Dan**)   Do. What. She. Says.

Dan *takes his shirt off and throws it on the ground.*

Molly *gestures to* **Laura**.

Laura   More.

Dan *takes of his trousers and throws them on the pile.*

Molly *offers* **Laura** *the matches, she takes them and strikes one.*

Dan   No –

Actor 1   She lit a match –

Actor 3   – it was so nice!

Dan   Don't. Please. Don't.

Actor 1   It crackled so –

Actor 3   – it burned so clear –

ActorS   – exactly like the picture here.

Molly   Go on. Burn him.

Laura   Seriously?

Molly   He deserves it.

Laura   We'll get in trouble.

Molly   I'll do the rest. No one will find out. They won't know it was us.

Laura   What're you going to do?

Silence.

I can't.

Molly   Yes you can.

Silence.

You want to. I know you do. It will feel good. Make him hurt. I want to watch him hurt.

Laura *goes to throw the match on* **Dan** *but* **Molly** *grabs her hand and blows it out.*

Molly   You were really going to do it.

Laura   No, I wasn't.

Molly   You were.

Laura   Shut up.

Molly   You're sick.

Laura   Stop it.

She gives the matches to **Molly**.

Laura   Are you okay Dan?

Molly   Why do you care?

Laura   He's freezing.

Molly   So?

Laura *takes* **Dan**'s *jacket off and puts it over his shoulders.*

Molly   What are you doing?

Laura (*to* **Dan**)   Get dressed, Dan.

Molly   I didn't give you permission.

Laura *helps* **Dan** *into his clothes.*

Laura (*to* **Dan**)   Put these on.

Molly   I said –

Laura   I heard what you said.

She dresses **Dan**.

Laura (*to* **Dan**)   *Go home.*

Dan *exits.*

Laura   I didn't want to do that.

Silence.

We can't be friends anymore.

Molly   What? You're blaming me?

Laura *goes to leave.*

Molly   Stay.

Silence.

Please.

Laura   No more, Molly.

She exits.

Molly   You're evil.

The clock pauses.

Actor 2   Well done, Molly.

Actor 4   Water?

Actor 1   Let's give Molly a big round of applause.

Applause.

Molly *looks at* **Laura** *in the audience.*

Molly   It was quite an evening wasn't it, Laura?

Actor 4 *hands* **Molly** *some water.*

Molly   We haven't spoken since. I don't suppose you'd like to catch up over dinner now, would you?

As a little girl my environment wasn't always kind to me and –

(*To* **Actor 1**.) Sorry, can I. . .?

Actor 1 *gives* **Molly** *permission to speak.*

Molly   I want to end with a story. It's a story that Laura and I made up when we were little. We used to act out it for fun. We called it 'The Scorpion and the Frog'. Silly, I know. Laura always insisted that I play the part of the nasty scorpion and that she should take on the role of the friendly frog.

Typecast again, eh, Laura? Maybe you could come up here and we could tell it together, for old times' sake?

No? Suit yourself.

One day, a scorpion saw a frog sitting in the rushes on the other side of a river. 'Hellooo, Mr Frog!' called the scorpion across the water. 'Would you be so kind as to give me a ride on your back across the river?' 'Well now, Mrs Scorpion! How do I know that if I try to help you, you won't try to kill me?' asked the frog. 'It's in your nature.' 'Because,' the scorpion replied, 'if I try to kill you, then I would die too, for you see I can't swim!' Now this seemed to make sense to the frog, so he agreed to take the scorpion across the river. He swam over to the bank and the scorpion crawled onto the frog's back and the frog slid into the river. The muddy water swirled around them, but the frog stayed near the surface so the scorpion would not drown. Halfway across the river, the frog suddenly felt a sharp sting in his back and, out of the corner of his eye, saw the scorpion remove her stinger. A deadening numbness crept into his limbs. 'You fool!' croaked the frog. 'Now we'll both die! Why on earth did you do that?' The scorpion shrugged and did a little jig on the drowning frog's back. 'I couldn't help myself . . . like you said, it's in my nature.' And they both sank into the muddy waters of the swiftly flowing river.

A little girl who was *different* needed to be treated *differently*. They failed me. All of them. Dan, Miss Woods, Mum, Dad, Laura . . .

Yes, you as well, Laura.

It could have been you, you know . . . Standing here.

That night in the woods . . .?

Actor 3   Let's talk about Duncan.

Molly *looks at* **Actor 3**.

Actor 3   Duncan Robertson.

Molly   I told you I'm not talking about that.

Beat.

Actor 1   This isn't what we agreed. This is *my* story –

Actor 3   Yes, it is, and Duncan's a part of it is he not?

Duncan *enters.*

Duncan   Ready . . .?

Actor 1 *gestures and the clock fast-forwards rapidly.*

The **Actors** *prepare for the second part of the show;* **Molly** *didn't expect this.*

Actor 1   You want to give us an understanding of who you are don't you Molly? So we can find answers?

Duncan   Ready. Set.

Actor 1   'Discover what led to such tragic events so we can prevent more of the same.'

Molly   . . .

Actor 1 (*to the audience.*)   Ladies and gentlemen, at some point Molly Chambers decided Duncan Robertson *deserved* what he had coming to him. Let's find out *when*, as we take you through the events that led to Molly's infamous confrontation with Duncan Robertson.

The clock lands.

Scene Ten

Eight years later. **Molly** *is twenty-two years old. The offices of Empire Solutions.*

Molly, **Jessica** *and* **Amy** *wear labels.*

Duncan   Ready. Set. Go.

Duncan *starts a timer.*

Amy   Great. So. I'm a doctor. Everybody needs doctors. It's pretty obvious that I'm an asset to our survival. You'll need my medical expertise if you want to survive the journey back to shore. So I should definitely be on the boat. It just makes sense. Agreed?

Jessica   Well –

Amy   Good.

Jessica   Sorry, but we didn't actually agree.

Amy (*to* **Molly**)   You agree don't you, Molly?

Molly   I think we should hear what Jessica has to say.

Jessica   Well, I have to survive for the sake of my children. If you leave me behind, they'll grow up without a mother. Their future depends on my survival.

Amy   Sorry, but I don't think that's a valid reason.

Jessica   Why not?

Amy   You need to bring something to the table.

Molly   Amy's right.

Jessica   Well, I'm a teacher. That means I'm intelligent and a strong communicator. I have a logical mind. We'll need good communication and clear thinking if we want to keep our wits about us.

Amy   What subject do you teach?

Jessica   That's not important.

Amy   I think it is.

Jessica   The point is I have skills you need. I should be on the boat.

Duncan   Pause there. I forgot to mention whichever two make it onto the boat will join us for the next interview round tomorrow. Carry on.

Amy   We don't need teachers on the boat.

Jessica   Stop acting like you're in charge.

Amy   I never said I was in charge.

Molly   Jessica does have a point.

Amy   What?

Molly   You're trying to control everything.

Amy   No, I'm not –

Jessica   Yes, you are –

Amy   This is a group decision –

Jessica   Yes, it is. So, as a group, can we agree that I should survive for the sake of my children?

Amy   Nobody cares about your children.

Jessica   Wow.

Amy   They're not relevant to the exercise.

Jessica   You can't even swim.

Amy   I don't need to swim, I'm on a boat.

Jessica   No, you're not. Not yet. We haven't agreed –

Molly (*to* **Amy**)   Are you really willing to let Jessica drown?

Amy   This is about survival. That's the whole point.

Molly   She has two kids waiting at home. What happens to them if she doesn't make it?

Amy   That's not my problem.

Molly   Well, I think that forfeits your right to be on the boat.

Amy   Don't be ridiculous.

Molly   I think Jessica should get on the boat.

Amy   Why?

Molly   My mother died when I was a little girl.

Beat.

Jessica   Oh, I'm sorry.

Amy   Sorry.

Molly   It's fine. It was a long time ago. But I'd never want a child to go through that experience. You're too important to be left behind. I think Jessica should get on the boat.

Amy   Me too.

Jessica   That was a sudden change of heart.

Amy   Well, I've thought about it and I think it's the right decision.

Duncan   So, you're agreed, Jessica is first onto the boat?

Molly   That's right.

Jessica *steps onto the boat.*

Duncan   Two minutes remaining.

Amy   It only makes sense that I'm next on the boat.

Molly   Why?

Amy   It's obvious, isn't it? You're an ex-criminal.

Molly   But I'm also a navigator.

Amy   Sure, but there's no way we can trust you. Why should a criminal take priority over a medical professional? It doesn't make any sense. Logic dictates that it has to be me.

Molly   I agree.

Beat.

Amy   What?

Molly   I agree that you should be on the boat.

Amy   Brilliant.

She goes to join **Jessica** *on the boat.*

Jessica *steps off the boat.*

Jessica   Wait, no, what?

Duncan   You're leaving the boat, Jessica.

Jessica   That's not how the game works.

Amy   It doesn't matter. We made it.

Jessica   You can't change the rules because you feel like it.

Molly   I've made up my mind.

Jessica   But we're supposed to be fighting to get on the boat?

Molly   You're a teacher. Amy's a doctor. You're pillars of society. There's no way I can compete with that. The survival of the many takes priority over the survival of the few. You both have what's needed to make it back safely. I'd only slow you all down.

Silence.

There's no room for self-interest when the survival of the tribe is at stake.

Jessica   She's twisting it.

Amy   What?

Jessica   She's trying to come across all self-sacrificing, so she'll look better than us.

Amy *steps off the boat.*

Amy   Molly should get on the boat.

Jessica   What?

Amy   I've thought about it, and if anyone stays behind it should be me.

Jessica   Why?

Amy   You have children, Molly is a navigator. You should both be on the boat together.

Duncan   So now nobody is on the boat.

Jessica   Alright, fine, Molly gets on the boat.

Molly *steps onto the boat.*

Amy   Great.

Jessica   But I'm staying behind.

Duncan   Thirty seconds remaining.

Amy   What? No, we already said –

Jessica   You're a doctor. You're so much more important than me. You said so yourself.

Amy   What about your children? You have to live for them.

Jessica   I think it's best for everybody if you get on board.

Amy   Well, I've already decided to stay behind, so –

Jessica   Well, we haven't agreed, so –

Duncan   Ten.

Amy   You have a navigator now, so get on board.

Duncan   Nine.

Jessica   Don't give me orders.

Duncan   Eight.

Amy   I'm not moving.

Duncan   Seven.

Jessica   Well, neither am I.

Duncan   Six.

Amy   There has to be two people on the boat.

Duncan   Five.

Jessica   Why don't you get on then?

Duncan   Four.

Amy   Because I'm sacrificing myself for you.

Duncan   Three.

Jessica   So noble.

Duncan   Two.

Amy   Opportunist.

Duncan   One.

Jessica   Coward.

The timer ends.

Molly *is the only one on the boat.*

Duncan   Congratulations, Molly.

Scene Eleven

Two years later. **Molly** *is twenty-four years old. The offices of ZipFast Deliveries.*

Molly   You're late.

Duncan   Five minutes.

Molly   *Six.*

Duncan   Six doesn't count.

Molly   We're on the clock here.

Duncan   Double espresso.

He hands **Molly** *a coffee.*

Molly   Your tie.

Duncan   What about it?

Molly   The knot. It's crooked.

Duncan   So?

Molly   Give it here.

She fixes **Duncan**'s *tie.*

Molly   Nervous?

Duncan   No. Should I be?

Molly   You're sweating.

Duncan   Thank you for noticing.

Molly   Have you showered?

Duncan   A few of the boys went out on a late one.

Molly   I can smell it.

Duncan   Don't worry, I'm stone cold sober. Just give me the gun and tell me where to aim.

He mimes cocking a shotgun.

Molly *finishes fixing* **Duncan***'s tie.*

Molly   There.

She takes deodorant from her handbag and hands it to **Duncan***.*

Duncan   Where would I be without you, eh?

Molly   Out of a job.

Duncan *sprays himself with deodorant.*

Duncan   How many today?

Molly   Twenty-three.

Duncan   Christ.

Molly   I'll get the ball rolling then you take over.

Duncan   Sounds good to me. (*Gesturing to* **Molly***'s notes.*) I see you've done your homework?

Molly   Front to back.

Duncan   If you keep this up you'll have that partner position sewn up.

Molly   Has Angela said anything to you?

Duncan   You're a shoo-in, Molly. Trust me. You've got nothing to worry about.

Molly   Not tempted to go for it yourself?

Duncan   Ha. You must be joking. Way too much responsibility.

Molly   More money.

Duncan   True, but I happen to enjoy my weekends.

Beat.

Seriously though. Angela would be insane not to snap you up.

Molly   Sometimes I forget you're not a completely heartless bastard.

Duncan   Only when it's necessary.

Beat.

So. Ready for the first hit?

He sits and opens a file as **Molly** *opens the door.*

James *enters.*

James   They told me to come to this room?

Molly   Yes, come in. It's James, isn't it?

James   Who are you?

Molly   My name's Molly. And this is Duncan.

Duncan *extends his hand;* **James** *ignores it.*

Duncan   Can we get you anything?

James   You could start by telling me what this is all about.

Molly   Tea? Coffee? Water?

James   Not for me.

Molly   Right. Well, if you change your mind . . .

James   Mmhm.

Molly   Great. Duncan?

Duncan   Yes?

Molly   Shall we begin?

Duncan   Yes. Of course. Erm. As you'll already be aware, James, your company is going through some changes. It's what we refer to as a restructuring –

James   Yes, I know what restructuring is.

Duncan   Right. Yes. Well, as a result of this restructuring process, we've been called upon to advise on the future vision of this company. To guide it –

James (*to* **Duncan**)   Have you been rehearsing this?

Duncan   Excuse me?

James   Because it sounds to me like you've rehearsed this.

Duncan   We're here to talk *with* you, about –

James   You're not bumping me over to commercial again, are you?

Duncan   No, James, we're not –

James   Well, at least that's something. The last thing we need is more interference from Head Office.

Duncan   We're not from Head Office, James.

James   You're not?

Duncan   No. We're separate.

Beat.

James   Are you here to sack me?

Duncan   . . .

James   You are, aren't you?

Duncan   Your company is undergoing –

James   You're sacking me.

Duncan   There's a range of factors –

James   Why?

Duncan   If you'll just let me finish –

James   Why me?

Duncan   We've conducted a thorough review and after consultation with our client, it is clear the others on your team have outperformed you.

James   Fuck. Oh fuck.

Silence.

Duncan   Take all the time you need.

Silence.

James   You can't get rid of me. Not like this.

Duncan   I'm afraid the decision's already been made.

James   I won't go. You can't make me.

Duncan   This isn't a negotiation, James.

James   I have kids. Does it say *that* in your file?

Duncan   That isn't relevant to this conversation.

James   'Isn't relevant'?

Molly   Duncan –

Duncan   What I mean is . . . Look, perhaps we should –

James   Tell them to give me a second chance. Please. I can do better. I can –

Duncan   We've taken a look at your figures, James. You've consistently failed to hit your targets in the last quarter. Not to mention the marked increase in your absences –

James   I was sick. You can't boot me out for being ill.

Duncan   We're not booting anyone. We've assessed –

James   This is discrimination. Plain and simple. You won't get away with this.

Duncan   This has nothing to do with your . . .

James   What?

Duncan   Condition.

James   Jesus. Who the fuck are you to assess anything?

Molly   Duncan, maybe I should –

Duncan (*to* **James**)   Perhaps that was the wrong choice / of words.

James   Where's Clive? I want to speak with my boss. It should be him standing in front of me, not you.

Molly   We're here on Mr Richard's behalf.

Duncan   I'm afraid you're stuck with us.

Molly (*to* **Duncan**)   Rein it in, Duncan.

Beat.

James   Didn't have the courage to tell me himself did he? Had to send in the shock troops.

Duncan   Listen to yourself, James. This is crazy –

James (*to* **Molly**)   Did you hear that? Did you hear what he just said?

Duncan   Now wait a second –

James   He just said I was crazy.

Molly   He didn't actually say *you* were –

James (*to* **Duncan**)   Well, I might be crazy, mate, but you're a fucking clown.

Duncan   That's enough –

Molly   Listen to me, James. I won't sit here and pretend to know exactly what you're going through. You have every right to be upset. And angry. But I've been where you are. I've sat in the chair you're sitting in now and I can honestly say – hand on heart – that the best way forward is to *engage*. You can hate us. You can despise us. By all means. But it won't do you any good. Because the truth is, James, we've not come here to punish you. As hard as it may be to accept, it's our job to make sure you're treated with the respect and dignity you deserve. Not just as an employee, but as a human being. Are you willing to engage with us, James?

Silence.

James *nods.*

Molly   Thank you, James. Duncan?

Duncan *hands* **Molly** *a document.*

Molly *puts it on the table in front of* **James**.

Molly   We've negotiated a severance package that I'm sure you'll agree is very generous.

Silence.

James *looks at the document.*

Molly   But before we can start that process, we need you to sign.

Molly *gives* **Duncan** *a look.*

Duncan *passes* **James** *a pen.*

Molly   James?

James *looks at* **Molly**.

Molly *mimes a scribbling gesture.*

Silence.

James *signs.*

Molly   We do offer complimentary career counselling if that's something you might be interested in?

James   No.

Beat.

Is that it then?

Molly   Unless you have any questions for us?

James (*to* **Duncan**)   Do you like your job?

Duncan   I beg your pardon?

James   Do you find what you do fulfilling?

Molly   Come on, James –

James   Bet you sleep like a baby, don't you?

Molly   This isn't helping.

James   I bet you're rolling in it as well.

Duncan   Not nearly enough to listen to this.

Molly   Duncan. That's enough.

James   People like you. You're cruel. You're –

Molly   That's enough, James.

Silence.

James *exits.*

Molly *looks at* **Duncan**.

Duncan   What?

Beat.

What?

Scene Twelve

Three days later. The offices of Empire Solutions.

Angela *withdraws a file.*

Angela (*to* **Molly**)   On Tuesday of this week, you accompanied Duncan to a redundancy meeting at ZipFast Deliveries. Is that correct?

Molly   Yes, that's right.

Angela   Can you confirm that one of the candidates you met on that day was James Muswell?

Molly   Yes, he –

Angela   I have a report of the meeting here. Can you take a look and confirm the details please?

She produces the report and hands it to **Molly**.

Molly   Sorry, I'm confused. Whose report?

Angela   I asked Duncan to file a report on the candidate. To assess the process.

Molly (*to* **Duncan**)   You never mentioned a report.

Angela   It's routine.

Molly *reads.*

Angela   Well?

Molly   Yes, that's the candidate. But I still / don't –

Angela   Very good.

She takes the report back.

How would *you* describe the meeting?

Molly   Normal. Straightforward.

Angela   How do you mean?

Molly   It was a good hit.

Angela   Excuse me?

Molly   I said I think it was a / good hit.

Angela Yes, I heard what you said. That's not a very *empathetic* way of describing someone who's just lost their job.

Molly What I meant was –

Angela Empathy is one of our core principles, Molly.

Molly *looks at* **Duncan**.

Angela Under no circumstances must you refer to the work we do here as a 'hit'. It sends entirely the wrong message. Is that clear?

Molly Yes. Of course. Sorry.

Angela Now, could you walk me through it from your point of view?

Molly It didn't last that long. Duncan introduced me. I spoke with James, and he agreed to sign the package we'd negotiated.

Angela How did he respond to the news?

Molly He was distressed.

Angela How?

Molly I don't know. Emotional? Sorry, I'm confused, what has this got to do with the partner position?

Angela Partner?

Molly That's why I'm here, isn't it?

Angela We're not here to discuss that, Molly.

Molly What?

Angela This isn't an interview.

Molly But I thought –

Angela Let's stick to the topic at hand, shall we?

Molly What topic is that supposed to be?

Angela He's dead, Molly.

Molly Who?

Angela James.

Beat.

Molly How?

Angela They found his body this morning. Suicide. Carbon monoxide poisoning.

Molly (*to* **Duncan**) Did you know about this?

Angela I brought the matter to Duncan's attention yesterday.

Molly   So, how does this affect us?

Duncan   Jesus, Molly –

Angela   Someone is dead.

Molly   What I mean is, yes, it's terrible, obviously, but how do we know that was the reason? He did have a history of illness. Maybe that's why he did it? We can't blame ourselves because he lost his job.

Duncan   They found him at work.

Molly   What?

Angela   He wanted his job back. They had to escort him from the building. Someone found his car in the warehouse car park.

Molly   That doesn't mean it had anything to do with us.

Angela   It's about to go public. Our client issued a statement this morning. They're pointing the finger in our direction. We have to respond.

Molly   What are they saying?

Angela   We're in blame game territory now, Molly. And since we're the evil ones that do all the sacking, they're trying to turn us into public enemy number one.

Molly   But that's what they pay us for. That's the job. They didn't have a problem with it before.

Angela   That's because we didn't have blood on our hands. (*Reading.*) 'Molly's brusque delivery and inability to strike a cordial tone resulted in the client becoming distressed.'

Molly   What?

Angela   It goes on. (*Reading.*) 'While Molly attempted to salvage the conversation, she struggled to make a meaningful connection and it showed through in her performance with the candidate.'

Molly (*to* **Duncan**)   Did you write that?

Angela (*reading*)   'It was at this point that Molly told the candidate his children were irrelevant.'

Molly (*to* **Duncan**)   Are those your words?

Angela   Is this accurate, Molly?

Molly   No. That's not how it happened. Duncan could barely string a sentence together. He was useless.

Duncan   It was my job to assess your performance, Molly. It's not personal.

Molly (*to* **Angela**)   If he thought things were going wrong, why didn't he step in? He could have intervened, but he didn't. If he thought there was a risk, he should have taken control of the situation.

Angela   Perhaps he felt uncomfortable.

Molly   Uncomfortable? (*Laughing.*) You must be joking!

Angela   I don't find the situation particularly funny, Molly. A man has lost his life. If I were you, I'd think very carefully about the words you're using.

Silence.

Molly   He's twisting it.

Angela   Are you suggesting Duncan has fabricated this report?

Beat.

Molly   I'm saying that's not how it happened.

Angela   I see.

Silence.

Look, this isn't going away. We have to put this story to bed. The board's recommendation, and I agree, is that someone goes. If it was up to me, things would be different, but my hands are tied. Whoever it is, you can rest assured that there won't be any fanfare. Just a quiet announcement. With any luck, that'll be enough. I really am very sorry it's come to this.

Silence.

Duncan   It should be me.

Molly   What?

Duncan   I should go.

Beat.

Molly is right. Molly did her best in a difficult situation, and I failed to step up.

Angela   What do you have to say to that, Molly?

Silence.

Molly   I agree with Duncan. He should go.

Duncan (*to* **Angela**)   You'll be receiving my letter of resignation later this afternoon. If that's everything, I should get back to my desk.

Duncan *stands.*

Thank you. I've really enjoyed my time here.

He goes to leave.

Angela   No. I'm sorry, but no. Come back, Duncan.

Duncan *sits.*

Angela   Thank you.

Beat.

This isn't an easy decision. I know that everybody says that when someone has to do something horrible, they say 'this isn't an easy decision', as if that makes it better somehow. It doesn't. Still. We are where we are. And it's my job to do what I think is best for the future of this company. And my employees.

Beat.

Duncan.

Duncan Yes?

Angela I want to thank you for all your hard work. You're an asset. Nevertheless, in light of recent events I think some time off is in order. To give you the opportunity to recuperate. To process what has happened. And as recompense for the ordeal you've been through.

Beat.

But I want you to stay.

Beat.

Molly –

Molly Oh come on –

Angela You've done good work –

Molly You can't do this.

Angela Some very good work indeed –

Molly He's lying to you.

Angela But an incident like this cannot stand.

Molly You're making a mistake.

Angela So it's time for you to do the right thing.

Molly You can't let him get away with this.

Angela As I've already explained –

Molly How can you not see what he's doing?

Angela What I see is a total lack of accountability. The truth is, Molly, that despite showing promise, you've acted entirely inappropriately towards a fellow employee and put the company's reputation at stake.

Molly He's lying to you.

Angela You're sloppy, Molly.

Molly How dare you –

Angela   This isn't the first slip-up you've made and I doubt it'll be the last.

Molly   I'm good at my job.

Angela   You dropped the ball. Considering the circumstances, I'd recommend immediate dismissal, but I'm willing to let you serve out your notice.

Molly   You can't do this.

Angela   We're done here. (*To* **Molly**.) In the meantime, I strongly advise you two give each other a wide berth.

She stands and prepares to leave.

Duncan *stands and extends his hand to* **Molly**.

Duncan   No hard feelings?

Molly *looks at* **Duncan**.

Actor 1   Pause.

The clock pauses.

Rewind.

The clock rewinds and the moment replays.

Duncan *stands and extends his hand to* **Molly**.

Duncan   No hard feelings?

Molly *looks at* **Duncan**.

The clock pauses.

Actor 1   There. That flicker in her eye.

The clock rewinds and the moment replays.

Duncan *stands and extends his hand to* **Molly**.

Duncan   No hard feelings?

The clock pauses.

Actor 1   There.

Actor 3   Was that the moment, Molly?

Molly   . . .

Actor 1   Yes, this is the part.

Actor 2   This is the part where Molly feels sixteen again.

Actor 3   This is the part where it all comes flooding back.

Actor 4   This is the part where Molly decides.

The clock fast-forwards.

Actor 2   A week passes.

Actor 3   Five days to be exact.

Actor 4   And Molly does her usual thing . . .

Actor 1   She brushes her teeth, puts on her suit and goes to work.

Actor 4   As usual.

Actor 2   She parks her car in the normal spot, takes the elevator to the sixth floor and sits at her desk.

Actor 4   As usual.

Actor 3   She eats her tuna, cucumber and sweetcorn sandwich in the canteen at lunchtime.

Actor 4   As usual.

Actor 3   She meets her deadlines, responds to emails and punches out at the end of each day.

Actor 4   As usual.

Actor 1   Breaks are spent alone.

The clock lands.

Voices whisper while backs are turned. Word spreads fast. All eyes are on Molly.

The clock fast-forwards.

Actor 4   Teeth.

Suit.

Car.

The clock lands.

Actor 3   She thinks about Duncan.

Actor 2   She thinks about Angela.

Actor 1   She thinks about James.

Actor 3   Mostly Duncan. She mostly thinks about Duncan.

The clock fast-forwards.

Actor 4   Teeth.

Suit.

Car.

Emails.

The clock lands.

Actor 1   Colleagues later testified to what they described as 'Molly's simmering and barely perceptible rage'.

The clock fast-forwards.

Actor 4   Teeth.

Suit.

Car.

Emails.

Lunch.

The clock lands.

Actor 1   But she stifles it. She forces the rage down into the pit of her stomach.

The clock fast-forwards and lands.

Scene Thirteen

The offices of Empire Solutions.

Actor 3   Friday 7 June. It's a bright day. Summer.

Actor 3   Molly's packing up her desk.

Actor 2   The office is empty. It's Jessica's birthday and everybody from the office has left for the pub to celebrate.

Actor 3   Molly, of course, is not invited.

Actor 2   She switches off her computer for the last time and heads for the elevator.

Actor 1   No farewells.

Actor 4   No goodbyes.

Actor 1   No good luck cards.

Actor 2   She presses the button. It arrives immediately.

Actor 1   She steps inside and presses the button for the underground car park.

Actor 2   The doors close.

Molly   I remember concentrating on my reflection in the glass.

I remember feeling the urge to scream.

I remember opening my mouth and nothing coming out.

I remember . . . I . . .

I don't want to do this.

I can't breathe.

I need to get out.

Let me out.

Ping.

The doors open to reveal **Duncan**.

Duncan *gets into the elevator.*

The doors close.

Silence.

Molly   What were you doing on the sixth floor?

Beat.

Duncan   There was a meeting.

Molly   A meeting?

Silence.

What kind of meeting?

Beat.

Duncan   Just your average meeting.

Silence.

Molly   Who was at this meeting?

Duncan   It was a board meeting.

Molly   A board meeting?

Silence.

Angela's office is on the sixth floor. Was she at this meeting?

Silence.

So, you were at a board meeting with Angela . . .

Silence.

Angela was scheduled to select the new partner today.

The penny drops.

Silly Molly.

Ping.

Congratulations, Duncan.

The doors open.

Duncan   No hard feelings.

He goes to leave.

Molly   Duncan.

Duncan *turns back to* **Molly**.

Molly   Have you ever wondered what it would feel like to lose your family?

The doors close.

Actor 1   This is the part where it all comes flooding back.

Actor 2   This is the part where Molly decides.

Actor 4   This is the part where Molly makes her plan.

The clock fast-forwards.

Actor 3   Basement.

Actor 1   Car.

Actor 4   Boot.

Actor 2   Ignition.

Actor 3   Gate.

The clock lands.

Molly   I remember Duncan's smug grin.

I remember his perfectly sculpted hair, perfect dark suit and perfectly crafted enamel grin.

I remember feeling the urge to slam his arrogant face into the glass until his jawbone shattered and his tongue turned to pulp.

(*To* **Actor 1**.) Can we stop?

The clock fast-forwards.

Actor 1   Days pass.

Actor 2   Months.

Actor 3   Two months and three days. To be exact.

Actor 4   During this period, Molly's neighbour – Tom Chapman, a primary school teacher – reported seeing Molly leave her apartment on three occasions.

Actor 1   On Monday 15 August Molly returned home carrying a bag of items from a nearby hardware shop. The store receipt showed; a large shovel, six reams of duct tape and two shower curtains.

The clock lands.

Scene Fourteen

A hardware shop.

Duncan *has a trolley full of camping gear.*

Duncan   What do you want, Molly?

Molly   A shovel.

Duncan   What?

Molly   Something big enough to dig a grave with.

Duncan (*quietly*)   Threatening me is one thing, but showing up while I'm with my family, that's crossing a fucking line, Molly.

Molly   Steady on, Duncan, you'll pop that vein in your forehead. (*Noticing the camping gear.*) Going camping?

Duncan   You've had your fun.

Molly (*noticing someone down the aisle*)   Is that your daughter?

Beat.

Abi, isn't it? How much does she weigh? Fifty-five, sixty pounds?

Duncan   Do yourself a favour and leave us alone.

Molly   Or what?

Actor 1   This is the part where she gets into Duncan's head.

Actor 2   This is the part where Duncan knows it's only her word against his.

Actor 4   This is the part where she gets him right where she wants him.

The clock fast-forwards.

Actor 3   Friday 19 August. Mr Chapman wakes to the sound of a car pulling away at one-thirty in the morning.

Actor 2   Cobbled driveway.

Actor 1   Flowerbeds.

Actor 4   White SUV.

Molly   Duncan's house.

The clock lands.

I remember walking through the side gate.

I remember the children's trampoline.

Actor 1   Shed.

Actor 3   Summer house.

Actor 4   Patio.

Molly   I remember checking for movement.

I remember avoiding the security light.

I remember the feel of the gloves.

I remember trying the back door.

Actor 3   Locked.

Molly   I remember the open window.

I remember slipping my arm through the gap.

I remember standing in the kitchen.

I remember dirty plates and wine glasses.

I remember children's toys.

Actor 3   She listens for noise.

Actor   Nothing.

Molly   I remember picking up the carving knife from the kitchen counter.

Actor 3   Hallway.

Stairs.

Landing.

Bedroom.

Molly   I remember the door being ajar.

I remember edging my way in.

I remember seeing her asleep.

Actor 3   No Duncan?

Molly   He's already left for his camping trip.

Beat.

I remember approaching the bed.

I remember the rise and fall of her breathing.

Molly *breathes with her.*

The clock fast-forwards.

Actor 3   Hallway.

Next bedroom.

Night light.

Actor 1   Walls covered with colourful drawings.

The clock lands.

Molly   I remember Abigail sleeping soundly.

I remember the brown teddy bear under her arm.

I remember holding the blade inches from her throat . . .

The clock fast-forwards.

Landing.

Hallway.

Front door.

Car.

Home.

The clock lands.

Actor 3   No trace.

The clock fast-forwards and lands.

Actor 1   Tuesday 28 August. Mr Chapman sees Molly load the boot of her car with what looks like a shovel and a large duffel bag.

Actor 2   Are you watching?

Actor 3   Are you sitting comfortably?

Actor 4   This is the really good part.

Molly   I drive.

I remember voices in the car that are not mine.

I remember voices on the radio floating through the air.

I remember voices on the news talking about me. They slither into my head like little worms.

Actor 1   Change the station.

Molly   I remember that song playing.

I remember my reflection in the mirror. My face looks strange. It doesn't look like my face. It's someone else's face. This is a face that I've borrowed. I've stolen this face.

Actor 2   Imagine you're in a movie.

Actor 3   You're the director of your very own thriller.

Actor 4   You see it all happen before it happens.

Actor 1   In celluloid.

Actor 2   High definition.

Actor 3   Surround sound.

Actor 4   Close-up.

Actor 1   Steadicam.

Molly   The engine roars.

Actors   Sharp left.

Molly   Exit motorway.

Dim headlights.

Actors   Sharp right.

Molly   Forest.

Trees.

Find clearing.

Actors   Stop car.

Molly   Boot.

Bag.

Shovel.

Actor 1   You're walking.

Molly   I imagine peeling off my face.

I imagine the bone and cartilage underneath.

I imagine the network of muscle and sinew.

I imagine the layers of soft flesh protecting my skull.

Actor 1   You're walking to the spot in the photo.

Molly   I imagine clawing at it.

I imagine digging at it.

I imagine scraping it away and reaching the cranium.

I imagine the brain pulsating inside.

Actor 1   You're walking to the spot in the photo on Duncan's Facebook.

Molly   I imagine reaching into my skull.

I imagine retrieving the lump of grey, vibrating muscle.

I imagine holding it in the palm of my hand.

I imagine crushing it.

Actor 1   You see a light.

Torchlight blinds **Molly**.

Scene Fifteen

King's Wood.

Molly *holds a bag and shovel.*

Duncan   What's in the bag?

Molly   . . .

Duncan   What's in the bag, Molly?

Molly *throws the bag onto the ground.*

Molly   Abigail.

Beat.

Duncan   What did you say?

Molly   You asked what was in the bag.

Duncan   . . .

Molly *throws Abigail's teddy bear to* **Duncan**.

Molly   She sleeps with a night light. Moon and stars on the ceiling. Baby ducklings on her duvet.

Duncan   How . . .?

Molly   With a knife. It was very quick.

Beat.

See for yourself.

Duncan *looks at the bag.*

Molly   Open it.

Duncan *goes to the bag.*

He unzips the bag.

He looks inside the bag.

Molly   Surprise.

Duncan   You're fucking –

Molly   Now we're even.

She goes to leave.

Duncan *lunges for* **Molly** *and they both fall to the ground.*

Duncan *spots the shovel.*

Molly *spots the shovel.*

Duncan *and* **Molly** *both go for the shovel.*

Molly *picks up the shovel and hits* **Duncan** *over the head.*

Duncan *falls to the ground.*

Molly *raises the shovel and prepares to crush* **Duncan** *'s skull.*

Duncan   Don't, please, don't! Please –

Molly *beats* **Duncan** *repeatedly with the shovel until his skull is crushed.*

The clock arrives at 00:00:00:00:00:00.

Actor 1   No, Molly. That's not how it happened.

Beat.

Rewind.

The clock rewinds to 00:00:00:00:00:29.

Duncan *goes to the bag.*

He unzips the bag.

He looks inside the bag.

Molly   Surprise.

Duncan   She's . . .?

Molly   Alive. The word you're looking for is alive.

Duncan   . . .

Molly   I wanted you to feel what it's like to lose something you love.

Duncan   You're fucking –

Molly   Now we're even.

She goes to leave.

Duncan *lunges for* **Molly** *and they both fall to the ground.*

Duncan *spots the shovel.*

Molly *spots the shovel.*

Duncan *and* **Molly** *both go for the shovel.*

Molly *picks up the shovel and hits* **Duncan** *over the head.*

Duncan *falls to the ground.*

Molly *raises the shovel and prepares to crush* **Duncan's** *skull.*

Actor 1   Pause.

The clock flickers between 00:00:00:00:00:01 and 00:00:00:00:00:00.

Molly *is frozen with the shovel hovering over* **Duncan***.*

Dan *enters.*

Dan   They're saying you're dangerous. They're saying no one should approach you. They're saying you were born this way. Is that true?!

Molly   Some of it.

Dan   Do you think they'll make films about you?

Molly   Probably.

Dan   Do you think they'll get Charlize Theron to play you?

Molly   Who?

Dan   You'll be famous, Molly!

Molly *raises the shovel and prepares to crush* **Duncan's** *skull.*

Miss Woods *enters.*

Miss Woods   Oh dear, oh dear, you've got yourself into a pickle haven't you, Molly?

Molly   Miss?

Miss Woods   What face is this?

She takes out a card with an image of a smiley face on it.

Molly   A smiley face?

Miss Woods   And how do people feel when they're smiling?

Molly   Happy?

Miss Woods   Exactly. Well done, Molly.

She takes out a card with an image of a sad face on it.

What about this face?

Molly   That's a not-happy face.

Miss Woods   And how do people feel when they're doing an unhappy face?

Molly   They feel sad.

Miss Woods   Good, Molly. And we don't want to make people sad do we?

She turns **Molly**'s *attention back to* **Duncan**.

Miss Woods   Now what do you think we should do?

Beat.

Dan   What are you going to do, Molly?

Molly *raises the shovel and prepares to crush* **Duncan**'s *skull.*

Dad *enters.*

Dad   Don't, please, don't! Please –

Molly   Dad?

Dad   What are we going to do with you, my little 'Molly Mischief Maker'.

Molly   Do you hate me?

Dad   Of course not.

Molly   Does Mummy hate me?

Dad   Mummy loves you.

Molly   Is she in heaven?

Dad   On a big fluffy cloud looking down on us.

Molly   Mummy used to say when we do bad things, we should tell someone to make it better.

Dad   Well, we can't tell anyone about this can we, darling? If we tell people, they might get scared and take you away. You don't want that do you, Molly?

Molly *shakes her head.*

Dad   You want to stay with Daddy?

Molly *nods.*

Dad   We'll tell a story. But we have to pretend it's real. It's important we make people believe the story.

Molly   How do we do that?

Dad   Can you cry?

Molly   No.

Dad   Make yourself feel sad.

Molly   But I don't feel sad.

Dad   Think about Mummy.

Molly *tries to make herself sad.*

Dad   What do you feel, Molly?

Molly   Nothing.

Dad   Try harder.

Molly *tries to make herself sad.*

Molly   Nothing.

Dad   Come on, Molly.

Molly *tries to make herself sad.*

Dad   You look so much like her. It makes me feel better to look at you. It gives me great relief to know there's nothing of me in you.

Molly *lowers the shovel.*

The clock arrives at 00:00:00:00:00:00.

Duncan *slowly stands.*

Police lights glare.

Molly *and* **Duncan** *look at each other.*

Actor 3   Let's give Molly a round of applause.

Actor 1   At ten past nine on Tuesday 28 August, Molly Chambers was arrested in King's Wood for the attempted murder of Duncan Robertson. Molly was taken into custody and charged with attempted murder, breaking and entering, and threatening behaviour. Molly maintains her innocence and claims she was 'defending herself'.

Epilogue

Actor 3   We know that was hard for you, Molly.

The **Actors** *present* **Molly** *with her prison clothes.*

Molly *begins changing her clothes.*

Molly (*to* **Actor 1**)   What happens now?

Molly *looks at the audience.*

Molly   Shall I scream?

She screams.

Shall I go on the lam?

She pretends to make a run for it.

Shall I beg? Go down on my hands and knees and tell you how sorry I am.

She pretends to beg for forgiveness.

Don't send me away.

I didn't mean to hurt anyone.

I'm sick.

I need help.

Will you help me?

Help me to be better.

Help me to be *good*.

How was that?

(*To* **Actor 4**.) Too much?

Molly   You aren't looking for a redemption story, are you?

She looks at **Laura** *in the audience.*

Hi, Laura . . .

Remember that day in the woods . . .?

You nearly went through with it. If that day had turned out different, you'd be the one standing here.

She is dressed; the **Actors** *wait for her at the exit.*

Molly   I've spent my whole life lying to people. I don't know when it started but I've been doing it since I was a little girl. It's as easy as breathing for me . . .

Sometimes I lie to get what I want. Sometimes I lie to cover my tracks. Sometimes I lie for fun because I like how it feels. I always know when I'm lying. I make the choice and I'm in control.

But you . . . you've been lying for years, and you don't even realize it. You lie to yourself.

Look at her. 'Lovely Laura'. A perfect angel. Never late for class. Always has a shiny new pencil case at the start of term. Hands in homework early. 'Hi, miss', 'Thanks, miss', 'See you tomorrow, miss'.

I used to ask myself, why does she want to be my friend?

If we're so different, if you're so good and I'm such an awful bitch, why do you want to be my friend? I think I know now . . .

You needed the perfect excuse.

You got tired of pretending to be perfect, you couldn't hack the goody-two-shoes routine and you wanted to do something – anything – to feel alive for a change, but you needed someone to blame when things got out of hand, so you kept me around to give yourself permission to be cruel.

But don't forget it was *me* who stopped *you* in the woods that day. You lit the match, turned around and blamed me but the hilarious thing is that if it wasn't for me you'd have killed him. If you really think about it, *I* rescued *you*.

But where were you when I needed rescuing, Laura?

I know what I am. I know my insides are all wrong. But maybe if you're being honest with yourself, you'd see that you're just as bad. Maybe even worse.

Maybe you're the scorpion and I'm the frog.

She looks at the exit where the **Actors** *are waiting.*

Molly *looks at the audience.*

Molly   Ribbit.

Blackout.

The Incredible True Story of the Johnstown Flood

This play was first performed to an invited audience at Ugly Duck, London in April 2021.

Created by Lee Anderson, Adam Foster and Andrew Whyment
Text by Lee Anderson and Adam Foster

Actor 1/Ken | Daniel Adeosun
Actor 2/Manager/Ruff | Natalie Radmall-Quirke
Actor 3/Heroine/Sally/Sallamina | Alice Vilanculo
Actor 4/Clown/Pearson | Martin Quinn
Actor 5/Musician | Philippa Hogg

Director | Andrew Whyment
Writers | Lee Anderson, Adam Foster
Movement Director | Kane Husbands

Stage Manager | Lavinia Serban

Characters

Actor 1/Ken
Actor 2/Manager/Ruff
Actor 3/Heroine/Sally/Sallamina
Actor 4/Clown/Pearson
Actor 5/Musician

Notes

The action takes place inside the Johnstown Opera House in the weeks after the Johnstown Flood in 1889. The action of the play-within-the-play takes place at South Fork Fishing and Hunting Club, fourteen miles upriver from Johnstown, eight years before the Johnstown Flood, in 1881.

The actors' own characteristics should bleed through in specific moments; deliberate slippage between actor and character is encouraged.

The text in brackets should be replaced with material created by the actors performing the play.

Prologue

Actor 1 *enters.*

Actor 1   [Rahhh.

It's proper sick to see so many of you here.

Thanks for coming.

The Incredible True Story of the Johnstown Flood.

Wow. Sick.

My name's Daniel, I'm twenty-two and I'm from East London. Barking and Dagenham's finest.

I'm playing the role of Ken.

I was introduced to Squint – the company who made this show – via a Zoom call. It was a bit mad cos Covid locked off my drama school's final-year performances and we had to have lessons online. Still. I'm here now. So it weren't all bad.

The play you're about to see is based on the real events of the Johnstown Flood.

Johnstown is a small town in Pennsylvania.

In 1889 it flooded. That's because the dam up at the rich white people's Disneyland – the South Fork Fishing and Hunting Club – split open. The torrent killed over two thousand people. Some say it was more. Maybe tens of thousands.

At the time, it was the biggest natural disaster in American history.

They held a trial – a trial to find out whether the Club owners were to blame for all those people losing their lives – and surprise-surprise, no one was held accountable.

Thousands died and the rich guys got away with it.

When I started working on this play, I tried to keep in mind that even though the story is based on real events, Ken – the central character, *my* character – isn't real. Squint made him up as a way of telling the story.

So . . . who is Ken?

Well, let's see.

Ken's a labourer. He's lived in Johnstown his whole life, never been nowhere else, and he's been scraping by on manual jobs ever since he was a young'un.

So I guess Ken must be strong, right? Because he's got to carry around raw materials all day long.

Actor 1 *explores* **Ken***'s physicality.*

So I started asking myself . . . what does that kind of job do to your body?

To your shoulders?

Your knees?

What about the texture of Ken's hands? They must be rough. Proper dry. Cracked.

How about the way he breathes? Like, does Ken have shallow breathing because of all the dust he kicks up working outdoors?

Actor 1 *breathes as* **Ken**.

And then I started thinking, Ken must be one of the few Black people in Johnstown. So how does Ken walk around town?

Does he walk with his chest deflated, so he's not seen by all those white folks as a threat?

Or does he walk in his power because he knows his worth?

But shit. *Is* Ken Black?

Cos maybe Squint wrote him as a white fella and I'm only here to fill a quota?

Nah, Ken is Black. Cos I'm Black.

So what about my accent?

Actor 1 *explores* **Ken**'s *accent*.

Is there such a thing as a Pennsylvanian accent?

A Pennsylvanian African American accent?

The majority of African American accents have a lil' southern something in them – but damn! – how far is Pennsylvania from the South?]

Actor 1 *locks into an accent*.

What's Ken afraid of?

What does he yearn for?

What do I do next?

Actor 1 *is now* **Ken**.

My town's driftwood.

I've lost my home.

My livelihood.

Everything.

I try to get some rest in the doorway outside the Opera House.

Ken *lies down*.

I'm cold.

I'm hungry.

I'm alone.

A Chance Encounter

The Johnstown Opera House, one day after the flood.

Actor 2 *enters.*

Can you help me, ma'am?

Please.

Please.

Please.

Please.

Please.

Actor 2 *becomes* **Heroine.**

We head inside the Opera House.

Turns out she's not from around here.

Turns out she's an actress.

Turns out she was doing a play here before she got caught up in all this.

Tells me her troupe's getting on the first train outta town.

Heroine *hands* **Ken** *a violin.*

Ken   I help her get her things together.

Heroine   Everybody, say hello to Kenneth! He's been assisting me with my little retrieval effort. A perfect gentleman.

Musician   You found it!

Musician *takes the violin and plucks a few strings.*

Heroine   Isn't he a darling?

Ken   I appreciate you folks letting me catch a ride with you.

Manager (*to* **Ken**)   I beg your pardon?

Heroine (*to* **Manager**)   I might have promised Ken he could come with us.

Clown (*to* **Heroine**)   What did you do that for?

Heroine (*to* **Clown**)   He asked me!

Clown (*to* **Heroine**)   And you didn't think to check with us first?

Heroine (*to* **Clown**)   His entire home's been washed away.

Musician (*to* **Manager**)   He did do us a favour.

Clown (*to* **Musician**)   You mean he did *you* a favour? I'm still missing half my wardrobe.

Manager   Enough.

Silence.

Let's maintain some perspective here. The boy's clearly desperate. What harm can it do?

Beat.

Ken can join us until the next town.

Heroine   The problem is . . . he doesn't have enough money for a ticket.

Clown   Here it comes . . .

Heroine   So I said we'd pay.

Clown   And there it is.

Musician *finds some change in her pocket and gives it to* **Heroine**.

Heroine   Thank you.

Manager *finds some change and gives it to* **Heroine**.

Heroine (*to* **Clown**)   We're still a little short.

Clown *finds some change but holds onto it.*

Heroine   There's enough here to get you to the next town.

Manager   We'll pay for your ride to Lewistown and then we'll go our separate ways.

Ken   Can't I come with you?

Clown   Sorry, we're broke enough as it is.

Musician   He could be useful.

Clown   Oh could he?

Ken   I work a lot with my hands. I can build you things.

Clown   Gee, really?

Musician   We are one down since Marsha blagged her way onto a stagecoach . . .

Heroine   Maybe we could find a temporary spot for him?

Clown   No way!

Ken   You mean I could join your band?

Clown   We're not a band. And you don't *join*, you *audition*.

Manager   Do you have any talents, Ken?

Ken   . . .

He does a small thing.

Clown   What was that?

Musician   Not bad.

Manager   Have you got anything else?

Ken *does a bigger thing.*

Manager   We could work with that . . .

Musician   I like it!

Manager   But I'm sorry, Ken, we can't just go offering places out willy-nilly. This is a craft. A *profession.*

Clown   You need range, or else people get bored.

Beat.

Ken   I can tell you a story.

Musician   What kind of story?

Ken   A true story.

Clown   How long is it?

Heroine (*to* **Clown**)   I think we can spare the time, don't you?

Beat.

Ken   You ever heard of Benjamin Ruff?

Manager   Rich chap who's been in all the papers?

Ken   Me and my old man used to work for him.

The **Troupe** *exchange glances.*

Manager   What kind of work?

Ken   This was some years back.

Me and my old man are crossing Broad Street – I'm helping him load up the truck – and we see this carriage hit a pothole.

Now what you got to understand about my old man is he made it his business to look out for people. That's the way he was. Some of the fellas who worked with him up at the Mill, well, they were good people, but they liked to talk tough and keep to themselves. My old man did things different. He trusted people. Saw the best in 'em. And he weren't afraid of a little conversation either.

So he offers to help.

And would you believe it? That fella in the carriage is Mr Ruff himself.

And the second we've patched up his wheel, Ruff's offering my old man work. He needs help building a carriageway up at his Club. A carriageway over the top of the dam so all those fancy rich folk can ride in and out.

They shake on it and next thing I know, I'm on a train heading up to South Fork with my old man.

Three weeks we was up there. Three weeks, before . . .

First day working there I bump into this girl. Didn't know it at the time but this girl – Sally, her name was – she's Ben Ruff's daughter. She's around my age, so we become friendly some and – me and Sally – we start noticing all this . . . *stuff*.

This *change* comes over my old man. Used to be you couldn't stop him talking but now you're lucky if you can squeeze two words outta him. He'd shoot you a look and it'd mean 'good job' or 'get outta my sight'.

Something was eating at him.

Anyways, we're three weeks in, the carriageway's good as done and the Club's set to open and Sally shows up. She gives me this letter.

Some engineer fella who's been inspecting the dam says it ain't safe. Says Ruff and my old man are involved in something rotten.

Now I'm *really* thinking something ain't right. I'm thinking my old man's in some kinda trouble!

So I march up to the clubhouse – it's opening night so all these rich folks are milling about – and I rush into Ruff's study, and there's my old man . . .

Just stood there.

He looks tired. More tired than I've ever seen him.

I say to Mr Ruff, 'If you don't stop what you're doing I'll take this letter and tell everyone in town what kinda danger you're putting them in!'

And my old man . . .

He's silent.

He ain't saying a word.

And he ain't looking at me.

He shot himself.

You forget a lot of things in eight years. But you don't forget a thing like that. Stays with you. Like a stain you can't scrub out.

You know, I've been doing a lot of remembering these past few days. Looking back at that time, trying to get a different angle on it. If you ask me, this flood, all the people they're pulling out the water, it ain't no coincidence or wrath of God, freak of nature, like they're sayin'. This is no accident.

It's the same as my old man; it's cos of that place and those folks up there. It's cos of *him up there*, Benjamin Ruff, and his precious carriageway!

Silence.

Clown *applauds.*

The **Troupe** *flash* **Clown** *a look.*

Clown *stops clapping.*

Manager   Ken, that was . . .

Clown   Unbelievable.

Heroine   I'm so sorry, Ken.

Ken *notices* **Musician** *is crying.*

Clown   Put that on stage and there won't be a dry eye in the house.

Beat.

Manager   Now there's an idea . . .

Ken   What?

Manager   Telling your story.

Ken   I just did.

Heroine   He means on a stage.

Manager   Here in Johnstown.

Beat.

Who else have you told?

Ken   No one.

Manager   You've kept that story to yourself all these years?

Ken   . . .

Heroine   Why?

Ken   Whose gonna believe me?

Heroine   We believe you.

Ken   You ain't from around here.

Heroine   People deserve to know the truth.

Ken   Look, if you folks wanna help, get me as far away from this place as possible.

Heroine   But Ken –

Manager   Let him run if he wants.

Ken   I ain't running.

Manager   Oh no? Then what would you call it?

Ken   You don't know the first thing about it.

Clown 'Thou shall have justice, more than thou desirest.'

Ken . . .

Clown Well, that's what you really want isn't it, boy?

Ken . . .

Manager Justice.

Ken . . .

Manager For your father. For this town. You won't find it by fleeing the scene of the crime.

Ken Maybe not. But I ain't gonna find it with some dumbass costumes and play-acting neither am I?

Manager Now you listen to me, young man. I've been in this 'play-acting' business a very long time. Too long. I've stood on hundreds of stages and looked out at thousands of people. I've seen grown men brought to tears. Sometimes it's a few words that does it. Sometimes it's little more than a gesture. But that's what the right story at the right time can do.

Take it from me, that story of yours, put it on stage and people will have no choice but to sit up and pay attention.

And I'll tell you something else. You'll make sure that this Benjamin Ruff fellow doesn't get another good night's sleep for the rest of his life.

Ken . . .

Manager Or you can run . . .

Beat.

Ken How does it work?

The First Rehearsal

Twelve weeks until opening night. **Ken** *and the* **Troupe** *rehearse a scene set on his first day at South Fork, eight weeks before the opening of the Club.*

Ken *stands with his eyes closed while* **Musician** *plays something soft.*

Ken I see us pulling out the station.

I see some guys smoking and playing cards.

I see the town getting real small as we go up into the hills.

I see my old man . . . sitting . . . staring out the window.

I see the train slowing.

I see a sign that says 'South Fork'.

He opens his eyes.

Heroine   Go on . . .

Ken *closes his eyes.*

Ken   We're walking down the path.

I see the sun shining through cracks in the trees.

I see insects, birds, acorns, flowers.

I see the lake as we come out the forest.

I see the footpath curling round the lake.

I see the door to the clubhouse.

I step inside.

Warm stale air rushes across my face.

I see the hallway.

I see a chandelier above the stairs.

I see paintings of rich old men.

I see the stairs.

I see a seat outside the study.

I sit.

I sit and I wait.

I see a sign that says 'Club President'.

I see light coming in through the window at the end of the hall.

I see a picture of the Mill in town.

I see it's not hung straight.

I see a scratch in the paint.

I see a crack running down the wall.

I see where the crack disappears behind a grandfather clock.

I see the big hand ticking.

I see it tick.

I see it tick.

I see it tick.

I see it tick.

I see it tick.

I see my old man come out the study.

He doesn't look at me, he just tells me to follow.

We walk along the lake path and I follow behind with my tool bag.

He walks.

He walks.

He walks.

I stop to tie my shoelace.

I look up.

He's gone.

I walk and I walk and then I run and I run and a girl jumps out and says –

Manager *gestures to* **Musician**.

Casting

Eleven weeks until opening night. **Ken** *and the* **Troupe** *rehearse a scene set in the woods, six weeks before the opening of the Club.*

Musician/Sally (*becoming* **Sally**)   Hey!

Ken   What are you – ?

Manager   Keep going, Ken.

Ken   Say, 'You do realize you're trespassing?'

Musician/Sally   You do realize you're trespassing?

Ken (*to* **Manager** *quietly*)   I don't like it.

Manager (*to* **Musician**)   He doesn't like it. (*Gesturing to* **Heroine**.) [Alice].

Heroine *walks around the space as* **Sally**.

Heroine   What do you want to see Ken?

Ken   She's confident.

Heroine *walks confidently.*

Ken   She's a bit of a show-off.

Heroine *walks performatively.*

Ken   But she can be shy.

Heroine *finds some inner life.*

Heroine/Sally   You do realize you're trespassing?

Ken   Say, 'You're standing on private property.'

Heroine/Sally   You're standing on private property.

Ken   'You can't be here without a licence!'

Heroine/Sally   You can't be here without a licence!

Ken   Who says?

Sally   Present the relevant papers or vacate the property immediately.

Ken (*to* **Musician**)   You're kidding.

Sally   Failure to produce the relevant papers will result in a fine and being escorted from the premises.

Ken (*to* **Musician**)   She didn't say that.

Sally   Refusal to leave the premises in a peaceful and orderly fashion will mean the proprietor will invoke their right to shoot the trespasser on site.

Ken *looks to* **Manager**.

Manager   Go with it, Ken . . .

Ken *reluctantly plays along*.

Ken   Oh I'm so scared, please don't shoot me! Get out of my way.

He goes to leave but **Sally** *gets in his way*.

Sally   If you don't turn around in three seconds, I'll be forced to take drastic measures. One . . . two –

Ken *walks past* **Sally**.

Sally *takes a tool out of* **Ken**'*s bag*.

Ken   Hey, do you mind?

He snatches **Sally**'*s fishing rod*.

Sally   Put that down.

Ken   (*inspecting the hook*)   You call that a hook?

Sally   As if you know.

Ken   You won't catch a cold with a knot like this.

Sally   Oh thank you, I've been waiting for a big strong clever man to come along and explain things I already know.

She goes to throw the tool into the lake.

Ken   Whoa, be careful with that!

Sally (*impersonating* **Ken**)   'Oh, look at me. I'm a big dumb stupid gristle head with a big bag of tools and all I do is trespass on other people's property and mess with stuff that doesn't belong to me.'

Ken (*to* **Heroine**)   I tell her to cut it out.

Silence.

Heroine/Sally   I tell him to make me.

Ken *sees something in* **Heroine**'s *performance.*

Ken   I ask her name.

Heroine/Sally   I tell him that's none of his business.

Ken   I say, 'Me and my old man are fixing up the carriageway'.

Sally   Over the dam?

Ken   That's right, so if you don't mind –

He goes to leave but **Sally** *gets in his way.*

Sally   Wait, did you say you're here to work on the carriageway?

Ken   Yeah, so I ain't got time to be standing around here explaining myself to you.

Sally   Huh . . . So you're the new guys.

Ken   There were fellas here before us?

Heroine/Sally   Well, sure.

Ken (*to* **Manager**)   That's Sally!

Beat.

I ask her when.

Heroine/Sally   I say, 'Few weeks ago'.

Ken   I ask where they went.

Heroine/Sally   I tell him they just up and left.

Ken   What, they just downed tools?

Sally   That's right.

Ken   I say, 'Well it sounds like the fella who runs this place is dumber than a bag of hammers'. (*To the* **Troupe**.) Stupid thing to say.

Heroine/Sally   I say, 'How come?'

Ken   I say, 'You got to be pretty dumb to hire a bunch of fellas who don't know their assholes from their elbows, pay them to do a shitty job, then turn around and pay a whole new bunch of fellas to fix the shitty job that the first bunch of fellas did'.

Sally   Well, you sound like you've got it all figured out.

Ken   How do you know all this anyway?

Sally   Because my daddy's the fella who owns this place.

Beat.

Ken   Oh, shit. I mean, not shit. Shit. Sorry. I didn't know . . . Your old man owns this place?

Sally   Well, sure.

Ken   The whole Club?

Sally   Uh-huh.

Ken   Sorry.

Sally   You said that already.

Beat.

You do know I could have my daddy fire you just for looking at me?

Ken   Please don't do that.

Sally   He's got a gun you know . . .

Silence.

Get lost before I change my mind.

Ken *gives* **Sally** *her fishing rod.*

Sally *gives* **Ken** *the tool.*

The **Troupe** *applaud.*

Manager   Bravo, Ken!

Heroine   He's a natural!

Acting Class

Ten weeks until opening night. **Ken** *and* **Heroine** *tidy the space.*

Ken (*to* **Heroine**)   How do you do that?

Heroine   What?

Ken   Act . . . like that. You're good at being Sally.

Heroine   You think?

Ken   You're so . . . *realistic.*

Beat.

Seriously, how do you do that?

Heroine *stops tidying.*

She goes over to **Ken**, *puts her hands on his shoulders and relaxes him.*

She turns him out towards the audience.

Heroine   Now speak in your own voice.

Ken   'Speak in my own voice.'

Heroine   From here . . .

She places a hand on his diaphragm; he flinches, then relaxes into it.

Ken   'Speak in my own voice from there.'

Heroine   Good. 'If she be false, O, then heaven mocks itself!'

Ken   What?

Heroine   Say, 'If she be false, O, then heaven mocks itself!'

Ken   'If she be false, O, then heaven mocks itself!'

Heroine   Okay, now imagine it isn't for a big audience. It's for one person.

Ken (*quietly*)   'If she be false, O, then heaven mocks itself!'

Heroine   Don't lose the energy.

Ken (*loudly*)   'If she be false, O, then heaven mocks itself!'

Heroine   But the audience still needs to feel, 'Ah, he's speaking to us'.

She guides **Ken** *to the lip of the stage.*

Ken   So I'm talking to them?

Heroine   *One* of them.

Ken (*to one person in the audience*)   'If she be false, O, then heaven mocks itself!'

Heroine   Exactly!

Ken   What's 'O'?

Heroine   It's an expression. Like 'O'.

Ken (*to one person in the audience*)   'If she be false, O, then heaven mocks itself!'

Heroine   Good.

Ken   Will there be people right at the back?

Heroine   Hope so! Now speak it to me . . .

Ken *and* **Heroine** *stand opposite each other and make eye contact.*

Ken   'If she be false, O, then heaven mocks itself!'

Heroine   Told you you were a natural.

Artistic Differences

Eight weeks until opening night. **Ken** *and the* **Troupe** *rehearse a scene set at the pavilion, four weeks before the opening of the Club.*

Manager   So you're working away on the dam . . .

Ken   That's right.

Manager   And you know nothing about the dangers of the work you're doing at this point?

Ken   Nothing.

Beat.

Nothing until the inspection.

Clown   Ah yes, the inspection!

Ken   We're a few weeks into the job and my old man moves me off the dam.

Clown (*searching for inspiration*)   Go on . . .

Ken   He comes over and says, 'Move'.

Clown   Right . . .

Ken   He goes, 'Get the paint and come with me.'

Clown   'Get the paint and come with me.'

Ken   He's never talked to me like that before, so I'm like, 'What the f –'.

'Cept I don't curse cos –

So I'm following my old man over to this pavilion in the woods when we see this carriage arriving . . .

This fella in overalls steps out, flanked by a couple of other fellas. Official lookin'.

Soon as my old man sees 'em heading for the dam he just –

Clown/Pearson   Paint it.

Ken (*to* **Clown**)   What?

Clown/Pearson   I need that pavilion paintin'.

Ken (*to* **Manager**)   What's he doing?

Clown/Pearson   This ain't no child's play, boy. Are you good for this work?

Ken (*to* **Clown**)   Stop it.

Clown/Pearson *squares up to* **Ken**.

Clown/Pearson   Well, are you?

Ken (*firmly*)   Stop.

He and **Clown/Pearson** *hold eye contact.*

Clown   Okay.

He drops it.

Manager   It's the day of the inspection. You're painting the pavilion.

Heroine *fetches a tin of paint and two brushes and hands them to* **Ken**.

Sally *enters and finds* **Ken** *painting a wall.*

Sally (*picking up the tin of paint*)   What's this?

Ken   Paint.

Sally   What sort of paint?

Ken   Blow de France.

Sally   'Blow de France'? It's Bleu de France . . .

Ken   That's what I said.

Sally   My daddy asked you to paint the pavilion?

Ken   Well, your old man asked my old man who asked me.

Sally   Why?

Ken   Cos that's what he's paying us for.

Sally   I thought he was paying you to build the carriageway?

Ken   He is.

Sally   Oh, so you got demoted . . .

She laughs.

Did you fall off your ladder, crack open your skull and now Daddy doesn't trust you with tools anymore?

Ken   We had to stop.

Sally   How come?

Ken   Some fella's up there inspecting it.

Sally   What fella?

Ken   Big ol' engineer fella with a face like thunder.

Sally   Well, that don't sound too good.

Ken   Over there, see.

He points towards the dam.

Sally   Uh-oh. That's Mr Fulton.

Ken   . . .

Sally   He looks mad.

Ken   . . .

Sally   Maybe you'll get fired and then you won't follow me around anymore.

Ken   Very funny.

Clown (*to* **Heroine**)   Pick up a brush and dunk it in his tin . . .

Heroine/Sally *picks up a brush and dunks it in* **Ken**'s *tin.*

Ken *gives* **Clown** *a look.*

Clown What?

Sally *starts painting as* **Ken** *keeps painting.*

Sally   Have you ever been to France?

Ken   Well, sure.

Sally   Really! '

Ken   Sure, we travel the world on what your old man pays us. Could be up the Eiffel Tower right now but we just can't get enough of painting pavilions and building carriageways!

Beat.

No, I ain't been to France.

Manager *gives* **Ken** *a thumbs-up.*

Sally   I have.

Ken   Well, good for you.

Beat.

(*To the* **Manager**.) I keep painting cos my old man could be back from the inspection any second –

Clown   You keep *pretending* to paint.

Ken   No, I keep *painting*.

Clown   You're pretending to paint and stealing looks at Sally.

Ken   What? No –

Clown (*to* **Heroine**)   Dab his face with paint.

Sally *dabs* **Ken**'s *face with paint.*

Ken   Hey, cut it out!

Sally   Sorry, I slipped.

Beat.

Clown   Do it again.

Sally *dabs* **Ken***'s face with paint.*

Ken   Stop!

Sally (*French accent*)   Oh *pardon*, I was not paying attention.

Clown   And again.

Sally *dabs* **Ken***'s face with paint.*

Ken   I mean it, stop that!

Clown (*to* **Sally**)   Now pretend your brush is a sword.

Sally *strikes a fighting pose.*

Ken   What?!

Sally (*French accent*)   *En garde, monsieur.* Draw your weapon! I challenge you to open combat.

Ken *gives* **Sally** *a look.*

Clown   Go with it, Ken . . .

Beat.

Ken (*reluctantly*)   I draw my weapon.

Sally   We sword fight with our brushes!

Ken *and* **Sally** *fight.*

Ken   I'm better than her!

Sally   I'm winning!

Ken   I smear paint on her dress!

He smears paint on **Sally***'s dress.*

Sally   Oh no!

Ken   Surrender!

Sally   It's not funny, Ken. My daddy's gonna be mad!

Ken   It was an accident.

Sally   You're such an idiot!

Ken   It's just a little paint.

Sally   Do you know how much this dress cost?

Ken   I dunno, fifty cents?

Sally   Try fifty dollars.

She attempts to untie the back of her dress.

Musician *whispers to* **Heroine**.

Ken   Fifty dollars?!

Sally   He'll flip his lid when he sees this.

Ken   Your old man paid fifty dollars for a *dress*?

Sally   Shut up and help me get it off.

Beat.

Ken   You want me to. . .?

Sally (*seductively*)   Well, I can't reach the back by myself, can I?

Ken   How do you put it on if you can't reach the back?

Sally   Can you just help me get it off?

Beat.

Please.

Ken *goes to* **Sally** *and loosens her dress.*

Sally *turns and faces* **Ken**.

Ken   What are you doing?

Sally   Have you ever kissed a girl before?

Ken (*to* **Manager**)   We never kissed.

Clown   But you wanted to?

Ken   No.

Heroine   [Martin]!

Clown   Are you honestly telling me there was no attraction between you?

Ken *looks at* **Heroine**.

Ken   Maybe a little –

Clown   I knew it!

Ken   But we never kissed.

Clown   If you could go back in time and kiss Sally right now, would you do it?

Ken   . . .

Clown   I don't hear a no.

Ken   This ain't no love story.

Clown   Ah, the pangs of dispriz'd love . . .

He acts out a love story in mime.

Musician *plays.*

Clown (*presenting a bouquet on one knee*)   Poor boy falls in love with unattainable rich girl . . .

He switches roles and accepts the flowers.

It's a love story as old as time.

He spins joyfully with the flowers.

He throws the flowers over his shoulder, as if he's the bride at a wedding.

Ken *impulsively catches the flowers.*

Clown *cheers.*

Musician *plays climactically.*

Ken   Are you done?

The Suicide Scene (v. 1)

Six weeks until opening night. **Ken** *and the* **Troupe** *rehearse* **Pearson**'s *death.*

Ken   Smoke. Burnt meat.

Manager   What can you hear?

Ken   The fire . . . crackling . . . in the living room . . .

Manager   Follow that sound . . .

Ken   I walk into the living room. It's all over the floor . . . across the chairs . . . up the walls . . . He's . . . He's his front . . . face down . . . on the floor . . . in front of the fire . . .

Manager *gestures to* **Clown**.

Clown *lies down on the floor in front of* **Ken**.

Manager   Open your eyes.

Ken *opens his eyes and stares at* **Clown**.

Interventions

Four weeks until opening night. **Ken** *and the* **Troupe** *rehearse a scene set in* **Ruff**'s *study, two weeks before the opening of the Club.*

Sally   Quit being a baby!

Ken   My old man told me to wait outside.

Sally *pulls* **Ken** *inside.*

Sally   You'll catch your death if you stand out there all night.

Ken   I'll catch a beating if he finds me in here.

Sally   Five minutes.

Ken   . . .

Sally   We got a fire.

Beat.

Ken   I guess five minutes can't hurt.

He enters and takes in the room.

What's this room for?

Sally   It's my daddy's study.

Ken   No kidding.

Beat.

It's kinda spooky. Fancy, but spooky.

Sally   You want to see something neat?

Stage Managers *wheel a diorama into the middle of the room.*

Ken (*to* **Manager**)   What's this?

Sally   Impressive, right?

Ken   Yeah, that sure is something. I mean I ain't that into doll's houses, but . . .

Sally   It's not a doll's house, stupid. It's the Club. It's a model of this place.

Ken *looks closer.*

Ken   Huh. So it is.

Sally   Would you care for a guided tour of the premises, Mr Pearson?

Beat.

Ken   Don't mind if I do, Miss Ruff.

Sally *takes* **Ken** *by the arm and shows him around the diorama.*

Sally   This is the entrance that leads to the hall. To the left you'll find the drawing room, for reading and taking tea, and to your right, you'll find the veranda with a frankly spectacular view of the lake.

She leads **Ken** *to a window and points to the real veranda outside.*

Sally   See?

Ken   Magnificent!

Sally   Through the hall, you'll find the entrance to the boathouse, but head upstairs and we'll arrive at the games room on your right, that's where you'll find me beating everyone at billiards, draughts and cribbage.

Ken   Splendid!

Sally   And on your left, there's the dining hall. I chose the table and chairs. They're dark oak, see? That's what your daddy'll be sitting on right now.

Ken   Did your old man build this himself?

Sally   Nah, he paid someone else to do it.

Ken   So, what, it's somebody's job to make toy models of real-life places?

Sally   It's not a toy.

Ken   So what's it do then?

Sally   It's not supposed to *do* anything.

Ken   So what's it for?

Sally   It's an object of contemplation.

Silence.

The sound of raised voices upstairs.

That's not good.

Ken   They're really going at it, huh?

He and **Sally** *listen.*

Sally   Your daddy's got a temper on him.

Ken   Yeah, well your old man's giving as good as he gets.

He and **Sally** *listen.*

Ken *goes to some photos on the wall.*

Ken   Your old man sure has met a lot of people.

Sally   Oh yeah. My daddy loves shaking hands and taking photos with important people.

Ken (*pointing to a framed photo*)   I recognize this fella.

Sally   That's the Egg Man.

Ken   The Egg Man?

Sally   Andrew Carnegie. We call him the Egg Man.

Ken   Your old man knows Andrew Carnegie?

Sally   Well, sure. He's helping pay for this place.

Ken   You serious?

Sally   Well, sure.

Ken   Jeez. Talk about rubbing elbows.

He notices a revolver mounted on the wall.

What's that?

Sally   Ergh. *That.*

Ken   You don't like it?

Sally   Hunk of junk. Papa won it at auction. Belonged to some general.

Ken   Your old man paid top dollar for this and then stuck it on a wall?

Sally   Well, sure.

Ken   Why do you always say 'sure' like it don't mean nothing?

Sally   What?

Ken   You always say 'Well, sure' like all this stuff ain't even s'posed to be important.

Sally   What do you want me to say?

Ken   I dunno. But you can't pretend like your old man shaking hands with Andrew Carnegie and buying up old shooters ain't a big deal . . .

Sally   Well, it's not.

Ken *looks at the revolver.*

Ken   Whose side?

Sally   Hm?

Ken   Whose side was the general on?

The altercation upstairs becomes even more heated.

Whatever that Fulton fella found, don't sound like good news.

Sally   It never is.

Ken   You think there's some kinda trouble?

Sally   Something ain't right.

Ken *and* **Sally** *listen.*

Ken *goes to the drinks cabinet, picks up a glass and searches the room.*

What you doing now?

Ken   Gimme that chair.

Sally   What? Why?

Ken   So I can hear what they're saying.

Sally   Just ignore it.

Ken   Can't ignore a racket like that.

He grabs a chair and moves it to the centre of the room.

He stands on the chair, holds the glass to the ceiling and listens.

Sally   Well?

Ken   Hold on.

He listens.

Your old man keeps shouting about the lake.

Sally   What about the lake?

Ken *listens.*

Ken   Can't make it out.

Stage Managers *wheel on a piano.*

Sally   Why don't I play us something?

Ken *gets down from the chair and puts the glass down.*

Heroine *gestures for* **Ken** *to join her.*

Ken *and* **Sally** *sit together at the piano.*

Sally *takes out some sheet music and places it on the stand.*

Sally When I nod, you turn the page okay?

She plays something beautiful; **Ken** *turns the sheet music.*

As the commotion upstairs intensifies so too does **Sally**'s *playing.*

The commotion upstairs subsides.

Sally *stops playing.*

Sally Sorry. I lost it.

Ken   No, that was good. You're really good.

Sally *smiles at* **Ken**.

Silence.

Clown *smashes a glass.*

Ken *jumps to his feet.*

Sally   Where are you going?

Ken   My old man's been acting strange since we got here –

Sally *gets in* **Ken** *'s way.*

Sally   You can't.

Ken   Why not?

Sally   You'll get us in trouble.

Ken   Move out the way, Sal.

Sally   What good will it do if you barge in there all guns blazing like some hothead?

Ken   Ain't you worried?

Sally   They're just rough necking. It was probably just an accident.

Ken   Well, if it was an accident, then you won't mind if I go up there and see for myself.

Sally   I won't let you.

Ken   Why are you always getting in my way? Do you have any idea how annoying you are? What's your deal anyway?

Sally   Excuse me?

Ken   You heard me. Do you get off on tormenting me or something?

Sally   No!

Ken   Well, then –

Sally   I'm trying to protect you.

Ken   Protect me? (*To* **Heroine**.) What the hell have you got to protect me from?

Sally   You and your daddy should get as far away from here as possible.

Ken (*to* **Manager**)   What?

Sally   You'd both be a lot better off if you quit this job and got away from the Club and never come back here again ever.

Ken (*to* **Manager**)   Where's all this coming from?

Sally   It's not a good place to be around, Ken. It's like it's got a curse on it or something.

Ken (*to* **Manager**)   This ain't the time for one of your silly games. This is supposed to be a serious scene.

Sally   I'm serious, Ken.

Ken   There ain't no such thing as ghosts.

Sally   I didn't say ghosts, I said cursed.

Ken *barges past* **Sally**.

Sally Someone got killed up here.

Ken (*to* **Manager**)   What?!

Sally   . . .

Ken   Killed?

Sally   . . .

Ken   What are you – ?

Sally   A fella just like you who used to work up at the dam. Luca, his name was.

Ken   Luca?

Manager *gestures to* **Musician**.

Musician *plays and a spotlight picks out* **Sally**.

Sally   A few months back, I started taking walks up there. Up by the dam. Not for any reason, I was just bored, and it was something to do.

I'd watch the workers camped out on the edge of the lake. Sitting outside their tents. Eating. Drinking. Talking. I'd keep my distance. Watch from the trees.

Anyway, this one night I'm up there, in the woods looking towards the clearing where they're all camped out and I make out this little yellow light. Like a lamp. And sitting next to it, there's Luca. Everyone's sleeping but he's sitting alone by the edge of the lake. Fishing.

I move in for a closer look and he sees me coming, but he doesn't chase me away or anything. He just waves. Smiles. And shows me how to catch fish. He doesn't speak English, but that doesn't matter. He shows me how to tie a hook. How to read the ripples on the water. When to stay quiet. How to reel them in.

I start going up there a couple of times a week. He's always there. Same time. Same spot . . .

Until one night he's gone.

They found him washed up on the shore of the lake. I saw them drag him out. He'd tied rocks to his hands and feet. Must have jumped in when the water was high.

There was a little funeral up at the Club. Daddy didn't go.

Work on the dam fell behind after that. The workers started asking questions about the work they were doing on the dam. A lot of them were family too and I guess they just couldn't get it together after Luca, so my daddy got rid of them. 'Drinking on the job,' he said, but it could have been anything.

I went back down to the clearing and there was no trace of them. No tents. No fires. No tools. It was like they'd vanished. Started to think maybe I imagined them – dreamt them all up – so, I walked around looking for proof, proof they were real. That's when I found Luca's fishing rod. It was just lying there in the water.

And then you showed up.

Musician *stops playing and the lights restore.*

Ken (*to* **Manager**)   What was that?

The Suicide Scene (v. 2)

Three weeks until opening night. **Ken** *and the* **Troupe** *rehearse* **Pearson**'s *death.*

Manager   Look, I know this is very sensitive. But we're going to do it night after night, so we need to do it in a way that's safe for you emotionally.

Clown/Pearson *turns.*

Clown/Pearson   What are you doing here, son?

Ken   . . .

Clown/Pearson   How did you know I was here?

Ken   . . .

Clown/Pearson   What's wrong?

Ken (*to* **Manager**)   It didn't happen in the study.

Musician   We can't have you going all the way home, we'll lose the tension.

Ken   But that's where it happened.

Manager   You're right – it didn't really happen in the study – but it's not real. That's the point; it'll be safer for you whilst *feeling* real for the audience.

Ken *is pacing, visibly agitated.*

Heroine *goes over to* **Ken** *and comforts him.*

Heroine   What do you think, Ken, could it happen in the study?

Ken (*pulling away from* **Heroine**)   No.

Beat.

Manager   Ken, I promise you, if we have to take the action away from the Club, it'll spoil the effect.

Ken   It happened at home.

Never Get Someone to Do a Job You Can Do Yourself

Nine days until opening night. **Ken** *and the* **Troupe** *rehearse a scene set at the dam, the day before the opening of the Club.*

Clown/Pearson   'Where've you been?'

Ken   I think I better tell him the truth, so I say, 'I been with Miss Ruff.'

Clown/Pearson   'Miss Ruff?'

Ken   'Yeah. We've been hanging out some.' And I think he's gonna blow his top but he . . .

Manager   He . . . ?

Clown   What does he do, Ken?

Ken   He just . . . walks away . . .

Clown   That's it?

Ken   Yeah, he just walks away so I chase after him and I'm like . . .

'Dad! Dad!'

He turns around.

Clown/Pearson *turns to* **Ken**.

Ken   My cheeks are hot. My hands are shaking.

And I'm looking at him and saying nothing.

And he's looking at me and saying nothing.

Clown/Pearson *squares up to* **Ken**.

Ken   And he's got these glazed eyes. Scared eyes. I ain't never seen his eyes like that before . . .

Musician (*making notes*)   This is good.

Ken   That's when I know something's not right. Something's eating at him. It's been eating at him since the day we got here.

'Stay away from Sally Ruff,' he says.

Clown/Pearson   'Stay away from Sally Ruff.'

Ken   No explanation. Nothing. Just, 'Stay away.'

Clown/Pearson   'Stay away.'

Ken   I thought I must have blown it. Thought maybe I was the whole reason the job wasn't workin' out. Why him and Ruff were arguing. Blamed myself.

So I keep away from Sally and, me and my old man, we keep working on the carriageway.

For a few days, everything's fine. Business as usual, you know?

Manager   But then . . .

Musician   Sally shows up!

Clown   She's holding a report!

He hands **Heroine** *a prop report.*

Heroine *enters as* **Sally**.

Manager   But wait, she stops!

Sally *stops.*

Manager   She waits. She listens. She hears Ken talking to himself.

Ken? Could you . . .

Ken   What?

Manager   You're talking to yourself.

Ken   Am I?

Clown   Improvise something.

Manager   You're tired, hungry, cold, your father's been away for a few hours and you're wondering when he'll be back.

Ken *talks to himself.*

Manager   Sally listens. She looks at the report. She's having second thoughts. She knows this piece of paper will change everything. She asks herself . . . how will Ken react? Will he be angry? Bitter? Sad?

She changes her mind. She can't go through with it. She goes to leave.

Sally *goes to leave.*

Manager   But Ken spots her!

Ken   What you got there?

Manager   Sally hides the report.

Sally   Oh, it's nothing.

Ken   How long you been standing there?

Sally   Oh, I um . . .

Manager   Sally tries to change the subject.

Sally   . . . long enough to hear you confessing your secret love for me.

Ken   Fancy that.

Sally   'Sally Ruff is the most fantastically beautiful girl in the whole wide world.'

Ken   Don't remember saying that.

Sally   'If I never get to see her again there'll be nothing left for me but to drown myself in the lake as an expression of my unquenchable passion!'

Ken   Nope, doesn't sound like me.

Manager   Very good! They laugh.

Sally *laughs;* **Ken** *doesn't.*

Manager   They laugh, Ken.

Sally *and* **Ken** *laugh.*

Manager   They share a moment.

But the moment passes.

Ken goes back to work.

Sally goes to say something.

But she can't.

She lingers for a moment before . . .

Sally   There's something I need to show you . . .

Manager *gestures to* **Musician**.

Musician *plays something melancholic.*

Ken (*to* **Manager**)   Sorry, can we stop?

Musician *stops playing.*

Manager (*frustrated*)   What now?

Ken   Something don't feel right.

Heroine   Is it me?

Ken   No, I just think maybe we're rushing ahead a little fast?

Clown   Good time to get cold feet.

Manager   Last-minute jitters! That's all it is.

Heroine   Always happens.

Ken   I'm just not sure we've got everything.

Manager   We have. Let's pick up from, 'There's something I need to show you.'

Ken *goes back to work.*

Sally   There's something I need to show you.

Manager   Sally shows Ken the report.

Sally   It's from Mr Fulton . . .

Ken   . . .

Sally   It's what our daddies were arguing about.

Manager   Sally offers the report to Ken.

Sally *offers the Fulton report to* **Ken**.

Manager   Ken takes it . . .

Ken *takes the Fulton report.*

Manager *gestures to* **Musician**.

Musician *plays something tense.*

Manager   Ken looks at the envelope. His hands are shaking. He reaches inside and fingers the paper. He unfolds the report. A storm rumbles in the distance . . .

Clown *makes storm sounds.*

Manager   This is the moment.

This is where all the pieces come together for Ken.

The strange inspections. The arguments. The glazed eyes.

It's the moment he realizes his father isn't the man he thought he was.

It's his coming of age. Loss of innocence.

Tears roll down his cheeks.

Tears roll down his cheeks.

Tears roll down his cheeks.

Musician *and* **Clown** *stop playing.*

Manager   Tears roll down his cheeks.

Ken *thrusts the Fulton report back to* **Sally**.

Ken   I think I'm remembering this wrong. Getting things mixed up.

The **Troupe** *eye* **Ken** *with suspicion.*

Ken   Can we go back a bit? Look at the script again.

Heroine *offers the Fulton report to* **Ken**.

Heroine   This is where you read the report, Ken.

Silence.

Ken *takes the Fulton report.*

Manager   Nice and loud now, there's a good chap.

Musician *and* **Clown** *play.*

Ken *looks at the Fulton report.*

Ken (*reading*)   'There appear to me two serious elements of danger in this dam. First, the want of a discharge pipe to reduce or take the water out of the dam for needed repairs. Second, the unsubstantial method of repair, leaving a large leak, which appears to be cutting the new –'. (*To himself.*) No.

Musician *and* **Clown** *stop playing.*

Ken (*to the* **Troupe**)   No, Ruff was in a bind. The Club was s'posed to open in a month and he's gotta find someone to finish the job. When he met my old man, he couldn't believe his luck. Sure, he weren't an engineer but –

Clown   Ah, so you admit it?!

Ken   Admit what?

Clown   He botched it!

Ken   You putting me and my old man on trial now?

Heroine   No one's doing that, Ken.

Manager   Ease off, [Martin].

Ken   He needed the money.

Musician   So?

Ken   So Ruff took advantage of that.

Heroine   That's right.

Manager   But your father agreed to the work?

Ken   He didn't have a choice.

Clown   Yes he did.

Ken   What?

Clown   He could have said no.

Ken   You make it sound simple.

Clown *does a knockabout version of a* **Ruff** *and* **Pearson** *dialogue.*

Clown   'Hello there, Mr Ruff. What can I do for you?'

'Well, Mr Pearson, how would you like to build a carriageway? I'll pay yer well.'

'Why sure, Mr Ruff. Is it safe work?'

'Not in the slightest.'

'Then no. Good day to you, sir.'

See. Easy.

Manager   That's enough, [Martin].

Silence.

Heroine   Look, Ken. This is bigger than one man now. We have a responsibility to all those families with lost loved ones. Lost homes. Lives . . .

Ken   Doesn't mean you have to paint my old man as a villain.

Heroine   That's not what we're doing. It's just . . . The truth is complicated.

Ken *is visibly upset, crippled by the idea that* **Pearson** *might have been complicit.*

Ken   You're saying he's to blame.

Heroine   Well, isn't he?

Ken   . . .

Heroine   Can you stand there and tell us with a straight face his hands are clean?

Silence.

Ken   You wanna know the first thing I noticed when I met you? *Your* hands. I noticed the palms of your hands. Smooth. Not rough like mine or my old man's – he had hands like canyons – *smooth.* You lot ain't never done a hard day's work in your lives. My old man used to say never get someone to do a job you can do yourself. 'Cause it'll always turn out wrong. It won't ever be like you wanted it.

Throughout the remainder of the play, **Ruff**'*s study is assembled piece by piece. At first it's just a door, then an oak desk, a leather chair, a bookcase, a chaise longue, framed portraits and windows giving way to the painted backdrop of a vast lake. Lighting and sound elements are also added gradually. The trappings of melodrama gradually imprison* **Ken**.

Who's in Charge?

Eight days until opening night. **Ken** *and the* **Troupe** *rehearse the introduction to the final scene.*

Musician   There's banners and balloons.

Manager   The rich and well-to-do of Pittsburgh are arriving in their droves.

Musician   Men with top hats and canes.

Heroine   Women in outrageous hats.

Manager   Laughter and gossip fills the room –

The **Troupe** *laugh.*

Musician   It's here, on this fateful night, where a rotten truth is submerged beneath the lake at South Fork, never to be dredged up . . . or so they thought!

Manager   Report in hand, Ken heads for the clubhouse.

Clown   Run, Ken!

Ken *stands still.*

Musician   He's Johnstown's last and only hope.

Manager   But time isn't on his side.

Heroine   His father's about to accept Mr Ruff's cheque.

Clown   Faster, Ken!

Ken *remains still.*

Heroine   Everything rests on him.

Manager   He has to put a stop to this.

Musician   Before it's too late!

Manager   You see the lake as you come out the forest.

Musician   You see the hills.

Clown   You see the footpath curling round the lake.

Heroine   You see the door to the clubhouse.

Clown   You hear the laughter.

Musician   You step inside.

Ken *doesn't move.*

Heroine   Warm air rushes across his face.

Clown   The Club is teeming with people –

Manager   A throng of activity –

Musician   The clink of glasses –

Manager   The swill of cigarette smoke –

Clown   The swapping of business cards –

Heroine   The dance of the waiters –

Manager   Lobster tail –

Heroine   Caviar –

Clown   Shrimp –

Troupe   Wash it all down with champagne!

The **Troupe** *laugh.*

Ken   I see the hallway.

Clown   But you don't know where you're going.

Ken   I see the door to Mr Ruff's study.

Clown   But you're not sure it's the right one –

The Final Showdown (v. 1)
Seven days until opening night. **Ken** *and the* **Troupe** *rehearse a scene set in* **Ruff**'*s study, on the night of the opening of the Club.*

Ken *enters.*

Ken   Dad?

Clown   He wouldn't just barge in like that would he?

Ken   Wouldn't he?

Clown   He'd be shot!

Ken   Would I?

Manager   So *quieter* then?

Beat.

Clown   *Much* quieter.

Manager   You hear that, Ken? Stealthy.

Ken *exits.*

The Final Showdown (v. 2)

Six days until opening night.

Ken *enters, stealthily.*

Ken   Pssst.

Pearson *ignores* **Ken**.

Ken   Pssst. Pa.

Pearson *turns to* **Ken**.

Pearson   What are you doing here?

Ken   *Underplayed.* What are *you* doing here?

Musician   Sorry, but the moment Ken sees his dad standing there, it should be like he sees the future stretching out in front of him. The suicide. The flood. The destruction of the town. All of it.

Ken *exits.*

The Final Showdown (v. 3)

Five days until opening night.

Ken *enters, urgently.*

Pearson *turns to* **Ken**.

Ken *falls to his knees, raises his hands and screams melodramatically.*

Ken   DAAAAAAAAAAAAAAAAAAAAAAAAAAAAAD!

The **Troupe** *stares at* **Ken**.

Ken (to **Musician**)   Too much?

Blackout.

The Final Showdown (v. 4)

Four days until opening night.

Ken *enters with canned laughter.*

Ken   Pa! I thought I might find you here!

Pearson   Shoot me dead and call me Lincoln – what a surprise!

Canned laughter.

Ken   What brings you to Mr Ruff's place, Pa?

Pearson   Well gee wiz, son, I was just gonna ask you the same thing!

Canned laughter.

Ken   Golly, we sure are a pair of knuckleheads!

Pearson   Your ma used to say the same thing!

Canned laughter.

Ken   Right before she left us and fled town!

Pearson   She sure got sick and tired of all our foolin', huh!

Ken   That she did, Pa!

Pearson   It's just like she used to say . . .

Clown *and* **Ken** *ready themselves for the big catchphrase moment.*

Pearson   Like father like son!

Clown *commits physically and vocally to the catchphrase but* **Ken** *doesn't join in.*

Ken *and* **Clown** *stare at each other.*

Blackout.

The Final Showdown (v. 5)

Three days until opening night.

Ken *enters.*

Pearson *turns and puts the revolver to his head.*

Clown/Pearson   Is this what you want?!

Ken   . . .

Clown/Pearson   Well is it?!

Ken   . . .

Clown/Pearson   Is it son?!

Ken *bolts for the door, but it's locked; he frantically wiggles the handle.*

He turns back and finds **Pearson** *has transformed into a monster.*

Musician *plays something horrifying.*

Clown/Pearson   WHAT'S THE HURRY, SON?

Ken *presses his back into the door as* **Pearson** *advances.*

Clown/Pearson   STAY AWHILE!

SPEND A LITTLE TIME WITH YER OLLLLLLD MAAAAAAN!

Ken *cowers in the corner and puts his hands over his eyes.*

Ken   ARGHHH!

Blackout.

The Final Showdown (v. 6)

Two days until opening night.

The space has been reset but **Ken** *is still cowering in the corner.*

Ken *cautiously opens his eyes and finds* **Pearson** *standing in the middle of the study looking at the revolver mounted on the wall.*

Clown *plays* **Pearson** *with subtlety and integrity for the first time.*

Pearson   What are you doing here, son?

Ken   . . .

Pearson   How did you know I was here?

Ken   . . .

Pearson   What's wrong?

Ken (*Cautiously*)   What are you doing up here?

Pearson   Business.

Ken   With Mr Ruff?

Pearson   You better skedaddle.

Ken *stands and joins the scene.*

Ken   What kind of business?

Pearson   Ain't nothing to worry about.

Ken   Dad?

Pearson   Go wait outside.

Ken   You ain't got to pretend.

Pearson   Listen to your father.

Ken   I know.

Beat.

Pearson   What do you know?

Ken *shows* **Pearson** *the Fulton report.*

Thunderclap; the door swings open to wind and rain.

Clown *switches into melodrama while* **Ken** *tries to retain realism.*

Pearson   Where did you get that?

Ken   . . .

Pearson   I said, where did you get that?!

Ken   How long you known about this?

Pearson   You turned thief now!

Ken   Is this why you're here?

Pearson *closes the door; the wind and rain quietens.*

Pearson *turns to* **Ken**.

Pearson   Hand it over!

Ken   Tell me the *truth*.

Pearson   What truth?

Ken   The truth about why you're here. Tell me. Tell me that you're here to warn him, Dad. Tell me that you've come out here to put this right.

Pearson (*Coming down to* **Ken***'s level*)   Look son, we can talk about this later. I promise. But please. I need you to hand that piece of paper over to me. It's important.

Thunderclap.

Ruff *enters as an archetypal old man with a walking stick.*

Ken *pockets the Fulton report.*

Ruff   Now, Mr Pearson, where were we! (*Raising his monocle.*) Who is this?

Pearson   This here is my son, Mr Ruff!

Ruff   Is it indeed?

Pearson   He came all the way out here to reprimand you for your dodgy dam, sir!

Thunderclap.

Ruff *throws a shocked look to the audience.*

Blackout.

The Final Showdown (v. 7)

One day until opening night.

Ruff *enters as a cowboy.*

Musician *plays something Western.*

Ruff   Now, Mr Pearson, where were we!

Pearson   Your move, Mr Ruff.

Ruff   I can see you brought the cavalry.

Ken   I guess you could say that.

He and **Ruff** *circle each other like animals.*

Ruff   You better be packing some serious firepower, kid.

Ken   More than you know, Mr Ruff.

Pearson   What you planning son?

Ruff   Well . . . what are you waiting for?

Ken *reveals the Fulton report like a revolver from a holster.*

Ruff   Oh. So that's how we're playing it, huh? Well, alrighty then. Looks like this is gonna get real messy.

Ken and Ruff *stare each other down.*

DRAW!

Blackout.

The Final Showdown (v. 8)

Twelve hours until opening night.

Ruff *enters as an upbeat industrialist.*

Ruff   Now, Mr Pearson, where were we? (*Seeing* **Ken**) Ah! Another visitor. Good golly, it is starting to get rather crowded in here isn't it? And you are?

Pearson   This here is my son, Mr Ruff, Kenneth. He came all the way out here to wish you good luck with your grand opening.

Ken   No, I didn't.

Pearson   You . . . didn't?

Ken   I came out here because I know about the dam. I know it's gonna split. And I have all the evidence I need to prove it.

Ruff   Is that so? I seriously doubt that.

Ken   Oh yeah. Well, try doubting this!

Ken *searches his pockets for the report but can't find it.*

Ruff   I don't even need to read it! I would only be wasting my time! I know precisely what it says before I even set eyes on it! Let me guess. It's a slew of accusations from that good-for-nothing, two-bit inspector Fool-ton, levelling all kinds of crazy allegations against me and my Club. Well, am I right or am I right?

He reveals the report.

Ken   How did you – ?

Ruff *throws the report on the fire.*

Ken   Nooo!

Ruff (*to* **Pearson**)   Get out.

Pearson   Sir?

Ruff   I want a minute alone with your son.

Beat.

Run along now. Your boy's safe with me.

Pearson (*to* **Ken**)   Proud of you, son.

Pearson *exits.*

Ruff   Take a seat, Ken.

Ken *doesn't move.*

Suit yourself.

Ruff *lights a cigar and sits.*

Ruff   That was mighty brave. Barging in here like that. Making demands. There ain't many people who would have the guts to stand up to me like that. I don't know why. I'm a pussycat.

He blows out a big puff of cigar smoke.

You look a lil' nervous all of a sudden.

Ken   I ain't nervous.

Ruff   You sure?

Ken *stares out* **Ruff**.

Ruff *stares back.*

Ruff   You blinked.

Still, I'm mighty impressed. And I want to thank you.

Ken   Thank me?

Ruff   For bringing me that report. See, I need people like you on my side. People with guts. Initiative. That crook Fulton is obsessed with trying to ruin me. He won't be happy until he destroys my Club. But hey, I guess some folks can't stand it when other folks have something good going on. Men like Fulton aren't like us, Ken. Tell me, how many fellas like yourself do you think I've got working in my kitchen?

Ken   In your kitchen, sir?

Ruff   Take a wild guess.

Ken   Uh –

Ruff   Six! Now, do you have any idea how many I'm training to carry golf clubs?

Ken (*to* **Manager**)   That's enough.

Ruff   You're damn right it's enough! If I took on anymore, I'd be overrun! But you see, what I *really* need is someone on the ground. Someone to keep an eye on things. Someone to watch out for the snakes slithering in the grass, trying to strangle off the work I'm doing for Johnstown. Because I love this place.

Beat.

Were you born here, Ken?

Ken   You know I was.

Ruff   Well, I might not be born here, but I sure as hell do care about this place and I want to offer you a job.

Ken   I already have a job.

Ruff   I'm talking something proper.

Ken   Proper?

Ruff   Being my right-hand man.

Ken   What?

Ruff   I can see you in a tie. Crisp white shirt. Dark suit. Polished shoes. Nice pair of shiny silver cufflinks. Something tailored. Fresh. Clean. Civilized.

Ken   'Civilized'?

Ruff   You got to look the part if you want to help me run this place.

Beat.

Well, what do you say?

Ruff *extends a hand to* **Ken**.

Gunshot offstage.

Ruff   What on earth was that?

Sally *enters, covered in blood.*

Sally   Oh my God, daddy –

Ruff   What is it, darlin'? What's wrong?

Sally   It's Mr Pearson! He's shot himself! There's blood everywhere!

Ken   No no no no no no –

He rushes to the lip of the stage and closes his eyes.

Sally   Ken, I'm so sorry.

Manager   Pause there!

Working lights flick on.

Heroine *cleans herself up.*

Clown *enters with the revolver.*

Clown   Don't we need to *see* the death? Do you know what I mean? Then it might be easier for Ken to imagine I'm his dad.

He places the revolver back on the wall.

Ken   You're not my dad.

Beat.

Clown   I am your dad.

Ken   You're not my dad.

Clown   I am your dad.

Ken   You're not my dad.

He squares up to **Clown**.

Clown/Pearson   I am your dad.

Ken   You're not my dad.

Clown/Pearson   You're not *my* dad.

Ken   You're not my dad.

Clown/Pearson   I am your dad.

Ken   You're not my dad.

Clown/Pearson   I'm your dad.

Ken   You're not my dad.

Clown/Pearson   I'm your dad.

Ken   You're not my dad.

Clown/Pearson   I'm your father.

Ken   You're not my dad.

Clown/Pearson   I'm your old man.

Ken   You're not my dad.

Clown/Pearson   I am your dad.

Ken *takes the revolver off the wall and aims it at* **Clown/Pearson**'s *head.*

Ken   You are not my dad!

Clown/Pearson   I am your dad!

Ken   You're not my dad!

Clown/Pearson   I'm your father, son!

Ken   You're not my *dad*!

He lowers the revolver, bolts to the corner of the room and calms himself.

Clown   Aye, you didn't shoot him. He shot himself. Remember?

Blackout.

The Final Showdown (v. 9)

Eight hours until opening night.

Everything is played at double speed.

Ken *enters.*

Ken   Dad.

Pearson *turns to* **Ken**.

Pearson   What are you doing here, son?

Ken   ...

Pearson   How did you know I was here?

Ken   ...

Pearson   What's wrong?

Ken   What are you doing up here?

Pearson   Business.

Ken   With Mr Ruff?

Pearson   You better skedaddle.

Ken   What kind of business?

Pearson   Ain't nothing to worry about.

Ken   Dad?

Pearson   Go wait outside.

Ken   You ain't got to pretend.

Pearson   Listen to your father.

Ken   I know.

Beat.

Pearson   What do you know?

Ken *shows* **Pearson** *the Fulton report.*

Thunderclap; the door swings open to wind and rain.

Pearson   Where did you get that?

Ken   How long you known about this?

Pearson   You turned thief now?

Ken   Is this why you're here?

Pearson *closes the door; the wind and rain quietens.*

He turns to **Ken**.

Hand it over.

Ken   Tell me the truth.

Pearson   What truth?

Ken   The truth about why you're here. Tell me. Tell me that you're here to warn him, Dad. Tell me that you've come out here to put this right.

Beat.

Pearson   Look, son, we can talk about this later. I promise. But please. I need you to hand that piece of paper over to me. It's important.

Ruff *enters.*

Everything is played at normal speed.

Ruff   Now, Mr Pearson, where were we . . .

Ken *pockets the Fulton report.*

Ruff (*seeing* **Ken**)   Ah! Another visitor. Good golly, it is starting to get rather crowded in here isn't it? And you are?

Pearson   This here's my son, Mr Ruff. Kenneth.

Ruff   Is it indeed?

Pearson   He made the long journey out here to wish you well for your grand opening, sir. He's been helping me with that carriageway of yours. Isn't that right, son?

Ken   . . .

Ruff   Ah, well. Pleasure to meet you.

He goes to his desk and sits.

Right, let's get down to brass tacks, shall we? Fair remuneration for a hard day's work.

He writes **Pearson** *a cheque.*

Pearson *can't look at* **Ken**.

Ruff *tears off the cheque and walks over to* **Pearson**.

Ruff   You're sure everything's in order, Mr Pearson?

Pearson   Yes, sir.

Ruff   Splendid. Well, it's been a pleasure doing business with you.

He holds the cheque out.

Pearson *goes to take it.*

Ken (*to* **Ruff**)   There's something I want to say.

Ruff *stops and pulls the cheque away from* **Pearson**.

Manager/Ruff   Oh?

Clown/Pearson   Be quiet, son.

Ken   I know about the dam.

Manager/Ruff   Yes . . . your father did a splendid job. First rate! It's thanks to him that we can open tonight.

Ruff *holds the cheque out again.*

Manager/Ruff   It's been a pleasure doing business with you!

Ken   I know it won't hold.

Beat.

Manager/Ruff   I beg your pardon?

Ken   It's gonna split.

Clown/Pearson (*to* **Ken**)   You're mistaken, son.

Ken   You know it. He knows it. Fulton knew it. And now I know it too. It will start small at first. But soon enough that split is gonna get bigger and bigger and one day it's gonna spring a leak and when that happens there won't be no plugging it.

Manager/Ruff   The dam is well fortified!

Ruff *holds the cheque out again.*

Manager/Ruff   Pleasure doing business with you!

Clown/Pearson   Hush your mouth son!

Manager/Ruff   Anyway, how can you possibly predict such a thing?

Ken *shows* **Ruff** *the Fulton report.*

Manager/Ruff   Ah. So that's where it disappeared to. (*To* **Pearson**.) Did you honestly believe you could get away with sending your son here to blackmail me?

Pearson   I swear I didn't know he was gonna show up like this!

Ruff   You are now both trespassers on my property. If you don't give me that report and vacate immediately, I will have to take matters into my own hands.

Ken   I wouldn't do that if I was you.

Manager/Ruff   One . . .

Pearson   That won't be necessary, Mr Ruff.

Ken   You're making a mistake.

Manager/Ruff   Two . . .

Pearson   Do as the man says.

Ken   Maybe I'll go show this to your guests . . . ?

Ruff   . . .

Ken   They might be interested . . .

Ruff   . . .

Ken   To know what's going on.

Manager/Ruff (*to* **Ken**)   Go ahead.

Ken   What?

Manager/Ruff   Please. After you.

Ruff *opens the door and gestures for* **Ken** *to walk through and join the party.*

Manager/Ruff   No? Very well.

Ruff *closes the door.*

Musician *and* **Heroine** *enter as country singers and begin singing a song with* **Ruff.**

Ruff   What do you think that piece of paper proves?

Musician & Heroine   [It proves nothing.

Ruff   You think that Fulton rules the roost?

Musician & Heroine   He knows nothing.

That mad old drunk came bargin' here, beggin' on his knees,
His friends had left him from far and near,
My Club's just what he needs.

Well, naturally, I refused,
This Club's no place for the likes of yous,
So sober up, dry out, come back,
When you're back off the booze.

So what do you know –
Oh!
What do I see?
That mad old drunk is back.

His yarn, this letter, a forgery,
He's here on the attack.

This report, in his own hand,
'Water will crash through Johnstown's land',
Ha!
It's a sack of lies, fat porky pies,
My wish is my command].

Ken   You really expect me to believe that?

Ruff   Ah, it doesn't matter what you believe!

Ruff *gestures to the guests in the next room.*

They'll believe it. Because it's your word against mine. And that's no competition at all, is it . . . *boy*?

Ken *springs towards* **Ruff**.

Ruff *tenses up.*

Pearson *steps between them.*

Manager/Ruff   . . . and besides . . . it was your father here who did the job in the first place. Any failing is his. So if you go out there you won't be shooting me. You'll be shooting him. Now. Hand it over.

Hand it over.

Hand. It. Over.

Ken *allows* **Ruff** *to take the Fulton report.*

Ruff *takes it to the fire and burns it.*

Ruff *turns to* **Ken** *and strikes him across the face.*

Pearson *goes to intervene but freezes when* **Ruff** *gives him a look.*

Ken *clutches his jaw and looks at* **Pearson**.

Ruff *rubs the back of his hand.*

Pearson *looks down at the floor and trembles.*

Manager/Ruff   Well, pleasure doing business with you!

Ruff *goes to leave.*

Ken *grabs the revolver from the wall.*

Manager/Ruff   Now don't be rash.

Ken (*to* **Pearson**)   Looks like I got his attention now.

Pearson   Son –

Ruff   Put that back. It's a collector's item.

Ken   Oh you hear that, Pa? This here is special. I bet it fetches a high price.

Manager/Ruff   You're only making things worse for yourself.

Ken   Let's start the bidding at one hundred dollars.

Ruff   Pearson! Control your son!

Ken   Going once!

Pearson   Ken, stop this!

Ken   Going twice!

Ruff   This is absurd.

Ken   Sold!

He goes to fire the revolver but **Clown** *intervenes.*

Clown/Pearson   We both know that's not how it happened, Ken.

Blackout.

The Final Showdown (v. 10)

Three hours until opening night.

Everything is played at double speed.

Ken *enters.*

Ken   Dad.

Pearson *turns to* **Ken**.

Pearson   What are you doing here, son?

Ken   . . .

Pearson   How did you know I was here?

Ken   . . .

Pearson   What's wrong?

Ken   What are you doing up here?

Pearson   Business.

Ken   With Mr Ruff?

Pearson   You better skedaddle.

Ken   What kind of business?

Pearson   Ain't nothing to worry about.

Ken   Dad?

Pearson   Go wait outside.

Ken   You ain't got to pretend.

Pearson   Listen to your father.

Ken   I know.

Beat.

Pearson   What do you know?

Ken *shows* **Pearson** *the Fulton report.*

Thunderclap; the door swings open to wind and rain.

Pearson   Where did you get that?

Ken   How long you known about this?

Pearson   You turned thief now?

Ken   Is this why you're here?

Pearson *closes the door; the wind and rain quietens.*

Pearson *turns to* **Ken**.

Pearson   Hand it over.

Ken   Tell me the truth.

Pearson   What truth?

Ken   The truth about why you're here. Tell me. Tell me that you're here to warn him, Dad. Tell me that you've come out here to put this right.

Beat.

Pearson   Look, son, we can talk about this later. I promise. But please. I need you to hand that piece of paper over to me. It's important.

Ruff *enters.*

Ruff   Now, Mr Pearson, where were we . . .

Ken *rushes to the door and holds it closed on* **Ruff**.

Ken *plays at normal speed.*

Ken (*to the audience*)   Listen. I know that any second now Mr Ruff's gonna offer to cut my dad a cheque and he's gonna want to take it. But we mustn't let him take that cheque. If he takes that cheque something bad's gonna happen. And I don't want it to happen like this. We can change that and do things different, but I need you to work with me –

Sally (*shouting, off*)   Papa! Papa?! Papa!

Ken   Please. *Please.*

Sally *enters downstage.*

Sally (*to* **Ruff**)   I can't find your cufflinks anywhere, Papa.

Ken *lets go of the door and* **Ruff** *enters.*

Ruff (*to* **Sally**)   What is it now?

Sally   The golden eagles . . . They're nowhere to be seen!

Ruff (*improvising*)   Ohhh. I see. Well, how appropriate that on tonight of all nights nothing can be found in its rightful place.

Sally (*noticing* **Ken**)   Oh hi, Ken!

Ruff   Ah another visitor! Pleasure doing business with you!

Ken (*to* **Sally**)   This is wrong. You're not supposed to be here.

Ruff (*to* **Ken**)   I beg your pardon!? You're the one standing in *my* study.

Pearson (*to* **Sally**)   Sorry, miss. Kenneth's not feeling too well.

Sally   Are you sick, Ken?

Ken   No I'm fine –

Ruff (*to* **Sally**)   Sally, do you know this roughneck?

Ken   No, I need you to go back out, [Alice]. Please. *Please!*

Heroine/Sally *exits.*

Ruff (*to* **Pearson**)   Now, where were we?

Ken   No, stop –

Ruff *goes to his desk.*

Ruff   Ah, yes. Brass tacks. Fair remuneration for a hard day's work.

He writes **Pearson** *a cheque and tears it off.*

Ruff   You're sure everything's in order, Mr Pearson?

Pearson   Yes, sir.

Ruff   Splendid. (*Offering the cheque.*) Well, it's been a pleasure doing business with you!

He holds the cheque out and **Pearson** *goes to take it.*

Ken (*to* **Ruff**)   There's something I want to say –

Sallamina *enters.*

Sallamina   There's summin' *I* wanna say!

Pearson   Sallamina!

Sallamina   That's right! I'm back, you piece o' shit husband!

Ken   You can't be serious?

Pearson   *I'm* the piece of shit husband?

Sallamina   Damn straight!

Pearson   It was *you* who walked out on *us*!

Sallamina (*to* **Pearson**)   Look at you! I can see you're still the same no good, two-bit, slack-jawed, fish-brained son of a bitch you ever was!

Pearson   And I can see you're still the same good for nothin' potty mouth I had the misfortune of marryin'.

Sallamina   Kenneth, get your things. You comin' home with Mama.

She takes **Ken** *by the arm.*

Pearson *grabs* **Ken** *by the other arm.*

Pearson   You let go of my boy!

Sallamina   *Your* boy? He's *my* boy!

Pearson   You gave up the right to be his mother when you walked out on us!

Sallamina   You didn't leave me no choice. What with all your whorin'!

Pearson   Oh, here we go again!

Sallamina (*to* **Ken**)   Let me tell you 'bout your Daddy. He used to stumble home in the middle o' the night, blind drunk, stinkin' out the place with cheap cologne and moonshine. And know what he do? He beat me black and blue! Just so he could feel strong. That's the kind o' man he is. I had to leave! I had no choice!

Ken   All right, quit it now –

Pearson (*to* **Ken**)   She drove me to it, son! I did all I could. I sweated, I bleded, I wrung every ounce o' strength I had in me. But it was never good enough! Your mama always found a way to make me feel small. So I drank! I gambled! And sure, I whored! Cos I needed to feel *alive*.

Sallamina (*to* **Pearson**)   Oh, quit your boo-hooing! This here is *my* boy! Look at him. [He Black and I'm Black! But you? Hell, you as white as a cracker! When was the last time you got some vitamin D! Oh, and speakin' of D, look at your peeny-weeny!].

Pearson *releases* **Ken**.

Pearson   My . . . peeny-weeny?

Sallamina   Mmm-hmm! You know what all the gals you got cosy with used to call you? They called you Peeny-Pee-Pearson! Cos you ain't nothin' but a joke. Well, I got some advice for you, husband! Everyone in this town would be better off if you just went ahead and shot yourself. Cos you sure as hell as ain't good to no one while you still breathing!

Pearson *cries.*

He takes the revolver from the wall, cocks it and puts it to his head.

Ken *rushes towards* **Pearson**.

Ken   No –

Blackout.

The Final Showdown (v. 11)

Opening night.

The set of **Ruff***'s study is now fully rendered.*

Ken *enters.*

Pearson *turns to* **Ken***.*

Pearson   What are you doing here, son?

Ken   . . .

Pearson   How did you know I was here?

Ken   . . .

Pearson   What's wrong?

Ken   What are you doing up here?

Pearson   Business.

Ken   With Mr Ruff?

Pearson   You better skedaddle.

Ken   What kind of business?

Pearson   Ain't nothing to worry about.

Ken   Dad?

Pearson   Go wait outside.

Ken   You ain't got to pretend.

Pearson   Listen to your father.

Ken   I know.

Beat.

Pearson   What do you know?

Ken *shows* **Pearson** *the Fulton report.*

Thunderclap; the door swings open to wind and rain.

Pearson   Where did you get that?

Ken   How long you known about this?

Pearson   You turned thief now?

Ken   Is this why you're here?

Pearson *closes the door; the wind and rain quietens.*

He turns to **Ken***.*

Pearson   Hand it over.

Ken   Tell me the truth.

Pearson   What truth?

Ken   The truth about why you're here.

Pearson   What truth?

Ken   The truth.

Pearson   What truth?

Ken   The truth!

Pearson   Look, son, we can talk about this later –

Ken   Tell me the truth –

Pearson   I promise –

Ken   Tell me the truth –

Pearson   But please –

Ken   Tell me the truth –

Pearson   I need you to hand that piece of paper over to me, it's important.

Ken   Tell me the truth!

Clown/Pearson   What truth?!

Ruff *enters with a chequebook and a pen.*

Ruff   Now, Mr Pearson, where were we –

Ken   WE. DON'T. WANT. YOUR. MONEY.

Beat.

Ruff   Well, it's too late for that, boy. I've already cut your old man a cheque.

Pearson *takes the cheque from his pocket and holds it up to the light.*

Ruff   He's earned it. You both have! A fair remuneration for a hard day's work!

Ken   No –

Ruff   Pleasure doing business with you!

Ken   Stop –

Clown/Pearson   It's no use, Ken. This only ends one way.

Manager/Ruff   This is how things shake down.

Pearson (*to* **Ken**)   Time to head home now, son.

Ken   I ain't your son.

Pearson   This is for you. It's yours. Take it.

He holds out the cheque.

Ken *looks at the cheque.*

*He spits in **Pearson**'s face.*

Ken   Keep it. I'll bury it with you.

Pearson *folds the cheque and puts it in his pocket.*

Pearson   Me and my son will be heading home now, Mr Ruff.

Ruff   Nonsense! Stay and enjoy the celebrations.

Pearson   That's very kind of your sir, but –

Ruff   Do you dance, Mr Pearson?

Beat.

Pearson   Do I . . .? Well, sure. A little!

Ruff   You people sure are a jolly bunch. Great sense of occasion!

Pearson   I s'pose so, Mr Ruff . . .

Ruff   I took a trip to Boston last year and I had the good fortune to see a wonderful little fellow just like yourself . . . and he danced the most spectacular little number!

Pearson   I got a few numbers in me, that I do, Mr Ruff!

Ruff   Well, let's lighten the mood with a little dance shall we? Let's let bygones be bygones and go out on a happy ending. It is a party after all!

Sally *enters.*

Ruff   Ah! Sally! Play something on the piano, will you? And you can tap something out for us, Mr Pearson. I'll even throw in a little bit extra for you and young Kenneth here. What do you say, boy?

Ken   Please don't make me.

Beat.

Pearson   You got yerself a deal, Mr Ruff!

Sally *sits at the piano and plays a jig.*

Pearson *takes his position in the middle of the room.*

He dances.

Ruff *watches and claps along.*

Ken *watches helplessly.*

Ruff   Come now. Nobody likes a spoilsport, Kenneth. Why not join your father and add a little competition into the mix? Dance, Kenneth! Dance!

Ken *joins* **Pearson** *and jigs alongside him.*

Ken *goes to grab the revolver from the wall but* **Ruff** *gets in his way.*

Ken *spots a sharp letter opener on* **Ruff**'s *desk; he grabs it and holds it to his neck.*

Ken   Do I have your attention?

It's my turn to speak.

The **Troupe** *give* **Ken** *space; he turns to the audience.*

I'm going to tell you how it really happened.
The truth.
Are you sitting comfortably?
Are you listening?

I hear the sound before I know what's happened.
The sound of something cracking.

Muffled.
Far off.
Distant.

I was talking to Mr O'Malley at the time.

I'm explaining to Mr O'Malley I can't afford to pay my old man's tab.

He's telling me he won't have him in the bar 'til he settles the debt.

I tell him maybe that ain't such a bad idea.

He tells me if a man's determined to drink there ain't no one can stop him.

That's when I hear it.

That crack.

He closes his eyes.

I leave the bar and I walk back to our place.
I see a small crowd standing outside our door.
I see Mrs Adams knocking.
I see Mr Harrington trying to hurry his kids back inside.
I see Mr and Mrs Jones peering out their window.
I see them turn away when they see me coming.
I open the door.
I head inside.
I smell the powder in the air.
I head through the hallway.
I walk into the living room.
I squint in the dark.
I see the curtains drawn.
I see . . .

I see . . .

I see him.

He opens his eyes.

At first it looks like he's just sitting there in the dark.
Sitting there in one of his stupors.
I reach out my hand.
Hand comes back wet.

He ain't moving.

I nudge him.

He ain't moving.

I see the shooter in his hand.
He quiet.
He still.
He . . .

I don't shout.
I don't scream.
I don't collapse to my knees and start weeping.
I just watch him.

Coward.
Deadbeat.
I just . . .

After the funeral, word starts going round it was an accident.
People say my old man was polishing his gun and he slipped.
Slipped and hit the trigger.
Cos he was hitting the liquor.

'Accidents happen.'
'Ain't no rhyme or reason.'
'God works in mysterious ways.'
But it weren't no mystery.
Weren't no accident.
He didn't slip.
You been telling the wrong story.

The truth is my old man died way before he pulled that trigger.
He died the moment he took that cheque from Mr Ruff.
Faded away the second he folded it up and put it in his pocket.
I saw it happen.
I saw Ruff take my old man's hand and the spirit leave his body.
Ruff shook the spirit out of my old man.
He shook it loose and sucked it out.
When he left that room he was empty.

Drained.
Drained like the river up there at the Club.

I want to shout at him.

Scream at him.
'Don't let him do this. Stand up for yourself. Be a man.'
But I don't.

I want to take the whole chequebook and make him eat every page.

Stuff the paper down his throat.

Watch him choke on it.
But I don't.

I stand there.

I watch.

I watch and I keep my mouth shut.
I see it all happen like they're actors in a show.

When we hurt, they blame us.
They tell us it's our fault when we're hurting.
Our fault when we suffer.
Our fault when we die.
They make us blame ourselves.
But that ain't the worst thing.
Worst thing of all is that we do it.
We hate ourselves.
And we hate each other.
And it works.
And it keeps working.
It keeps happening.

I'm sick of it.
I've had enough of it.

Ain't you had enough of it?

Ain't it time we did something?

What are we gonna do?

Silence.

I'm really asking, I'm really asking the question.

Silence.

Well?

Silence.

Say something!

Manager *prizes the letter opener from* **Ken***'s hand.*

Sally *starts playing piano again.*

Pearson *dances.*

Ruff *watches and claps along.*

Ruff   Now dance, Kenneth, dance!

Ken *joins* **Pearson** *and jigs alongside him.*

Ruff   Faster!

Ken *and* **Pearson** *dance with greater ferocity.*

Ruff   Faster I say!

Ken *and* **Pearson** *dance even faster.*

Ruff *fires the revolver at* **Ken** *and* **Pearson***'s feet.*

Ruff   Ye-hah!

Ken *and* **Pearson** *dance faster still.*

Pearson *dances over to the revolver mounted on the wall and takes it.*

He puts the barrel of the revolver to his chin.

He looks **Ken** *in the eyes.*

Ken   Please.

Pearson *shoots himself.*

Blood sprays over **Ken***,* **Ruff** *and* **Sally***.*

Pearson *collapses and dies.*

Sally *and* **Musician** *stop playing.*

Ken *continues to jig despite what's just happened.*

Ruff   Great Scott!

Sally *runs to* **Ruff** *and hugs him.*

Sally   Oh no! It's horrible!

Ruff   Avert your eyes, dear.

Sally   It's all in my hair and my dress!

Ruff   Come with Papa, dear. Let the authorities handle this mess!

Ken*'s jig slows as reality settles in.*

He goes to **Pearson***.*

A spotlight picks out **Ken** *and* **Pearson***.*

Musician *plays something mournful.*

Ken   DAAAAAAAAAAAAAAAAAD!

Musician *plays climatically.*

The **Troupe** *speak to the audience.*

Musician   Many thousand human lives –

Heroine   Butchered husbands, slaughtered wives,

Manager   Mangled daughters, bleeding sons,

Clown   Hosts of martyred little ones,

Musician   Worse than Herod's awful crime,

Heroine   Sent to heaven before their time,

Manager   Lovers burned and sweethearts drowned,

Clown   Darlings lost but never found!

Musician   All the horror that hell could wish,

Heroine   Such was the price that was paid for fish!

Musician *plays climactically.*

Blackout.

The Aftermath

Ken *speaks to the audience.*

Ken   It's dark.

I can hear my own breath.
My heart beating in my ears.
Then. From the back of the theatre. A solitary clap.
Then, like raindrops, another, and another, and another, and . . .

The working lights flick on; the **Troupe** *are gone.*

I see the faces of the crowd.
The whites of their eyes.
The teeth in their mouths.
The furrow of their brows.
I see a man pumping his fist in the air shouting my name.
I see a man crying.
I see a woman looking at me, shaking her head.
I see a family making for the exit.

I step outside into the night.
There's a newspaper on the stand outside the Opera House with Ruff's face.
'Our misery is the work of man!'
A trial's coming.

I walk through flooded streets.
I see people untangling barbed wire and sweeping up dirt.
Bloated bodies being dragged from the wreckage.
Fires still burning.
Folks without homes.
I see Mr Willis the undertaker and his wife drive by in their carriage, counting their money.

I go to the bar on Main.
Order myself a drink.
'Don't worry, son, it's on the house.'

I drink.
I see sad faces propping up the bar.
Men without purpose.
Women without hope.
I hear whispered words.
Angry eyes.
Slow shakes of the head.
What do they think of me?

I stand.
Spit on the floor.
Leave.

I stumble through the night.
It's cold.
I see a little girl on the pavement smiling at me.
I see her mother pull her away.

I get home.
Or to where home used to be.
It's a shell now.
Walk into my old room.
Where I think it used to be.

Close my eyes.
And, finally, I sleep.

He sleeps.

Actor 1/Ken   Really?

'Ken sleeps.'
That's the best you got?

No.

He doesn't sleep.
He can't sleep.

Faces in crowds.
Staring faces.
Bloated faces.
His old man's face.

To some, he's a hero, to others, he's as guilty as Ruff and his old man . . .

Can you imagine what that feels like?
Walking around town . . .

So what does he do?

Silence.

Ken stirs.
Gets up.
Goes to the closet.

Opens the door.

There's his overalls.

Still smell like my old man.

Fit pretty good too.

That's not my face.
That's . . .
Go downstairs.
Light a fire.
Hear it crackle.
Pour a bourbon.
Sit in his chair.
Rock back and forth.
Back and forth.
Back and forth.

Then I see it.
Corner of my eye.
On the mantelpiece.

Walk over.
Pick it up.
Turn it over in my hand . . .

An envelope.
Still sealed.
Unopened.

Actor 1/Ken *sits.*

What's inside?

Actor 1/Ken *opens the envelope.*

A cheque.

Mr Ruff's cheque.

Uncashed . . .?

Silence.

Burn it?

Actor 1/Ken *takes a lighter out his pocket and goes to burn the cheque.*

No.

Donate it?

Actor 1/Ken *looks for someone in the audience to receive the cheque.*

No.

Cash it.

Take the money.

Leave town.

Start again.

Actor 1/Ken *folds the cheque, puts it in his pocket and collects his things.*

No.

What do I do?

What do I do?

What do I do?

Silence.

Actor 1/Ken *places the cheque on the chair.*

Actor 1/Ken *exits.*

Silence.

Blackout.

The Squint Toolkit

Introduction

How to begin?

Whenever we start a new project, we're confronted with this question.

The early stages of a project's development are a bit like metal detecting. Artists, like metal detectorists, spend a lot of time scanning about in search of something shiny. We know it's out there, but we can't quite see it. We remain patient and alert, fighting back feelings of self-doubt that threaten to derail our search until – maybe, finally – we get a signal and alight upon hidden treasure.

But what happens once you've found that shiny new idea? What do you do with it? How do you make something of it?

Each of our projects sprung from different ideas and were made in distinct circumstances. *Long Story Short* emerged from extensive research, *Molly* was born from a question and *The Incredible True Story of the Johnstown Flood* was inspired by a specific event. We don't approach new projects with a fixed methodology, but we do have hundreds of exercises that help us write and devise.

We call them our tools. They enable us to take an idea and turn it into something tangible. Something that physically exists on the page or in the rehearsal room and, eventually, as a piece of theatre. They make abstracts concrete.

The Squint Toolkit offers up several of our tools, explores how each of them contributed to the creation of *Long Story Short*, *Molly* and *The Incredible True Story of the Johnstown Flood* and unpacks how you can use them to make your own plays. The exercises have all been applied and developed practically on our projects and have since been finessed through our *Get Writing* and *Get Devising* education workshops.

Whether you're constructing characters, structuring narrative, unlocking ideas, scripting dialogue, editing scenes, approaching research or connecting with personal experience, these tools are here to help you.

Some incite impulsivity and instinct while others encourage thoughtful planning. Individual artists are often predisposed to one of these approaches more than the other. Some take in the lay of the land from above like birds, getting a sense of the whole before swooping down to catch their prey. Others intuitively move through the dirt like worms, wriggling around blindly before popping through the topsoil into the light. We find we need both these approaches to make good work and encourage you to bounce between the two on any given day of making. A dynamic process that combines both approaches will better serve both you, and the diversity of brains you have amongst your collaborators.

So, you've got an idea for a project and all these tools up your sleeve, but how do you know what to use when?

When writing and devising we plan and manage our time rigorously. It helps us stay focused, productive and, most importantly, creative. We guide each day of work in the writers' room or the rehearsal room with a question.

Sometimes it centres on story and character:

– How might Neil persuade Jamie to do a live television interview? (*Long Story Short*).

- What story events might the Hare Psychopathy Checklist inspire? (*Molly*).
- What story events might occur between Ken and Sally? (*The Incredible True Story of the Johnstown Flood*).

Sometimes it centres on form:

- How do we give Red's arrival into London the energy of a 'media circus'? (*Long Story Short*).
- How does the reality television show format alter how Molly's story is told? (*Molly*).
- How might the Troupe use the trappings of melodrama to ensnare Ken? (*The Incredible True Story of the Johnstown Flood*).

We find 'what' and 'how' questions more useful than 'why' questions. 'Why' questions get us in our heads and often hinder practical discoveries.

Whether you're sitting down to write or going into a rehearsal room to devise, we recommend identifying a question to centre your day around before finding the tools you need to tackle it.

There are some key principles that underpin all our work as a company. Before diving into the tools, it's worth having a read through the following tips; they'll help you use them effectively and give you more fruitful outcomes:

1. ***Embrace failure***. Enjoy failure as much as success. Relish being in the shit. It's when we're stuck that the best and purest ideas emerge.

2. ***Find the game***. There's a game to be found in everything. They're called *plays* for a reason.

3. ***Apply pressure***. Restrictions clear the way for imagination and get you started. Limitations breed creativity; use them.

4. ***Follow your North Star***. Whatever your starting point is, make it your guiding light. Befriend it, interrogate it, keep returning to it, trust it. It'll keep you on the straight and narrow.

5. ***Work expressively***. Literalism is not the only way. Express literal things in extraordinary and imaginative ways and the audience will fill in the blanks.

6. ***Use the 'four elements of drama'***. We learnt from Stephen Jeffreys that action, character, place and time are the essential building blocks of any scene. Get those ingredients in place and you can't go wrong.

7. ***Get off your seat and onto your feet***. Don't talk for too long. Conversation can kill the energy of a new idea. Try first, discuss after.

8. ***Take care of your collaborators***. The joy of collaboration is finding solutions together. Nurture a culture of trust and take questions instead of answers into the rehearsal room.

9. ***Ignore the gremlins***. The first idea might be the only one you need. Don't censor. Silence your inner critic and don't knock it until you've tried it.

10. ***Keep moving forward***. Whether you're writing or devising, behave like a person walking backwards; have an eye on what's behind you, but don't stop moving forward. Take the brakes off and trust your instincts.

We've tried to keep the toolkit jargon-free, but have defined a few terms below to make the exercises as user-friendly as possible. When facilitating any of these tools with a group, we often offer relevant definitions at the top of the session to get everyone on the same page:

- Action - the stuff the characters are 'doing' in a scene.
- Antagonist - a character who possesses something the protagonist wants.
- Draft/Redraft - we believe there can be many interesting versions of a moment/ scene and a 'draft' is just one of them; when redrafting we'd encourage you to start from a 'blank page' and embrace new ideas.
- Event - a moment in a scene/play where something changes for all the characters present.
- Protagonist - a character with a desire which the story centres on.
- Free-Write/Speak Aloud - this instruction encourages you to write/speak 'with the brakes off'; keep your pen moving, fingers tapping or lips moving and trust your instincts.
- Game - an activity which creates the possibility of failure and incites tactics from it's player(s).
- Improvisation - something created spontaneously; sometimes with preparation, sometimes without.
- Provocation - something to stimulate ideas.
- Text/Dialogue - the words the characters speak.
- Subtext - the underlying, unspoken stuff that exists beneath a scene/play.
- Write/Draw - every brain is different; this instruction gives you the choice to use words, images or a combination of both.
- Write/Improvise - this instruction allows you to use an exercise for writing at a desk or improvising in a rehearsal room.

Some tools in this book are our own inventions, others are variations on practice we've learnt from other artists. The genealogy of an exercise is often hard to pin down but, where possible, we've acknowledged the artists and companies that have inspired us so you can be inspired by them too.

In particular, we'd like to give a shout-out to Anne Bogart and Tina Landau, Brené Brown, Stephen Jeffreys, Toby Litt, the National Youth Theatre, Told by an Idiot and John Yorke who have all had a big influence on the way we make theatre. Also, contemporaries of ours Ned Bennett, Brad Birch, Chris Bush, Ashley C. Karaweigh, Rory Mullarkey, Ella Road and Ruby Thomas have inspired specific tools in this book. We're forever grateful to the people we've learnt from and continue to learn from.

Whatever stage you're at with whatever project you're working on, we hope there's something in here that'll help you bring your ideas to life and make your play the best version of itself.

Contents

Tools

1. FETCH

Use found objects to crystallize story ideas.

Participants: 2+

What You Need: An idea for a project, a selection of objects.

How We Use It: During early development on *The Incredible True Story of the Johnstown Flood*, we needed an exercise to help us transition out of our research phase and start making.

This exercise uses found objects – pieces of costume, props, personal belongings, etc. – to get out of our heads, inspire ideas and identify tangible building blocks for scenes.

Step 1: Individually, 'fetch' an object from the environment you're in, using one of the following provocations:

- Something red. *E.g. a red pen.*
- Something beginning with 'p'. *E.g. a piece of paper.*
- Something joyful. *E.g. A party popper.*
- Something sad. *E.g. a photo of a childhood pet.*
- Something throwable. *E.g. a pillow.*
- Something huggable. *E.g. a pillow.*
- Something powerful. *E.g. a megaphone.*

Step 2: Individually, study your object, identifying ten things you notice about it. Be both factual and interpretive. *E.g. a piece of paper; glossy, brand new, formal, embossed, shiny, yellow, stiff, stale, intimidating, clean.*

Step 3: Use your object to inspire ideas related to your project by responding to the following questions:

- What action could your object be involved with? *E.g. The signing of a contract.*
- What character could the object be used by? *E.g. The clubowner, Benjamin Ruff.*
- What place or time could the object be from? *E.g. Ruff's study, ten years before the flood.*

Step 4: As a group, share your ideas.

Step 5: List all the tangible ideas for action, character, time and place that have been shared by the group. Start making scenes with your ideas using **2. Building Blocks**.

Variation: In Step 1, try fetching objects directly related to your project, using the following provocations:

- Something related to one of your themes.
- Something related to one of your questions.

- Something related to the action of one of your scenes.
- Something related to one of your characters.
- Something related to the place/time your story is set in.

Tip: Keep the objects to hand and use them as starting points for writing and devising.

Note: We learnt a version of this exercise while working with the National Youth Theatre.

2. BUILDING BLOCKS

Build scenes inspired by the world of a project.

Participants: 1+

What You Need: An idea for a project.

How We Use It: Early in the development of *The Incredible True Story of the Johnstown Flood*, we explored the world of Johnstown in 1889. We understood the facts of what happened to the town, but we needed to start visualizing the community; their way of life, their jobs, their habits, their relationships, etc.

Inspired by our research into the world of Johnstown, we listed all our ideas for action, character, place and time, and put different combinations of these building blocks together to create scenes.

We use this exercise to start building and exploring robust scenes inspired by the world of our project.

Step 1: Choose a world related to your project to explore. *E.g. Johnstown, 1889.*

Step 2: On a piece of paper, draw four columns with the following titles at the top.

1. Action.
2. Character.
3. Place.
4. Time.

Step 3: List ideas for action, character, time and place in each of the columns, by responding to the following questions:

- Action – what things happen in this world? *E.g. Painting, waiting for a train, clearing up after the flood.*
- Character – what people are in this world? *E.g. Ken, an inspector, a troupe of actors.*
- Place – what locations are in this world? *E.g. The dam, the clubhouse, a train.*
- Time – when do things happen in this world? *E.g. Christmas Eve, midnight, the day after the flood.*

Step 4: Read through your lists and choose five favourites from each column. These are the building blocks of your world.

Step 5: Write your favourites from each column on small pieces of paper and put them into four piles; action, character, place and time.

Step 6: Randomly select one piece of paper from each pile to establish the four elements of drama for a scene. *E.g. Painting, Ken, the dam, Christmas Eve.*

Step 7: Write/improvise your scene. Take your characters on a journey, ensuring something changes. Focus on dialogue rather than stage directions and get to the end.

Step 8: Read through/reflect on your scene. Notice what you like/don't like. What did you discover? Is there anything that can be developed?

Step 9: Repeat Steps 5–7 several times to explore different combinations of building blocks that could make for dynamic scenes. Some will work better than others. Enjoy the randomness and embrace the unknown.

3. COLLABORATOR DIAMONDS

Explore who you are, what matters to you and what you bring to a project.

Participants: 2+

What You Need: A group of collaborators.

How We Use It: The lockdown of 2020 meant we couldn't work in-person. When we did get back into a rehearsal room together, our associates, Kane Husbands and Louise Roberts, co-facilitated this exercise to reconnect us as collaborators. It helped us create a more empathetic, resilient and creative working environment after a challenging period in our lives.

We use this exercise to make our collaborative relationships the best they can be.

Step 1: Individually, on a piece of paper, draw a diamond. Make the edges of the diamond meet the edges of the paper, creating four triangular corners.

Step 2: Fill the middle of the diamond with words/phrases describing who you are as a collaborator. Work freely from your own point of view, thinking about yourself and what you bring to a project in response to the following questions:

- What 'values' do you hold dear in yourself and others? *E.g. Honesty, humour, punctuality, loyalty, vulnerability.*
- What 'skills' do you have to offer? *E.g. Guitar playing, writing, debating, baking, acting.*
- What 'roles' do you play? *E.g. Director, clown, big brother, carer, fixer.*
- What 'taste' do you bring? *E.g. Handmade, melancholic, loud, jazzy, symmetrical, sky blue, a roaring lion, spoken word, twisted, horror.*

Step 3: Read through your words/phrases. Notice the descriptions that bring who you are to life.

Step 4: Identify the 'four corners of you' by sorting and distilling your words/phrases into the four corners of your page. Think about yourself in relation to the project you're working on and what you can bring to it, organizing your thoughts using the following provocations:

- Put the words/phrases that best describe your values in the top left corner.
- Put the words/phrases that best describe your skills in the top right corner.

- Put the words/phrases that best describe your roles in the bottom left corner.
- Put the words/phrases that best describe your taste in the bottom right corner.

Step 5: In pairs, present your diamonds. Ask each other questions, identify your similarities and celebrate your differences.

Step 6: Individually, write/draw three 'pledges' in response to the following provocations. They can be big or small, artistic or personal.

- A pledge to yourself. *E.g. To actively use my communication skills to help the collaborative process.*
- A pledge to your partner/group. *E.g. To play games with full commitment and competition.*
- A pledge to your project. *E.g. To facilitate a relaxing warm-down after a stressful rehearsal.*

Step 7: As a group, share your pledges and stick them on the wall so they're in view throughout your project.

Tip: Brené Brown's *Dare to Lead* features a comprehensive list of values that we find helpful for Step 2.

Variation: During Step 5, have a conversation about what you need to do your best work. Reflect on moments when you've been at your best and worst in a group and why that might have been. Use your discoveries to inform your pledges.

4. LOOKING IN, LOOKING OUT

Identify research tasks tailored to a project.

Participants: 1+

What You Need: An idea for a project.

How We Use It: We did a lot of research into broadcast news media for *Long Story Short*. We wanted to authentically depict the lives of professional journalists, while ensuring that the story resonated on an emotional level with an audience.

Our research involved looking out, to build a detailed picture of the world of the project, and looking in, to unlock its emotional core. We read books, interviewed journalists and visited broadcast news studios, but it wasn't until we read a tabloid news article about a fifteen-year-old boy who learned about his brother's death while live on television that we unlocked the crux of the project; the character of Jamie.

Too little research can result in a project that lacks detail and texture; too much, and the story can become smothered and stodgy. This exercise helps us strike the right balance.

Step 1: Look in. List all the 'inward' research tasks you could do for your project by responding to the following questions:

- What personal experiences could you explore?
- What people in your life could you speak to?

- What places in your life could you visit?
- What stories you already know could you use?

Step 2: Look out. List all the 'outward' research tasks you could do for your project by responding to the following questions:

- What places could you visit?
- What books could you read?
- What online research could you do?
- What people could you meet?
- What activities could you do?

Step 3: Read through your lists, noticing which tasks feel accessible and which feel less accessible.

Step 4: Choose two research tasks to carry out in response to the following provocations:

- A task that's accessible and you can do right away. *E.g. Interview a flatmate about their views on the nature of 'evil'.*
- A task that's less accessible and requires some groundwork. *E.g. Interview the Head of Criminal Psychology at Harvard University.*

Step 5: Identify a desired outcome for each of your chosen research tasks.

Step 6: Carry out your research tasks.

Tip: Research doesn't always have to happen at the beginning of your project, it can be done in parallel with writing and devising. We continue researching throughout a project and allow it to shape and refine our creative choices as we go.

5. THE UNANSWERABLE QUESTION

Identify the central question underpinning a project.

Participants: 1+

What You Need: An idea for a project.

How We Use It: Plays that centre on unanswerable questions can be uniquely thought provoking. They avoid easy answers and instead pose compelling problems to the audience. They bind the artist and audience together in a shared attempt to wrestle with a complex theme or topic.

For *Molly*, we centred our process around a set of questions. 'What drives someone to commit a seemingly random and atrocious act of violence?' 'What is evil?' 'Is evil the product of nature, nurture, or a combination of both?'

We use this exercise to identify a central question we can build a play around. On Molly, the question which became the locus of both story and form was simply, 'what makes someone evil?'

Step 1: On a piece of paper, draw three columns with the following titles at the top:

1. Questions for Me/Us.
2. Questions for the World.
3. Questions for the Audience.

Step 2: In each of the three columns, list as many questions related to your project as you can.

Step 3: Read through your lists, highlighting all the questions you don't have answers to.

Step 4: Choose one question that feels 'unanswerable'. Something that provokes your imagination and compels you to make your project. Pin the question above your desk or stick it on your rehearsal room wall. Keep returning to it and let it guide you; it's your North Star.

Tip: Sometimes the questions underpinning our projects change as the process unfolds. It's worth repeating this exercise multiple times throughout your process as a way of checking in with anything that might be changing or evolving.

6. USE WHAT YOU KNOW

Create a scene inspired by a memory.

Participants: 1+

What You Need: An idea for a project.

How We Use It: We are the sum of our lived experiences. This means, to some extent, we're always writing from experience.

When creating the childhood scenes in *Molly*, we used our own memories of childhood as starting points. We were telling the story of a burgeoning sociopath, but it was important that the play's exploration of adolescence was grounded in truth. To achieve this, we explored events from our teenage years that included bullying, peer pressure, and social anxiety, in order to identify potential story events.

We developed this exercise for our *Get Writing* workshops to help participants find project ideas from their own lived experiences.

Step 1: Free-write/speak aloud a series of memories in response to the following provocations:

- A moment that changed you.
- An environment you know well.
- A person you know who intrigues you.
- An event you witnessed that stuck with you.

Step 2: Read through/reflect on your memories, identify those with conflict and a clear beginning, middle and end.

Step 3: Choose one of your memories to work with. Make sure it has at least two characters.

Step 4: Free-write/speak aloud everything you recall about your chosen memory. Describe as much detail as you can, starting with the phrase 'I remember . . .'.

Step 5: Prepare a scene inspired by your memory by deciding the following:

- The title of the scene.
- The first line of the scene.
- The last line of the scene.
- The place the scene is set.
- The time the scene is set.

Step 6: Write/improvise your scene. Take your characters on a journey, ensuring something changes. Focus on dialogue rather than stage directions and get to the end.

Step 7: Read through/reflect on your scene. Notice where you've stuck to the reality of your memory and where you've invented.

Variation: Choose a moment of 'invention' in your scene – something that departs from the reality of your lived experience – and use it as a starting point for a new scene.

Note: We developed this exercise in collaboration with actor/writer Sid Sagar.

7. AMAZING SPACES

Create a story inspired by a space.

Participants: 1+

What You Need: An inspiring space.

How We Use It: During the development of *Long Story Short*, we visited the ITV News studios to research the world of television news journalism. We eavesdropped on meetings, watched live transmissions of news bulletins and spoke to reporters.

When we returned to the rehearsal room, we used our experience of this space to create a pivotal scene in the play.

We use this exercise to create story and build scenes inspired by physical spaces.

Step 1: Choose a space to respond to. It should ideally be a space you can visit, but a photograph of a space can also work. Perhaps it's a place that features in your story, or the space where your project will be performed, or just a location that you find interesting. Make sure it's a dynamic space with lots to explore.

Step 2: On a piece of paper, write/draw everything you notice about the space. Explore it, question it, study it, interrogate it. Capture the mood, the light, the architecture, the sounds, the smells, the temperature, the textures, the power. Describe it literally and expressively.

Step 3: Read through/reflect on everything you noticed, identifying potential starting points for story. What conflict could emerge in this space? What characters might exist there? What action could take place?

Step 4: Make some story decisions by responding to the following questions:

- What characters occupy your space?
- What are the characters doing in your space?
- How do the characters enter and exit your space?
- How do the characters interact with your space?
- What character(s) occupies the most powerful position in your space?
- What character(s) occupies the least powerful position in your space?
- How does your space change the characters?
- How do the characters change your space?

Step 5: Write/draw a 'storyboard' for a scene, summarizing the action using a minimum of three panes. Use the following provocations to inspire your three panes:

1. Things Kick Off. *E.g. Neil and the team assemble in the newsroom for a briefing.*
2. Everything Changes. *E.g. Neil learns that Amy is responsible for publishing Jamie's tweet.*
3. Things Climax. *E.g. Neil and the team decide to bring Jamie in for an interview.*

Step 6: Use your storyboard as a starting point for writing or devising.

8. AN OBJECT LESSON

Shape the action of a scene with a found object.

Participants: 1+

What You Need: A selection of objects.

How We Use It: Whether it's a briefcase full of cash, a lost wedding ring or a severed head in a bag, an object can be a great source of conflict in a scene.

In Scene Eleven of *Long Story Short,* Neil wants Jamie to sign a contract agreeing to a live television interview. The scene depicts a battle of wills and the contract's presence is integral to how both characters persuade or evade the other. Despite rarely being mentioned in the dialogue, the contract was a key to developing the action of the scene.

We use this exercise to anchor ourselves when drafting scenes.

Step 1: Choose an object to work with. It can be something completely random or something that has a relationship to your project. *E.g. A piece of paper.*

Step 2: Free-write ten things you notice about your object. Be factual and interpretive. *E.g. Glossy, brand new, formal, embossed, shiny, yellow, stiff, stale, intimidating, clean.*

Step 3: Free-write/speak aloud ideas for the role your object could play in a scene by responding to the following questions:

- How might this object be used as a gift? *E.g. It's a wedding certificate.*
- How might this object be used as a threat? *E.g. It's an incriminating photograph.*
- How might this object be used as a secret? *E.g. It's a list of CIA agents.*
- How might this object be used as a goal for one or more characters? *E.g. It's a contract that agrees to a live television interview.*

Step 4: Read through/reflect on your ideas, identifying those with the most dramatic potential.

Step 5: Choose one idea for a role your object could play to develop further. Are you using your object as a gift, threat, secret, or goal? *E.g. A goal; it's a contract that agrees to a live television interview.*

Step 6: Write/improvise a monologue from the perspective of your object. Use the monologue to imagine the scene your object is in. Your object speaks directly to the audience, describing its own significance and narrating the action of the scene it's in through present-tense monologue. Invent as much detail as you can relating to action, character, place and time.

Step 7: Read through/reflect on your monologue, noticing all the action you've invented.

Step 8: Create a 'storyboard' for your scene using the action invented through your monologue. The storyboard visually chart the beginning, middle and end of your scene and the journey of the object.

Step 9: Write/improvise your scene. Take your characters on a journey, ensuring something changes. Focus on dialogue rather than stage directions and get to the end.

9. WHAT IT IS, WHAT IT ISN'T, WHAT IT MIGHT BE

Define the parameters of a project.

Participants: 1+

What You Need: An idea for a project.

How We Use It: On *The Incredible True Story of the Johnstown Flood*, we spent a lot of time researching the history of Johnstown, talking to people with knowledge of the 1889 flood and exploring American forms of popular entertainment. The sheer abundance of history, ideas and interesting anecdotes was inspiring, but overwhelming.

We use this exercise to get organized and collaboratively agree on the direction of a project.

Step 1: On a piece of paper, draw three columns with the following titles at the top:

1. What It Is.
2. What It Isn't.
3. What It Might Be.

Step 2: Free-write everything you know for certain about your project in the 'what it is' column. *E.g. It follows Ken, it involves a melodrama, it has a cast of five, it'll be staged with minimal props, it tells the story of the Johnstown Flood.*

Step 3: Free-write everything you know your project won't be in the 'what it isn't' column. *E.g. It doesn't have an interval, it isn't a comedy, it isn't just naturalistic, it isn't overly wedded to historical fact, it isn't just for an American audience.*

Step 4: Free-write everything you know your project might be in the 'what it might be' column. *E.g. It might involve clowning, it might have live music, it might be as much about Sally as Ken, it might include a chorus, it might chart the duration of a rehearsal process.*

Variation: Instead of applying this exercise to your whole project, try using it on a specific element such as a character, a scene, design or music.

10. STORY WALL

Visualize the shape of a story.

Participants: 1+

What You Need: A story.

How We Use It: *Molly* depicts the titular heroine's journey from childhood to adulthood, exploring how Molly's personality is shaped through relationships with friends and teachers in a school setting.

We invented the story of Molly's childhood years (Scenes 1–9) by writing in prose to identify the events that could become scenes. With the events in hand, we created a story wall and used it to visually build the first half of the play.

We use this exercise to zoom out, organise our story and identify story holes.

Step 1: Identify the protagonist of your story. The character at the centre of your story who has a want of some kind.

Step 2: Free-write/speak aloud your entire story. Include as much detail as possible and get to the end. If you're speaking your story aloud, record it and transcribe it afterwards.

Step 3: Read through your story and highlight the 'events'. An event is something that changes the direction of the story. Some events are big and obvious – like Jamie learning his brother is dead on live television in *Long Story Short* – while others are small and subtle – like Molly lighting a match against her parents' wishes in *Molly* – try and identify all of them.

Step 4: Write each of the events you've highlighted onto prompt cards. Include everything you know about the event on the prompt card, responding to the following questions.

- – What's the event?
- – What characters are involved?
- – Where does the event happen?
- – When does the event happen?

Step 5: Stick your events on the wall.

Step 6: Write the following 'story ingredients' onto seven fresh prompt cards:

1. Set-Up.
2. Inciting Incident.
3. Lock-In.
4. Midpoint.
5. Crisis.
6. Climax.
7. Resolution.

Step 7: Stick the story ingredients on the wall in numerical order, pairing them up with your events where possible. Use the following definitions as a guide:

1. Set-Up – the event where your protagonist is introduced.
2. Inciting Incident – the event where your protagonist's world is disrupted, and your story is ignited.
3. Lock-In – the event where your protagonist passes the point of no return.
4. Midpoint – the event in the middle where everything changes.
5. Crisis – the event where your protagonist experiences the worst-case scenario your Inciting Incident has been leading towards.
6. Climax – the event where your protagonist experiences the battle/confrontation your Inciting Incident has been leading towards.
7. Resolution – the event that establishes your protagonist's new reality and ties up loose ends.

Step 8: Look at your story wall. Where do you have story ingredients without events? Where do you have events without story ingredients?

Step 9: Write a poster strapline for your story by combining the descriptions of your 'inciting incident' and 'climax'. Make your audience ask, 'What's going to happen?.'

Variation: Try drawing your story wall as a graph/shape to visualize the big picture of your narrative and its dynamics.

Note: We first explored a version of this exercise while working with writer Brad Birch and learnt some of the theory featured in it from practitioner John Yorke.

11. FAILURE!

Silence your inner critic and start making.

Participants: 1+

What You Need: An idea for a scene.

How We Use It: Whilst making *The Incredible True Story of the Johnstown Flood*, we landed on the idea that the story should culminate as a melodrama, with the Troupe taking control of Ken's story and transforming it into sensational entertainment. We wanted the scene to veer between the ugly and the sublime but were stuck on how to begin writing it. We overcame this block by writing an intentionally bad version of the scene, making a virtue of failure.

We use this exercise to overcome the fear of starting.

Step 1: Choose a scene to draft/redraft. Perhaps a scene you don't know how to start making or one you've been struggling to finish.

Step 2: Give your scene a title. *E.g. The Final Showdown.*

Step 3: Identify the characters in your scene. *E.g. Ken, Manager, Heroine, Clown, Musician.*

Step 4: Identify what each character wants in your scene. The simpler and more conflicting, the better. *E.g. Ken wants the Troupe to tell the story as a realistic drama, the Troupe want Ken to tell the story as a melodrama.*

Step 5: Write the first line of text of your scene. Don't overthink it, use the first thing that comes to mind. *E.g. 'Ken: You lot ain't never done a hard day's work in your lives.'*

Step 6: Write/improvise a bad version of your scene. Embrace cliché and on-the-nose dialogue, be as obvious as you can and get to the end.

Step 7: Read through/reflect on your scene. Notice what you like/don't like. What did you discover? Is there anything that can be developed further?

12. CHARACTER FROM VERBATIM

Create a character from an audio recording.

Participants: 1+

What You Need: An idea for a project, an interviewee, a voice recorder.

How We Use It: Whilst researching *Long Story Short*, we conducted a lot of interviews with journalists and academics. While the interviews themselves don't appear in the play, they shaped our thinking and broadened our knowledge of the key themes and enriched the project. The play's protagonist, Neil, was inspired by an ITV news editor we met and interviewed.

This exercise helps us transition from research to making, using real people we've met as a starting point for the creation of characters.

Step 1: Record a conversation with an interviewee related to your project. Prepare a list of questions or let the conversation play out organically. Try to engage their head and their heart.

Step 2: Listen to your recording. Notice the syntax, texture and tone of how the person communicates.

Step 3: Transcribe your recording, writing everything your interviewee said exactly as they said it. Include all their pauses, mistakes and idiosyncrasies. If your recording is long, select a ten-minute extract to work with.

Step 4: Read through your transcript. Choose two lines of text that represent two different parts of your interviewee's character.

Step 5: Explore your first line of text by speaking the line repeatedly. What does it make your voice do? What does it make your body do? Work expressively unpacking this side of your interviewee.

Step 6: Explore your second line of text by speaking the line repeatedly. What does it make your voice do differently? What does it make your body do differently? Work expressively, unpacking this different side of your interviewee.

Step 7: Write/draw three things you notice about your interviewee. Describe the two sides of them literally and expressively.

Step 8: Create two 'character portraits' representing the two sides of your interviewee. Each portrait should involve movement and be ten seconds in length. Include one object, one piece of music and one moment of stillness in each. Express your interviewee's character with a focus on feeling.

Step 9: Free-write a monologue from your interviewee's perspective in response to one of the following provocations. It should address the audience, confiding in them. At the beginning of the monologue, the character should have the energy of your first portrait, by the end they should have the energy of your second portrait. Take inspiration from the original person but don't feel bound to them. Engage with syntax, texture, tone and idiosyncrasies as much or as little as you like.

  – 'My desire is . . .'.
  – 'My strength is . . .'.
  – 'My weakness is . . .'.
  – 'My greatest fear is . . .'.

Tip: Use **4. Looking In, Looking Out** to help identify interviewees for your project.

Note: We learnt some of the language featured in this exercise from practitioners Anne Bogart and Tina Landau.

13. THE FOUR CORNERS OF A CHARACTER

Get to know a character inside and out.

Participants: 1+

What You Need: A character, a rehearsal room.

How We Use It: When creating the character of Molly, we spent a lot of time exploring the different layers of her identity; her relationships with family and friends, her fears, her secrets, her desires. Once we had a first draft of the play, we became interested in the gap between Molly's public and private selves.

This exercise helps us establish a deeper understanding of our characters and, in turn, empowers us to draft more dynamic versions of our plays.

Step 1: Choose a character to work with. *E.g. Molly.*

Step 2: On a piece of paper, draw a diamond. Make the edges of the diamond meet the edges of the paper, creating four corners.

Step 3: In the middle of the diamond, list your character's physical traits.

Step 4: In the middle of the diamond, list your character's psychological traits.

Step 5: In the middle of the diamond, list the roles your character plays.

Step 6: In the middle of the diamond, describe your character expressively by responding to the following questions:

- What animal represents your character?
- What object represents your character?
- What colour represents your character?
- What gesture represents your character?
- What emotion represents your character?
- What element represents your character?
- What texture represents your character?
- What shape represents your character?
- What smell represents your character?
- What music represents your character?
- What sound represents your character?
- What genre represents your character?

Step 7: Look at your diamond, noticing the words/phrases that best bring the character to life.

Step 8: Identify the four corners of your character by distilling the best words/phrases into the four corners of the page using the following provocations:

- Describe your character's 'mask' in the top left corner.
- Describe your character's 'true self' in the top right corner.

- Describe your character's 'strengths' in the bottom right corner.
- Describe your character's 'weaknesses' in the bottom left corner.

Step 9: Assign the four corners of your character to the four corners of a rehearsal room. With music playing, physically explore each of the four corners of your character. Work expressively, using body and voice to unpack your character's mask, true self, strengths and weaknesses.

Tip: If you've been exploring the protagonist of your story in this exercise you can use the discoveries you've made to explore their journey in **18. The Roadmap of Change**.

14. THE TWENTY-FOUR-HOUR CLOCK

Live a day in the life of a character.

Participants: 2+

What You Need: A character, a sound system, a rehearsal room.

How We Use It: On *Long Story Short*, we were working with a large ensemble of characters. We needed to make quick decisions about the characters' everyday lives to understand how the story was disrupting them and affecting their behavior.

Our associate Kane Husbands facilitated this exercise – a long-form improvisation which imagines twenty-four hours in the life of a character – to develop our shared understanding of *Long Story Short*'s characters.

We use this exercise to quickly create a shared reference palette for how our characters behave in public and private which we then apply in rehearsals and to redrafts.

Step 1: Choose a character to work with. Perhaps a character you want to embody for the first time or one that you want to make more three-dimensional.

Step 2: Create a twenty-four-minute music playlist. Choose dynamic music that isn't too prescriptive in terms of mood/feeling. We use tracks like Ludovico Einaudi's 'Nightbook' and Bickram Ghosh's 'Hands and Sticks'.

Step 3: Choose the place your character would be at 3 a.m. on an average day. Stand, sit or lie in your rehearsal room, imagining that you're the character in your chosen place.

Step 4: Improvise twenty-four hours in the life of your character – from 3 a.m. to 3 a.m. – whilst playing your music. Have someone facilitate by calling out the time of day – '4 a.m.', '5 a.m.', '6 a.m.', etc. – every sixty seconds. Work naturalistically, exploring both the public and private sides of your character. Focus on doing. Use voice and text as much or as little as you like. Embrace the whole space. Use/mime objects with specificity. Don't interact with other actors in the space; work individually, imagining any people your character meets throughout the day. Work with and against the music, explore your character's extremities.

Step 5: Reflect on your improvisation by responding to the following questions.

- What's your character's physical centre (where do they lead from when they move)?
- How does your character behave publicly?
- How does your character behave privately?
- How does your character's behaviour change around different people?

Variation: Repeat this exercise for different moments in your story to map an arc of change for your character. How does a day in your character's life at the beginning of the story differ from a day in the middle or the end of the story? How does your character's behaviour change?

15. OPPOSING FORCES

Create an antagonist.

Participants: 1+

What You Need: A protagonist, a rehearsal room (if improvising).

How We Use It: In *Long Story Short*, Jamie is on the run searching for his brother, Andy. The cinematic nature of Jamie's quest means that, with every scene, he faces a new obstacle. Films thrive on conflict between a character and the world they're in whereas, in theatre, conflict needs to be interpersonal. To create Jamie's obstacles, we unpacked what Jamie wants and put those wants into the hands of other characters, thus creating antagonists which we could build scenes from.

We use this exercise to unpack a protagonists inner and outer antagonisms and use them to create robust antagonists for scenes.

Step 1: Choose a protagonist to create an antagonist for. *E.g. Jamie.*

Step 2: Write/draw three things your protagonist wants by responding to the following questions. If you already have a story, answer the questions thinking about your protagonist at the beginning:

1. What does your character want by the end of the day? *E.g. To find his brother.*
2. What does your character want by the end of the year? *E.g. To get released from the young offender's institute.*
3. What does your character want by the end of their life? *E.g. To make a family.*

Step 3: Choose one of your protagonist's wants to work with. Select one that you're already building a story around or would like to grow a story from. *E.g. Jamie wants to find his brother.*

Step 4: List the 'inner antagonisms' that might stop your protagonist getting what they want by responding to the following questions:

- What personal beliefs might get in their way? *E.g. distrusting of authority.*
- What personality traits might hold them back? *E.g. hotheaded.*
- What values could become obstacles? *E.g. family loyalty.*

Step 5: List the 'outer antagonisms' that might stop your protagonist getting what they want by responding to the following questions:

- What people might get in their way? *E.g. his brother's ex-girlfriend, train passengers, journalists.*
- What environmental obstacles might they need to overcome? *E.g. The police are looking for him.*
- What time pressures are there? *E.g. The news cycle is moving on.*

Step 6: List ten antagonists who could exist in your story and respond to the following questions to flesh out each one. They should literally possess your protagonist's want or embody their want somehow. They might know your protagonist, or they might be a stranger.

- Who are they and what's their relationship to your protagonist? *E.g. Sarah; Jamie's brother's ex-girlfriend.*
- What do they possess/embody that your protagonist wants? *E.g. Sarah might have information about where Jamie's brother is.*
- Why might they stop your protagonist from getting what they want? *E.g. Jamie's brother has sworn Sarah to secrecy.*

Step 7: Choose one antagonist to work with and respond to the following questions:

- What's your antagonist's name?
- How long have the protagonist and antagonist known each other?
- How do they know each other?
- What does your protagonist want from your antagonist?
- What does your antagonist want from your protagonist?
- What do they openly like about each other?
- What do they openly dislike about each other?
- What do they secretly like about each other?
- What do they secretly dislike about each other?

Step 8: Clarify the 'four elements of drama' for your scene by responding to the following questions:

1. Action – What's the action? What are the characters doing?
2. Character – Who are the characters? What are their relationships? What do they want from each other? What do they get from each other?
3. Place – Where's it set? Is it a neutral place? Does a particular character own it or have a sense of owning it?
4. Time – When's it set? Time of day, month, year, etc.? Is there a time pressure?

Step 9: Write/improvise your scene. Take your characters on a journey, ensuring something changes. Focus on dialogue rather than stage directions and get to the end.

16. CHARACTER FIRSTS

Invent a character's backstory.

Participants: 1+

What You Need: A character, a rehearsal room.

How We Use It: While developing *Molly*, we used character 'firsts' to chart Molly's journey through her childhood years (Scenes One to Nine). We identified 'firsts' we could relate to from our own lives – first day at school, first kiss, first cigarette, etc. – and asked: what would Molly's version be? By grounding scenes in 'firsts' familiar to an audience, we could subvert expectations of how recognizable scenarios ought to play out.

A by-product of this exercise was a rich understanding of Molly's backstory. We now use it on all our projects to quickly and practically create character backstories, giving us a shared understanding of the events that shaped them before the play begins.

Step 1: Choose a character to work with. *E.g. Molly.*

Step 2: Identify the chapter of your character's life you want to explore. *E.g. Molly's childhood years, aged seven to fifteen.*

Step 3: List ten questions about your character you want to find answers to in that chapter of their life. *E.g. What were Molly's parents like? How was Molly different from the other children at school? When did Molly realize she was different?*

Part 4: List twenty 'firsts' relating to your character in that chapter of their life. *E.g. First time without her parents home, first friend, first fight, first kiss.*

Step 5: Improvise each of your firsts as short, thirty-second scenes. Have someone facilitate by reading out the 'firsts' and being strict with timekeeping. Work impulsively and don't plan anything before each improvisation. Remember, this isn't about perfect scenes or good acting, it's about making quick discoveries about your character.

Step 6: Reflect on your improvisations, noticing the answers you've found and identifying any scenes you'd like to do a longer improvisation of to find more answers.

17. ACTION!

Drive a scene with physical action.

Participants: 1+

What You Need: An idea for a scene.

How We Use It: Scene Nine of *Molly* sees Molly and Laura bullying Dan in the woods. More than any other scene in the play, it's driven by physical action. There's a moment that involves Molly and Laura playing catch with Dan's backpack (something involving an object), a moment that involves Dan accidentally striking

Laura (something involving physical contact) and a moment in which Molly makes Dan get undressed (something slow).

Many good scenes are action rather than dialogue led; this exercise allowed us to be true to that and create a more visceral and theatrical scene than it might otherwise have been.

We use this exercise early in the development of scenes to discover the physical action we could use and how it might drive the story.

Step 1: Choose a scene to draft/redraft.

Step 2: Clarify the 'four elements of drama' for your scene by responding to the following questions:

1. Action – What's the action? What are the characters doing?
2. Character – Who are the characters? What are their relationships? What do they want from each other? What do they get from each other?
3. Place – Where's it set? Is it a neutral place? Does a particular character own it or have a sense of owning it?
4. Time – When's it set? Time of day, month, year, etc.? Is there a time pressure?

Step 3: Write the following provocations for stage directions onto small pieces of paper (or choose your own) and put them in a pile:

1. Something involving an object.
2. Someone exits.
3. Something involving physical contact.
4. Something silent.
5. Something slow.
6. Someone gives a look.
7. Something repetitive.
8. Something involving all characters.
9. Something fast.
10. Something small.
11. Someone enters.
12. Something big.
13. Something loud.

Step 4: Write your scene, inserting a stage direction every three lines. You can invent a stage direction impulsively or pick a provocation from your pile and use it to inspire an idea. Allow each stage direction to inform the action/dialogue that follows. The stage directions will generate physical action and physical action is the fuel for your scene.

Step 5: Read through your scene, noticing how the dialogue is in service to the action.

Step 6: Redraft your scene, using stage directions at your own discretion. Only pick a provocation from your pile if you get stuck. There'll be things from the previous draft you retain and things you lose. Use your instincts to drive your scene with action.

Variation: Try a different rule in Step 3 by using one of the following provocations.

- Insert a stage direction every five lines.
- Insert a stage direction after every question.
- Insert three stage directions every three lines.
- Only write stage directions.

Note: This exercise was inspired by practice we learnt from writer Rory Mullarkey.

18. THE ROADMAP OF CHANGE

Chart a protagonist's change.

Participants: 1+

What You Need: A protagonist.

How We Use It: Ken is the protagonist of *The Incredible True Story of the Johnstown Flood*. It's his emotional journey that the narrative centres on.

As the play progresses, Ken's relationship to the Troupe undergoes a gradual, but radical shift. Ken begins the play as a desperate and vulnerable young man – a survivor who places his trust in a group of well-meaning strangers – but when he rejects their help, he finds himself at loggerheads with the very people he once trusted. Ken's behaviour significantly changes over the course of the play and by the end, he's a very different person to the one we met at the start.

We use this exercise to chart our protagonists' journeys of change and use the roadmap it creates to draft/redraft scenes.

Step 1: Choose a protagonist to work with. Perhaps it's a character who you plan to centre a play around or a character at the centre of a play you're already making.

Step 2: Get to know your protagonist by responding to the following questions:

1. What three words would people who don't know your character well use to describe them?
2. What is your protagonist's greatest fear?
3. What are your protagonist's three greatest strengths?
4. What are your protagonist's three counter-traits (the qualities that get them into trouble in their world)?
5. What characteristic does your character most detest in other people?
6. What characteristic does your character most admire in other people?

Step 3: List your protagonist's characteristics by inserting your answers from Step 2 into the following sentences.

1. Mask: [your answer to Question 1].
2. Greatest Fear: [your answer to Question 2].

3. Strengths: [your answer to Question 3].

4. Counter Traits: [your answer to Question 4].

5. Dark Self: [your answer to Question 5].

6. True Self: [your answer to Question 6].

Step 4: Create a 'roadmap of change' for your protagonist by inserting your responses from Step 3 into the following sentences:

1. At the beginning they're [wearing their mask].

2. Then they [experience their greatest fear] so they [use their strengths].

3. But [their strengths fail] so they [experience their counter-traits].

4. Which leads them to [their dark self].

5. Until they [find their true self].

Step 5: Illustrate your roadmap of change by adding visuals to the sentence which bring your protagonist's journey to life.

Step 6: Look at your protagonist's roadmap of change. How does your protagonist change? How does their journey map onto your story?

Note: We learnt a version of this exercise from writer Ashley C. Karaweigh, who learnt a version from actor/writer Arinzé Kene.

19. A RELATIONSHIP MONTAGE

Unpack a character relationship.

Participants: 2+

What You Need: A character relationship, a rehearsal room.

How We Use It: Midway through the development of *Molly*, it became clear that the relationship between Molly and Laura was integral to the dramatic arc of the play. We needed to understand this relationship in more depth.

We use this exercise to enrich our understanding of characters, flesh out their relationships and inspire ideas for scenes.

Step 1: Choose a character relationship to explore – two or more characters who you want to explore the relationship of.

Step 2: List five questions you have about this character relationship that you want to try and answer with this exercise.

Step 3: Free-write a timeline for the character relationship, identifying where it starts and where it ends.

Step 4: Identify ten scenes that chart the journey of your character relationship and give each one a title.

Step 5: Write/improvise your ten scenes including no more than five lines of text in each. The beginning of each scene should match or oppose the energy of the previous scene.

Step 6: Read through/reflect on your scenes.

Step 7: Make your 'relationship montage' including the following ingredients across the ten scenes:

- A fast moment.
- A slow moment.
- A long pause.
- A physically distant moment.
- A physically close moment.
- A loud moment.
- A quiet moment.
- A unison moment.

Step 8: Share your relationship montage.

Step 9: Reflect on your sharing and return to the list of questions from Step 2 to see what answers you've found.

Variation: Find a moment where you can slip into genre (romantic comedy, horror, western) and see how it enhances the montage. Your choice of moment will often reveal the emotional peak of a story.

20. MAKING TO MUSIC

Create a scene in response to music.

Participants: 1+

What You Need: An idea for a project, a sound system.

How We Use It: For *Long Story Short*, we wanted to create a scene which captured the energy of what we observed at ITV News whilst researching the project.

The characters and dialogue in Scene Nine of the play were directly inspired by people we met, but to capture the dynamics we found a piece of music that captured the essence of our experience in the newsroom – Trent Reznor and Atticus Ross's 'In Motion' from the film *The Social Network* – and used it as inspiration, literally drafting the scene to the music.

We use this exercise when we have an idea of what we'd like a scene to become, but don't know how to get there.

Step 1: Choose a piece of music around four minutes in length to work with. Make sure the music you choose has several movements and lots of changes in dynamics.

We like using Too Many Zooz's 'Missy', Bikram Ghosh's 'Hands and Sticks' and A Hawk and a Hacksaw's 'God Bless the Ottoman Empire'.

Step 2: On a piece of paper, draw a line through the middle of the page in landscape, dividing it into two halves. The line you've drawn represents the entirety of your piece of music – the beginning of the line is the beginning of the track, the end of the line is the end of the track – it's a timeline.

Step 3: Above the line, write/draw your first impressions of the music whilst listening for the first time. Notice the different movements and the changes in dynamics. Notice how it makes you feel.

Step 4: Thinking about the music in relation to the world of your project, choose a place and time to set your scene. What place and time does the music evoke?

Step 5: Above the line, write/draw the mood, atmosphere, tone and energy of the music, whilst listening for a second time. Describe the music literally and expressively. Draw vertical lines down the page to mark the movements.

Step 6: Thinking about the music and the world of your project, choose two or more characters for your scene. What characters does the music evoke?

Step 7: Below the line, write/draw ideas for action and dialogue, whilst listening for a third time. Be impulsive; don't try to connect things or tell a story at this stage.

Step 8: Clarify the 'four elements of drama' for your scene by responding to the following questions:

1. Action – What's the action? What are the characters doing?
2. Character – Who are the characters? What are their relationships? What do they want from each other? What do they get from each other?
3. Place – Where's it set? Is it a neutral place? Does a particular character own it or have a sense of owning it?
4. Time – When's it set? Time of day, month, year, etc.? Is there a time pressure?

Step 9: Write/improvise your scene, whilst listening for a fourth time. Use your action, character, place and time decisions as inspiration but try not to overthink; stay with the music, moving into each new movement of your scene as the track takes you there. Your scene is the music, and your music is the scene.

Step 10: Read through/reflect on your scene, thinking about what could be developed and by responding to the following questions:

- Could you respond more to the loudest moment?
- Could you respond more to the quietest moment?
- Could you respond more to the fastest moment?
- Could you respond more to the slowest moment?
- Could you respond more to the highest pitch moment?
- Could you respond more to the lowest pitch moment?

Step 11: Redraft your scene without the music playing. There'll be things from the previous draft you retain and things you lose. You'll have an internalized sense of the music by now; use it to guide your redraft.

Tip: Try performing your scene with a completely different piece of music playing and discover what juxtaposing it with an opposite piece of music does.

21. MARRIAGE COUNSELLING

Reconnect with a project.

Participants: 1+

What You Need: An idea for a project.

How We Use It: More than anything else we've worked on, *The Incredible True Story of the Johnstown Flood* tested and challenged us. The play kept slipping free of our grasp and we became overwhelmed by the complexity of the subject matter; we lost sight of what the story meant to us. We paused and asked ourselves: why are we telling this story and what does it mean to each of us on a personal level?

Sometimes, when developing a project, we go off on a tangent and lose sight of what we originally set out to make. Like a rocky period in a relationship, it's at these times when we risk falling out of love with a project and the prospect of divorce emerges. 'Marriage counselling' is required to rekindle the love.

We first facilitated this exercise at one of our *Get Writing* workshops to help participants connect/reconnect with their projects.

Step 1: Free-write/speak-aloud the 'points of connection' you have with your project by responding to each of the following provocations:

- 'This project matters to me because . . .'.
- 'I first became interested in this because . . .'.
- 'When I really think about this project, I feel . . .'.
- 'It involves me, because . . .'.
- 'Telling this story costs me . . .'.

Step 2: Read through/reflect on your points of connection, noticing discoveries you've made about your relationship to your project.

Step 3: Write/speak aloud three 'statements of intent' by responding to the following questions.

- What story am I telling?
- Why am I telling this story?
- How am I telling this story in a way that only I can?

Variation: If you're working with collaborators, share your statements of intent as a group. Ask each other questions and find further connections between you and your project.

Note: We developed this exercise in collaboration with actor/writer Sid Sagar.

22. POT LUCK

Explore scenes with games and conditions.

Participants: 1+

What You Need: A story, a rehearsal room (if improvising).

How We Use It: At the beginning of our process making *The Incredible True Story of the Johnstown Flood*, we created a story outline and went into a rehearsal room with actors to improvise scenes from it. These improvisations explored the Ken and Sally relationship and their attempts to uncover what is happening at the South Fork Fishing and Hunting Club.

We set up improvisations by applying games and conditions randomly to action we wanted to explore. The games and conditions created restrictions which liberated the actors to play. They took the scenes beyond the realm of naturalism and forced us into an imaginative space.

Whether writing or devising, this exercise allows us to begin identifying what the story might be and how we might tell it. It gets us out of our heads and helps us discover weird and wonderful possibilities for scenes.

Step 1: Prepare your action. Write ten ideas for action inspired by your story on small pieces of paper and put them in a pile. Each piece of paper should detail what the characters in the scene are doing; 'Ken and Sally break into Ruff's study', for example. Make your descriptions specific and concise; a good stimulus opens up possibilities and doesn't overly prescribe or endgame the scene.

Step 2: Prepare your games. Write ten games from the list below (or choose your own) on small pieces of paper and put them in a separate pile:

- Each line begins with the next letter of the alphabet.
- Each line begins with 'fortunately' or 'unfortunately'.
- Each line begins with 'yes and' or 'no but'.
- Each line begins with the last word/phrase of the previous line.
- Each line begins with 'sorry'.
- Each line begins with 'thank you'.
- Every line is a question.
- Every line rhymes with the previous.
- Every line contains a number.
- Every line is one word long.
- Every line is no more than three words long.
- Every line includes the letter 't'.
- Everything is repeated.
- Everything is reversed.
- The characters only speak to the audience.

- The characters cannot lie.
- The characters only lie.
- The scene is silent.
- The characters narrate what they're doing to the audience.
- The characters narrate their internal thoughts/feelings to the audience.
- The characters narrate other characters' internal thoughts/feelings to the audience.
- The actors must not move (improvisation only).
- The actors speak in a made-up language (improvisation only).
- The actors are always in motion (improvisation only).
- The actors can freeze the scene and speak to the audience (improvisation only).
- The actors can only sing (improvisation only).
- The actors are always at least five metres apart from each other (improvisation only).
- The actors must not make eye contact with each other (improvisation only).
- The actors are always making eye contact with each other (improvisation only).
- The actors can replay moments if they don't like them (improvisation only).
- The actors shut their eyes when anyone else is speaking (improvisation only).
- The actors are always in physical contact with each other (improvisation only).
- The actors can only whisper or shout (improvisation only).
- The actors play the characters furthest from their identities (improvisation only).
- The actors must not look at each other (improvisation only).
- The actors can switch characters during the scene (improvisation only).

Step 3: Prepare your conditions. Write ten conditions from the list below (or choose your own) on small pieces of paper and put them in a separate pile:

- One character has a plan.
- One character has millions of Instagram followers.
- One character has just had sex.
- One character never listens.
- One character has a problem with the opposite sex.
- One character is in love.
- One character hasn't showered.
- One character got no sleep last night.
- One character doesn't want to be here.
- One character loves gossip.
- One character has a cold.
- One character has eaten a lot of sweets.

- One character is hungry.
- One character doesn't have enough money.
- One character doesn't like reading.
- One character owns this place or has a sense of owning it.
- One character has somewhere else to be.
- One character doesn't like someone.
- One character is cold.
- One character is late.
- One character is early.
- One of the characters is about to leave for good.
- One character doesn't like this game.
- One character needs a hug.
- One character knows a secret.
- One character is sick with anxiety.
- One character is experiencing love for the first time.
- The characters haven't seen each other for a long time.
- The characters had an argument recently.
- The characters are meeting for the last time.
- The characters are from different worlds.
- It's the hottest day of the year.
- It's raining.
- It's the day of a funeral.
- It's the day the world is going to end.

Step 4: Randomly select one piece of paper from each pile to establish the action, a game and a condition for a scene.

Step 5: Write/improvise your scene with a strict time limit. Negotiate the action whilst committing to the game you're working with and feeding off the condition. Play hard and let the limitations breed creativity.

Step 6: Read through/reflect on your scene. Notice what you like/don't like. What did you discover? Is there anything that can be developed?

Step 7: Repeat Steps 4–6 several times to explore different combinations of action, games and conditions. Some will fly and some will flop. Enjoy the randomness and embrace the unknown.

Tip: If you're improvising, have someone facilitate by reading out the three ingredients before each scene begins and being strict with timekeeping. Work impulsively and don't plan anything before each improvisation. Remember, this isn't about perfect scenes or good acting, it's about discovering ideas for what your story is and how it might be told.

Variation: In Step 1, prepare events instead of action; 'Ken realizes Pearson is complicit in making the dam unsafe', for example. You might have an event in mind for a scene but be unsure how to get to get. Events are harder to use as starting points for writing and improvising as they tend to endgame the scene; be sure to discover action as you go, and you'll avoid arriving at the event too soon.

Note: We first explored this approach to improvisation whilst working with writer Chris Bush and we've learnt a lot about using restrictions from theatre company Told by an Idiot.

23. THE SHAPE OF A SCENE

Mould the action of scenes with shapes.

Participants: 1+

What You Need: A story, a rehearsal room (if improvising).

How We Use It: On *The Incredible True Story of the Johnstown Flood*, we wanted to explore how some of the scenes in our story might be told differently. We set up improvisations by applying scene shapes randomly to action from our story.

We use this exercise when we know what our scenes are, but we want to make them more dynamic. The shapes create restrictions which, in turn, force imaginative choices from the actors and allow us to quickly discover what scenes could be when a particular dynamic is applied.

Step 1: Prepare your action. Write ten ideas for action inspired by your story on small pieces of paper and put them in a pile. Each piece of paper should detail what the characters in the scene are doing; 'Ken and Sally break into Ruff's study', for example. Make your descriptions specific and concise; a good stimulus opens up possibilities and doesn't overly prescribe or endgame the scene.

Step 2: Prepare your shapes. Write/draw ten shapes from the list below (or choose your own) on small pieces of paper and put them in a separate pile:

- A triangle.
- A square.
- A circle.
- A diamond.
- A lightning bolt.
- A rectangle.
- A star.
- The event occurs at the beginning.
- The event occurs in the middle.
- The event occurs at the end.
- A big to small waveform.
- A small to big waveform.

- A big to small to big waveform.
- A small to big to small waveform.

Step 4: Randomly select one piece of paper from each pile to establish the action and a shape for a scene.

Step 5: Write/improvise your scene with a strict time limit. Negotiate the action whilst committing to the shape you're working with. Play hard and let the limitations breed creativity.

Step 6: Read through/reflect on your scene. Notice what you like/don't like. What did you discover? Is there anything that can be developed?

Step 7: Repeat Steps 4–6 several times to explore different combinations of action and shapes. Some will work better than others. Enjoy the randomness and embrace the unknown.

Tip: If you're improvising, have someone facilitate by reading out the two ingredients before each scene begins and being strict with timekeeping. Work impulsively and don't plan anything before each improvisation. Remember, this isn't about perfect scenes or good acting, it's about discovering ideas for what your story is and how it might be told.

Variation: In Step 1, prepare events instead of action; 'Ken realizes Pearson is complicit in making the dam unsafe', for example. You might know what event needs to happen in a scene but be unsure of how to get to it. Events are harder to use as starting points for writing and improvising as they tend to endgame the scene; be sure to discover action as you go, and you'll avoid arriving at your chosen event too soon.

Note: This exercise was inspired by practice we learnt from writers Ella Road and Ruby Thomas.

24. SURPRISE!

Build a scene around a moment of surprise.

Participants: 1+

What You Need: An idea for a scene, a rehearsal room (if improvising).

How We Use It: Scene Twelve of *Long Story Short* involves Jamie being interviewed on live television and ends with him discovering his brother has died. Something expected occurs (Jamie's brother's death) in an unexpected way (during Jamie's interview). The result is a surprise moment that disorientates the characters and shocks the audience.

Moments of surprise subvert audience expectations and raise the stakes. Surprises are most impactful when used sparingly to create narrative turning points, bring tensions to the boil and/or depict sudden changes in characters.

We use this exercise to identify moments that will, hopefully, surprise an audience and decide how to deploy them in a dynamic way possible.

Step 1: Choose a scene to draft/redraft.

Step 2: Clarify the 'four elements of drama' for your scene by responding to the following questions:

1. Action – What's the action? What are the characters doing?
2. Character – Who are the characters? What are their relationships? What do they want from each other? What do they get from each other?
3. Place – Where's it set? Is it a neutral place? Does a particular character own it or have a sense of owning it?
4. Time – When's it set? Time of day, month, year, etc.? Is there a time pressure?

Step 3: Free-write/speak aloud ideas for surprises by responding to each of the following provocations, imagining six different versions of your scene. Describe the action of each scene in prose, discovering how each surprise creates drama differently.

- A character is not who/what they appear to be.
- An object is not what a character expects it to be.
- The best possible thing happens.
- The worst possible thing happens.
- Someone does something extremely out of character.
- A place is not what it appears to be.

Step 4: Read through your free-writing/reflect on your ideas, noticing those with the most dramatic potential.

Step 5: Choose one of your scene ideas to work with, using the one that feels most dynamic.

Step 6: Choose where to deploy the surprise in your scene from the following three options:

- Beginning – the scene deals with the fallout of the surprise.
- Middle – the scene builds up to the surprise and then deals with the fallout.
- End – the scene builds up to the surprise and climaxes on a cliff-hanger.

Step 7: Write/improvise your scene. Take your characters on a journey, ensuring something changes. Focus on dialogue rather than stage directions and get to the end.

Variation: Try a redraft where you deploy the surprise at a different moment in your scene.

25. SECRETS REVEALED

Create subtext in a scene.

Participants: 1+

What You Need: An idea for a scene, a rehearsal room (if improvising).

How We Use It: Molly loses her job following a fatal workplace incident, while her colleague, Duncan, avoids punishment despite his culpability. This event invites the audience to look again at previous scenes and reinterpret ambiguous moments that reveal Duncan's attempts to sabotage Molly. Duncan's ability to disguise his true intentions and manipulate Molly becomes the subtext of these scenes.

Subtext is the name given to all the unspoken, less obvious, sometimes hidden stuff that simmers beneath the surface of a scene. Perhaps a character has too much to lose by being direct? Maybe you want your audience to be more active, like detectives piecing together clues? Subtext is a powerful tool for crafting a dynamic scene.

We use this exercise when redrafting to identify character secrets and create more sophisticated versions of scenes.

Step 1: Choose a scene to draft/redraft.

Step 2: Clarify the 'four elements of drama' for your scene by responding to the following questions:

1. Action – What's the action? What are the characters doing?
2. Character – Who are the characters? What are their relationships? What do they want from each other? What do they get from each other?
3. Place – Where's it set? Is it a neutral place? Does a particular character own it or have a sense of owning it?
4. Time – When's it set? Time of day, month, year, etc.? Is there a time pressure?

Step 3: List all the 'shared knowledge' your characters have at the beginning of the scene; everything that all your characters know before it begins.

Step 4: Read through your list, noticing any pieces of shared knowledge that you could turn into a secret to create drama.

Step 5: Choose one piece of shared knowledge from your list to turn into a secret. Give it to one character/group of characters as their secret. It's now knowledge that only they possess; at least one character in the scene is in the dark.

Step 6: Write your scene. The secret shouldn't be revealed but it should feed the drama of the scene; it can advantage or disadvantage the character(s) who possess it.

Step 7: Read through your scene, noticing how your secret fed the drama.

Step 8: Free-write/speak aloud ideas for how your secret could be revealed in a redraft of your scene by responding to each of the following provocations, imagining three different versions of your scene. Describe the action of each scene in prose, discovering how each type of revelation creates drama differently.

1. Overt Revelation – the secret is revealed, and the characters confront it openly. The secret is buried at the beginning of the scene and gets revealed during.

2. Hidden Revelation – the secret is revealed, but one or more characters hide their awareness of the new knowledge. The secret is buried at the beginning of the scene, and gets revealed during, but the characters conceal their new knowledge and don't deal with it openly.

3. Audience Revelation – the secret is revealed to the audience, but not the characters. The secret is buried at the beginning of the scene and gets revealed to the audience during, but the characters remain in the dark.

Step 9: Choose one version of your scene to write, using the one that feels most dynamic.

Step 10: Redraft your scene using your chosen secret and revelation to feed the drama.

26. THE PERFECT PROTAGONIST

Unpack a protagonist's wants and needs.

Participants: 2+

What You Need: A protagonist, a rehearsal room, a timer.

How We Use It: *Long Story Short*'s protagonist is Jamie – a sixteen-year-old boy who finds himself in the middle of a media storm whilst desperately searching for his soldier brother who's missing in Afghanistan.

We wanted the audience to connect with Jamie's vulnerability. Understanding Jamie's backstory and world view was key to achieving this.

We use this exercise to generate ideas for what makes our characters tick and discover their wants and needs.

Step 1: Choose a protagonist to work with.

Step 2: On a piece of paper, write your protagonist's name and spend a few minutes imagining them. If you already have a story, think about your protagonist at the beginning. Picture them, explore them, interrogate them, spend time with them.

Step 3: With fifteen minutes on the clock, list fifty memories your protagonist has.

Step 4: With ten minutes on the clock, list thirty beliefs your protagonist has.

Step 5: With five minutes on the clock, list ten things your protagonist would change about the world.

Step 6: Read through your lists, choosing one thing from each that you didn't know before the exercise.

Step 7: Write/improvise a conversation between your protagonist and an 'audience' by responding to the following questions. The audience's questions should help identify your protagonist's wants and needs. Think about how your protagonist would speak to an audience they've never met before.

- What memory would you like to share?
- What belief would you like to share?
- What thing you'd change about the world would you like to share?
- What makes you happy?
- What's missing from your life?
- What would make you happier than you are now?
- What do you desire most?
- What gets you up in the morning?
- What's your greatest fear?
- What secret have you never told anyone?

Step 8: Read through/reflect on your conversation, noticing any discoveries about your protagonist's wants and needs.

Step 9: List all the 'wants' your protagonist has. These wants should be things your protagonist is consciously aware of.

Step 10: List all the 'needs' your protagonist has. These needs should be things your protagonist is unaware of, but other characters/the audience may know about them.

Tip: The pressure of Steps 3–5 will make you impulsively draw on lived experiences. Embrace the overlaps between you and your protagonist; they will ground you and connect you to them.

Variation: Choose one of your protagonist's wants, list inciting incidents which could spark a story driven by it and identify the needs that lie beneath each want. *E.g. Jamie wants his brother home; his brother goes missing which sparks a story where Jamie discovers he needs to become an adult with his own agency.*

27. THREE TYPES OF DIALOGUE

Enrich the dialogue of a scene.

Participants: 1+

What You Need: An idea for a scene, a rehearsal room (if improvising).

How We Use It: In *The Incredible True Story of the Johnstown Flood*, there's a scene in which Sally invites Ken into her father's study. It's a fraught moment; Ken is scared to set foot in such a forbidding, elitist environment, but he craves the warmth and intimacy of Sally's company. We wanted Ken and Sally's dialogue to capture the shifting emotions of fear, desire and, eventually, anger.

Characters communicate their wants – either directly or indirectly – through dialogue. Dialogue can make characters articulate themselves in surprising or unexpected ways, enrich the meaning of a given exchange and create dynamic character relationships.

This exercise gives scenes a full body workout by applying three different types of dialogue.

Step 1: Choose a scene to draft/redraft.

Step 2: Clarify the 'four elements of drama' for your scene by responding to the following questions:

1. Action – What's the action? What are the characters doing?
2. Character – Who are the characters? What are their relationships? What do they want from each other? What do they get from each other?
3. Place – Where's it set? Is it a neutral place? Does a particular character own it or have a sense of owning it?
4. Time – When's it set? Time of day, month, year, etc.? Is there a time pressure?

Step 3: Write/improvise your scene using only 'fighting dialogue'. Fighting dialogue is where characters want to win and come out on top. The conflict escalates with each and every line. The characters never say anything to agree or placate. Each new line raises the stakes.

Step 4: Read through/reflect on your scene. How has your scene changed? What's successful/unsuccessful about the use of fighting dialogue in your scene?

Step 5: Redraft your scene using only 'masking dialogue'. Masking dialogue is where characters evade and/or cover up the truth. Characters never reveal what they want or feel; they only hint or imply. Characters might suspect the truth and probe to reveal it.

Step 6: Read through/reflect on your scene. How has your scene changed? What's successful/unsuccessful about the use of masking dialogue in your scene?

Step 7: Redraft your scene using only 'distracted dialogue'. Distracted dialogue is where characters' minds are elsewhere. Characters never address or respond directly to each other; they're caught up in their own worlds.

Step 8: Read through/reflect on your scene. How has your scene changed? What's successful/unsuccessful about the use of distracted dialogue in your scene?

Step 9: Redraft your scene using fighting, masking and distracted dialogue. A good scene often contains all three types of dialogue. There'll be things from the previous draft that you retain and things you lose. Allow yourself to freestyle.

Step 10: Read through/reflect on your scene, noticing how much more muscular your dialogue is.

Tip: When you've been working on a scene for a while, it can be worth doing a redraft using just one type of dialogue as a way of finding one or two new ideas that can be inserted back into your earlier draft.

Note: This exercise was inspired by the practice of novelist Toby Litt.

28. AND . . . CUT!

Edit a scene into the best version of itself.

Participants: 1+

What You Need: A draft script.

How We Use It: Whether we're writing, devising, or both, we always create a script. We write collaboratively, so the first draft tends to be a long, overwritten affair; the imperfect product of multiple voices. Cutting brings focus, shape and coherence to a draft.

As you redraft a script, you'll find yourself dispensing with dialogue, action or scenes that you like, but are no longer integral. You'll go back and forth, debating whether to retain some parts and lose others. Sometimes cutting is quick and intuitive; sometimes it's slow and calculated.

This exercise helps us edit scenes in a sensitive, considered and purposeful manner.

Step 1: Choose a scene to edit.

Step 2: Identify the 'event' of the scene. The event of a scene is the moment where something changes for all the characters; it's often the reason the scene exists in the story.

Step 3: Start late. How late can your scene begin? What could be cut from the top of the scene so there's drama from the very first line? Highlight potential cuts.

Step 4: Get out early. How early can your scene end? What could be cut from the bottom of the scene so there's drama until the very last line? Highlight potential cuts.

Step 5: Bury intention. Is there any dialogue in your scene where characters state their intentions? Where do characters say overtly what they want? Where do characters say overtly what other people want? Do they need to? Highlight potential cuts.

Step 6: Show don't tell. Is there any dialogue in your scene where characters reveal or explain things without provocation? Is there more exposition or information than there needs to be? Highlight potential cuts.

Step 7: Read through your highlights.

Step 8: Choose some cuts to make or notes to give. Be kind to yourself but be bold and remember, you can always undo!

29. MONOLOGUE LOTTERY

Jumpstart a monologue.

Participants: 1+

What You Need: A character, a rehearsal room (if improvising).

How We Use It: During development for *The Incredible True Story of the Johnstown Flood*, we did a version of this exercise with actor Daniel Adeosun, to generate the opening monologue of the play.

This exercise gets you writing a monologue instinctively and impulsively.

Step 1: Choose a character to write a monologue for.

Step 2: Write ten random words/phrases on ten small pieces of paper and put them in a pile. They should be the first ten words/phrases that come to mind when thinking about your character's voice.

Step 3: Randomly select one word/phrase from the pile.

Step 4: Write ten random lines inspired by your chosen word/phrase on ten small pieces of paper and put them in a new pile. They should be the first ten lines that come to mind when thinking about both your chosen word/phrase and your character's voice. It's up to you whether your lines include the word/phrase itself.

Step 5: Randomly select two lines from the pile.

Step 6: Write/improvise your monologue using your chosen lines as the first and last lines of the speech. Don't plan, just start writing/improvising and figure out who your character is speaking to and what they want as you go. Take your characters on a journey, ensuring something changes. Focus on dialogue rather than stage directions and get to the end.

Step 7: Read through/reflect on your monologue. Notice what you like/don't like. What did you discover? Is there anything that can be developed?

Variation: During Step 1, feed action, character, place and/or time decisions in, to create a monologue for a specific moment of story.

Note: We learnt a version of this exercise from writer Ella Road.

Acknowledgements

We'd like to thank the following individuals and organizations for everything they've done to aid the creation of these plays. We couldn't have done it without their support, creativity and generosity.

Adam Loxley
Alasdair Linn
Alex Harvey-Brown
Amit Lahav
Anne McNulty
Ashley C. Karaweigh
Avital Shira
Bart Lambert
Bianca Stephens
Brad Birch
Brandon Grace
Caroline Moroney
Chris Bush
Chris Jackson
Clare Shaw
Clive Foster
Damien Hasson
Daniella Isaacs
Danielle Frimer
David Bond
David Cann
David Goodhart
David Smith
Davina Moss
Deirdre O'Halloran
Douggie McMeekin
Edmund Digby-Jones
Eleanor McLoughlin
Elizabeth Bourne
Elizabeth Gaubert
Ella Road

Ellen Spence
Emily Maitlis
Eric Knopsnyder
Francesca Knight
Freddy Elletson
Gabriel Gatehouse
Garry Jenkins
George Cook
Glynn Jones
Grace Chilton
Grace Quigley
Grace Saif
Hana Walker-Brown
Helen Coyston
Henrietta Page
Holly Race Roughan
Jake Orr
James Sobol Kelly
Jenny Foster
Jason Houston
Jim Hustwitt
John Seaward
Joseph Potter
Judith Dimant
Kim Monney
Kimball Stroud
Laura Free
Laurence Anderson
Laurie Coldwell
Lewis Mackinnon
Liadan Dunlea

Lloyd Trott
Louis Landau
Lisa Houston
Lyndsey Turner
Marc Walsh
Marina Margarita
Matt Dwyer
Matt Mang
Maya Goodfellow
Michael Grandage
Michael Herrod
Michaela Moore
Michelle Ghatan
Mike McDavid
Mimi Ndiweni
Molly Vevers
Nancy Crane
Ned Bennett
Nick Jonczak
Padraig Cusack
Phil Gleaden
Polly Bennett
Rachel Parslew
Rebecca Benson
Rhys Lewis
Richard Burkert
Robyn Hoedemaker
Roger De Freitas
Roger Roberts
Ron McAllister
Ronke Adekoluejo
Rosalind Lailey
Rory Mullarkey
Rosie Sansom
Ruth O'Dowd
Ryan Desaulniers
Sam Page

Sarah Churchwell
Sarah Kosar
Sasha Wilson
Sid Sagar
Stanley Whyment
Steffan Cennydd
Stephen Bailey
Steve Winter
Stuart Campbell
Stuart Wilde
Tami Rain Knopsnyder
Tara Finney
Tara Gadomski
Tom Blyth
Tom Chapman
Tommy Aslett
Vicky Graham
Vincent Riotta
William Towler
Zachary Wyatt

Arizona State University
Arts Council England
Balance Restaurant
Bloomsbury Publishing
Carnegie Mellon University
Charing Cross Theatre
Complicite
Compass Collective
English Touring Theatre
Etch
Gecko
Guildhall School of Music and
   Drama
ITV News
Johnstown Flood National Memorial
Johnstown Tomahawks

Leeds Playhouse

Masterclass Theatre Trust

National Theatre

National Youth Theatre

New Wimbledon Theatre

North Carolina State University

The Old Vic

Open Door

Pleasance Theatre

Royal Academy of Dramatic Art

Royal Welsh College of Music and
    Drama

South Hill Park

Sparks

The Pennington School

The Really Useful Group

The Tribune Democrat

Town Hall Theatre

Ugly Duck

University of Johnstown Pittsburgh

Bibliography

Confessions of a Sociopath: A Life Spent Hiding in Plain Sight by M. E. Thomas
  (Sidgwick & Jackson).
Dare to Lead by Brené Brown (Penguin).
Into the Woods by John Yorke (Penguin).
Playwriting: Structure, Character, How and What to Write by Stephen Jeffreys
  (Nick Hern Books).
Story by Robert McKee (Methuen Publishing).
The Johnstown Flood by David McCullough (Touchstone Books).
The Viewpoints Book: A Practical Guide to Viewpoints and Composition by
  Anne Bogart and Tina Landau (Nick Hern Books).